05/23
STRAND PRICE
FOR $5.00 EACH

D0081437

HARMONY
AND
VOICE
LEADING 1

HARMONY AND VOICE LEADING 1

EDWARD ALDWELL

The Curtis Institute of Music
The Mannes College of Music

CARL SCHACHTER

Queens College of the
City University of New York

HBJ

HARCOURT BRACE JOVANOVICH, INC.

New York   San Diego   Chicago   San Francisco   Atlanta

Copyright © 1978 by Harcourt Brace Jovanovich, Inc.

All rights reserved. No part of this publication may be reproduced or transmitted in any form or by any means, electronic or mechanical, including photocopy, recording, or any information storage and retrieval system, without permission in writing from the publisher.

Requests for permission to make copies of any part of the work should be mailed to: Permissions, Harcourt Brace Jovanovich, Inc., 757 Third Avenue, New York, N.Y. 10017.

ISBN: 0-15-531515-3
Library of Congress Card Number: 78-52039

Printed in the United States of America

The excerpts from Josquin's *Ave Maria* and Dufay's *Ave Maris Stella* are reprinted from *Study Scores of Musical Styles* by Edward R. Lerner, copyright © 1968 by McGraw-Hill, Inc., with the kind permission of Edward R. Lerner and McGraw-Hill Book Company.

PREFACE

Harmony and Voice Leading is a textbook in two volumes dealing with tonal organization in the music of the eighteenth and nineteenth centuries. Both in content and in method it offers a new approach to the teaching of harmony. As the title suggests, the book emphasizes the linear aspects of music as much as the harmonic, with relationships of line to line and line to chord receiving as much attention as relationships among chords. In addition, large-scale progressions—both harmonic and linear—are introduced at an early stage so that students can gain an understanding of the connection between detail and broad, inclusive plan in a musical composition. They learn that "harmony" is not merely the progression from one chord to the next and that "voice leading" is much more than the way two consecutive chords are connected.

The book is suitable either for a self-contained course in harmony or for an integrated program combining harmony with other aspects of music. *Harmony and Voice Leading* touches on many of these aspects, including rhythm, melody, counterpoint, and form. It can function, therefore, as the basic text for an integrated program, and can serve as a convenient point of departure for systematic work in the other areas, with or without a supplementary text. Many theory programs are returning to the study of species counterpoint, usually at an early stage. This book would combine very well with work in species counterpoint; such a combination would provide an excellent basis for the understanding of tonal music. But counterpoint need not precede or accompany work in *Harmony and Voice Leading;* this is a completely self-contained and self-sufficient text.

In most theory programs, instruction in harmony or counterpoint usually follows a review of fundamentals: scales, key signatures, intervals, and so forth. This initial phase can pose difficult problems for instructors. Students vary widely—even wildly—in the quality of their previous training. And even those with a reasonably secure grasp of the fundamentals seldom understand the significance of the material they have learned by rote. The first three units of *Harmony and Voice Leading* attempt to deal with these problems. They offer both a review of the fundamental materials and a glimpse—a first glimpse for most students—of their significance for musical structure. Thus these opening units attempt to provide both a practical and a conceptual basis for the students' later work. For students deficient in their knowledge of fundamentals, we have provided a large number of written drills in the accompanying workbook as well as a smaller group in the text itself. Better prepared students will not need to devote much time to these drills, but they will profit from reading through the first three units and from classroom discussion of their contents.

If *Harmony and Voice Leading* is used for the harmony phase of a comprehensive theory program, four semesters will suffice to work through the two volumes; of course, other aspects of music would also be covered during that time. If the book is used for a self-contained harmony course, less time will be required—about three semesters depending on the number of class hours a week and the amount of time spent reviewing fundamentals. The remaining months could be devoted to an intensive study of form, to larger compositional projects, or to twentieth-century music. The two volumes of text and the workbooks contain far more exercise material than could be covered in any single course. Instructors can thus choose the number and type of exercises that best meet the needs of their particular class. The remaining exercises will provide valuable material for classroom demonstration, exams, and review.

The order in which important materials and procedures are presented differs from that found in any other text. After a discussion of chord vocabulary, chord construction, and voice leading (Units 4 and 5), the fundamental harmonic relationship between tonic and dominant is introduced, and the discussion then proceeds quickly to the most frequent linear expansions of tonic harmony. Confining students' work in these initial stages to a single harmonic relationship and to a number of closely related contrapuntal ones makes it much easier for them to *hear* what they are doing than if they are confronted immediately with seven root-position chords, each with a different sound and function. In subsequent units students learn new usages a few at a time, in a way that relates to and expands on the techniques they have already mastered. This order of presentation also makes it possible to show examples from the literature at a much earlier stage than in other approaches—and without including usages that students have not yet learned. Thus they develop their ability to hear in a logical and orderly fashion, and they can begin their analysis of music of the highest quality much sooner than in other approaches.

Although *Harmony and Voice Leading* probably covers more material than any comparable text, it does not require an inordinate amount of time to complete. Nonetheless, this book offers no shortcuts. There are no shortcuts in learning music theory—especially in the development of writing skills. If twentieth-century students wonder why they need to master such skills—why they need to take the time to learn a musical language spoken by composers of the past—they can be reminded that they are learning to form the musical equivalents of simple sentences and paragraphs. The purpose is not to learn to write "like" Mozart or Brahms, but to understand the language the great composers spoke with such matchless eloquence, the language that embodies some of the greatest achievements of the human spirit.

Late in the eighth decade of the twentieth century, no one can minimize the importance of a thorough study of twentieth-century music. But we believe that to combine in a single text an intensive study of tonal harmony with an introduction to twentieth-century techniques would fail to do justice to either subject. For one thing, some of the simplest and most fundamental principles of earlier music—the functioning and even identity of intervals, for example—become radically altered in twentieth-century usage, so that it is impossible to proceed directly from one kind of music to the other. And the twentieth century has seen the development of compositional styles that sometimes differ from one another so profoundly as to amount to different languages. To deal adequately with this disparate and often complex material requires a separate text.

Many readers will realize that this book reflects the theoretical and analytic approach of Heinrich Schenker, an approach many musicians recognize as embodying unique and profound insights into tonal music. *Harmony and Voice Leading* is not a text in Schenkerian analysis—no knowledge of it is presupposed for either instructors or students—but the book will lay a valuable foundation in Schenker's approach for students who wish to pursue it later.

We extend our thanks to the many colleagues, students, and friends—more than we could possibly mention—whose comments and suggestions helped us in writing this book. Gerald Krimm typed the manuscript while perusing it with a highly critical eye. Hedi Siegel prepared the indexes with unusual care and discrimination. Larry Laskowski contributed a few of the exercises—and excellent ones. Bertrand E. Howard, University of Arkansas; Roy Johnson, The Florida State University; Gordon R. Keddington, Diablo Valley College; and Gary E. Wittlich, Indiana University, read the manuscript and offered valuable advice. David Loeb, The Curtis Institute of Music and The Mannes College of Music, shared with us his vast knowledge of the literature and set us on the track of many excellent examples. Charles Burkhart, Queens College of the City University of New York, and John Rothgeb, State University of New York at Binghamton, gave generously of their time and their deep knowledge of music theory in subjecting the manuscript to careful and very helpful scrutiny. And Felix Salzer and the late Ernst Oster provided unfailing interest and encouragement.

We also thank the staff of Harcourt Brace Jovanovich—in particular Nina Gunzenhauser, who sponsored the project and gave us enthusiastic and discerning guidance; Albert Richards, who offered valuable support; and finally our editor, Natalie Bowen, to whom we owe a special debt of gratitude for the uncommon intelligence and dedication she brings to her work.

Edward Aldwell
Carl Schachter

CONTENTS

II I-V-I AND ITS ELABORATIONS

III $\frac{5}{3}$, $\frac{6}{3}$, AND $\frac{6}{4}$ TECHNIQUES

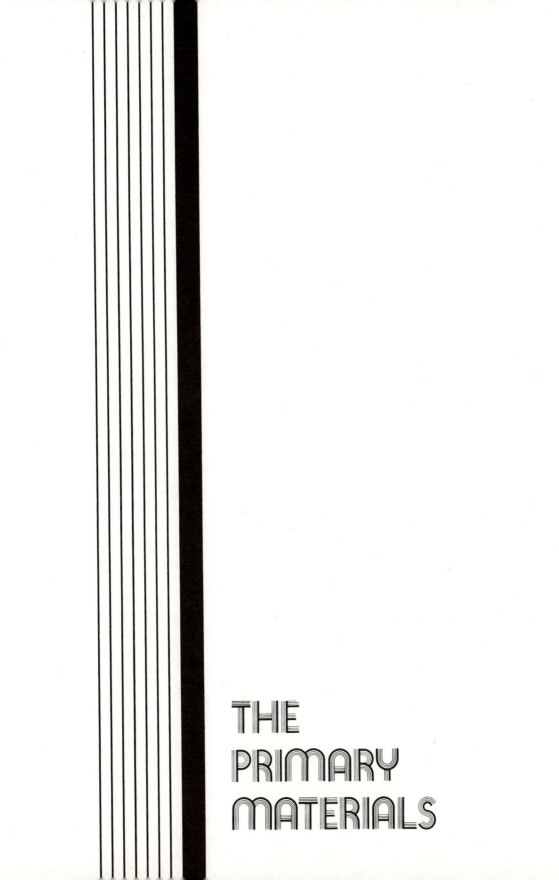

THE
PRIMARY
MATERIALS

ONE | KEY, SCALES, AND MODES

1-1 Mozart, Piano Sonata, K. 545, I

TONAL RELATIONSHIPS; MAJOR KEYS

1. Key. We'll begin by considering the opening of Mozart's familiar Sonata in C major, K. 545 (Example 1-1). The piece obviously contains many tones besides C. Why, then, do we call it a "Sonata in C major," or say that "it's written in the key of C"? Most people would answer that music is "in a key" when its tones relate to one central tone—the one that has the same name as the key—and when the functions of the other tones result from the ways in which they relate to the central one. According to this answer, the Mozart sonata is in C because C is the central tone; we hear the other tones as subordinate to C. (Why it's not simply in C but in C *major,* we'll discuss presently.)

This explanation of key is certainly correct as far as it goes, but it tells us little about the *kinds of relationships* that exist between the central tone and the others. (A definition of chess as "a game played on a board by two people, each with sixteen pieces" would be correct in the same way. But it wouldn't help anyone to learn to play chess.) Let's now look more closely at these relationships.

2. The tonic. We call the central tone of a key the *tonic.* In Example 1-1, both hands begin on the tonic, C. The left hand stays on C for most of bars 1-4 and moves on the C as the lowest point in the downward motion F-E-D-C, bars 5-8. The right-hand part does not return to C after the opening bars, but its subsequent course points to C as its eventual goal. Example 1-2 shows the most prominent tones of the melodic line. In bars 3 and 4, the melody moves from the high A down as far as E. The sixteenth-note scales that follow repeat, in varied form, the melodic line A-G-F-E but then carry it one step further, to D (bar 9). In listening to the melody, we are led to expect it to finish on C, to complete the circle by ending where it began. But it doesn't—not yet, at any rate. Instead the D is taken up again in bars 11 and 12; the first part of the piece closes without having arrived at its melodic goal.

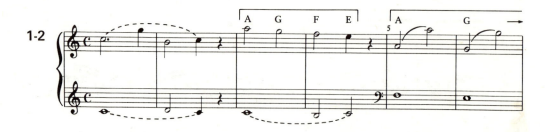

And, in fact, C's function as a goal is not fulfilled until almost the end of the piece (Example 1-3). Generalizing from the Mozart, we can state that the tonic, the central tone of the key, forms the *point of departure* from which the other tones move and the *goal* to which they are directed. As in bars 1-12, the music does not always reach its goal at the moment we expect it to; by ending a part of the piece in a state of suspense, a composer can enhance the feeling of finality at the very end.

1-3 Mozart, Piano Sonata, K. 545, I

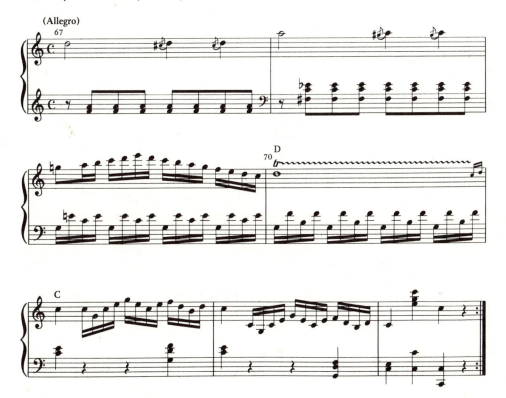

3. Scales. In Example 1-1, Mozart uses only some of the tones that the piano keyboard can produce. Almost all the sounds in these twelve bars result from playing the white keys; of the nearly 200 notes, the only exceptions are two C#'s (bar 9) and one F# (bar 10). And if we were to look at other pieces in C major, we would find similar tonal materials. For the most part the pieces would contain the tones C, D, E, F, G, A, and B, and any other tones would play a subordinate role.

When all the tones that belong to a key occur in consecutive order, each one next to those closest to it in pitch, the result is a *scale* (Latin *scala*, steps, staircase, or ladder). In bars 5-8 of the Mozart, C major scales occur beginning on A, G, F, and E. The basic form of a scale, however, is the one that begins and ends on the tonic. A scale in this basic form can be thought of as a symbol of, or abstraction from, the natural flow of music—at least of music that is written "in a key." For such a scale begins on the tonic as its point of departure and concludes on the tonic as its goal (Example 1-4).

1-4   scale degrees in C*

The capped numbers above the notes in Example 1-4 indicate *scale degrees* (sometimes called *scale steps*) and will be used for this purpose throughout the book. In addition to numbers, the following traditional names are used so often for the scale degrees that you should memorize them:

$\hat{1}$ tonic
$\hat{2}$ supertonic
$\hat{3}$ mediant
$\hat{4}$ subdominant
$\hat{5}$ dominant
$\hat{6}$ submediant
$\hat{7}$ leading tone

4. The octave. The beginning and ending tones of Example 1-4 are both C, but they are not one and the same tone. The last tone sounds considerably "higher" in pitch than the first. Yet despite this marked difference in register, the sounds of the two C's are very similar; that's why we call them both by the same letter name. When two tones are separated by an *octave* (Latin *octava*, eighth) they are equivalents—that is, they are variants of the same sound. This phenomenon of *octave equivalence* is one of the most important aspects of pitch organization in music. In technical writing about music, it is frequently helpful to indicate the register in which a tone occurs. Example 1-5 shows how this can be done.

1-5   registers

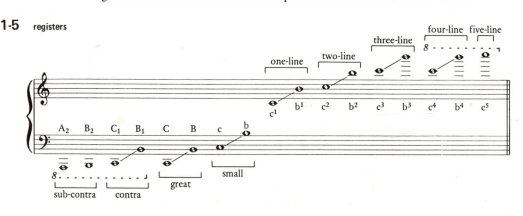

*Throughout the examples, the exercises, and the Workbook, capital letters are used for major keys and lower-case letters are used for minor keys. Thus, G and g indicate the keys of G major and G minor respectively.

5. Major scales; whole steps and half steps. If we play a white-key scale from C to C on the piano, we can easily see that there is a black key between most of the adjacent white keys—between C and D, D and E, F and G, and so on. However no black key appears between E and F or between B and C. The distance between one tone of a scale and the next is usually called a *step*. The scale from C to C contains two kinds of steps: small ones between E and F and between B and C, larger ones between the other adjacent tones. The small ones occur where there is no intervening black key; the larger ones where there is a black key.

We call the smaller steps *half steps* (or *semitones*) and the larger ones *whole steps* (or *whole tones*). The half steps occur between $\hat{3}$ and $\hat{4}$ and between $\hat{7}$ and $\hat{8}$; all the others are whole steps:

1 w 2 w 3 h 4 w 5 w 6 w 7 h 8

A scale with half steps and whole steps arranged in the above order is called a *major scale.* Only the major scale has half steps between $\hat{3}$ and $\hat{4}$ and $\hat{7}$ and $\hat{8}$. Any piece whose tones can be arranged to form such a scale is a piece in a major key.

The major scale is one kind of *diatonic scale.* All diatonic scales contain five whole steps and two half steps within the octave, but each of the different types of diatonic scale has the half steps in different places. From the time of the ancient Greeks through the nineteenth century, most Western art music was based on diatonic scales. Other kinds of scales are used in some Western folk music, music of non-Western cultures, and much twentieth-century music.

6. Intervals. Example 1-6a shows the tones that begin each of the first five bars of the Mozart sonata in both the left-hand and the right-hand parts. We call the relationship between two tones heard in a single context an *interval.* Intervals formed by simultaneously sounding tones are called *vertical* (because they are written one above the other). Intervals formed by tones that sound one after the other are called *horizontal* (Example 1-6b). The terms *harmonic* and *melodic* are sometimes used instead of vertical and horizontal.

1-6

(a) vertical intervals   (b) horizontal intervals

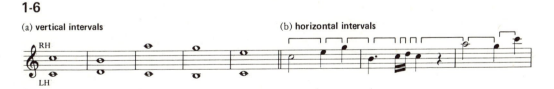

We can describe intervals by ordinal numbers arrived at by counting letter names up from the lower to the higher tone, or down from the higher to the lower. Thus C up to G is a *5th,* because it spans five letter names, C, D, E, F, and G. From B to C is a *2nd,* because it spans two letter names. From G to the next G above is an *octave* (not an "eighth," though it has the same meaning as "octave"). Finding the numerical size of an interval does not identify it completely. For example, B-C and C-D are both 2nds. Yet C-D (a whole step) is larger than B-C (a half step). Later on we will be specifying intervals more exactly; for now, it is enough to be able to determine the numerical size.

7. Chords; triads. Compare the first and last bars of the Mozart (Examples 1-1 and 1-3). Both bars contain the same three tones (with octave duplications); the tones are C, E, and G ($\hat{1}$, $\hat{3}$, and $\hat{5}$). These three tones are very closely associated, the basis of their association being membership in the same chord. A *chord* is a group of three or more tones that functions as a *simultaneity*—that is, the tones make sense played all at the same time. In essence a chord is a vertical unit; the simplest and most basic way to present it is as a *block chord,* with all the tones sounding at once (as in the last bar of the Mozart, second beat). But a composer can also present the tones one after the other, as Mozart does in bar 1. Because our ear and memory can group the tones into a unit, we still hear a chord. But not a block chord; it is a *broken chord* or *arpeggio.*

The chord C-E-G contains three tones; the upper two form the intervals of a *5th* and a *3rd* from C, the lowest. A three-tone chord formed in this way is a *triad.* The triad is the basic chord in Western music from the fifteenth through the nineteenth centuries. All other chords are derived from it. In every key the triad $\hat{1}$-$\hat{3}$-$\hat{5}$ has the tonic as its lowest tone. Since the lowest tone, called the *root,* functions as the basis of the chord, we call this triad the *tonic triad* or *tonic chord.*

8. Active tones; stable tones. Among the many mysterious powers of music is its ability to suggest *motion.* In listening to a piece of music, we do not hear a succession of static tones; rather, we hear tonal motions, one tone moving to another. In part this impression comes from rhythm, for musical rhythm has close relationships to some of the physical activities—walking, for instance—that form our primary experience of motion. But the impression of motion also arises from tonal organization. We have already seen that $\hat{1}$, the tonic, functions as the goal to which the other tones are directed. (And musical motion is essentially *directed* motion, motion to a goal.) We might say that all the other scale degrees, in different ways, are *active* in the direction of $\hat{1}$, that they tend to move to this stable, central tone. However $\hat{3}$ and $\hat{5}$ can also function as stable tones, though they are less stable than $\hat{1}$. They can serve as goals to which other, still more active tones can move because they are members of the tonic triad and thus closely associated with $\hat{1}$. Motion to $\hat{3}$ or $\hat{5}$ will not have the same finality as motion to $\hat{1}$.

Many melodies begin on $\hat{3}$ or $\hat{5}$ rather than on $\hat{1}$. If these melodies are harmonized, the tonic will almost always appear in the lowest part. Thus the music will still move from a tonic at the beginning to a tonic as final goal even if $\hat{1}$ does not serve as the initial *melodic* tone.

9. Passing tones; neighboring tones. Example 1-7 contains a diagram of the C major scale. The stable tones, $\hat{1}$, $\hat{3}$, $\hat{5}$, and $\hat{8}$, are shown as whole notes; the more active tones are written with black noteheads.

1-7

○ = stable tones   ● = active tones

As the diagram indicates, the active tones lead from one stable tone to another: up from $\hat{1}$ to $\hat{3}$, $\hat{3}$ to $\hat{5}$, and $\hat{5}$ to $\hat{8}$; down in the reverse order. A tone that moves by whole or half step between two stable tones is called a *passing tone* (abbreviation, P); the term clearly conveys the transitional character of these tones. We can readily hear this transitional character if we play the scale in the right hand while holding the tonic triad in the left. Note that a single passing tone connects $\hat{1}$ with $\hat{3}$ and $\hat{3}$ with $\hat{5}$ but that two passing tones are needed to connect $\hat{5}$ with $\hat{8}$.

Motion along the scale—that is, motion with passing tones—is by no means the only type of melodic progression, though it is the basic type. Example 1-8 shows another important possibility. Here the active tones decorate a single stable tone rather than move from one to another. A tone that moves by step away from and back to a stable tone is called a *neighboring tone,* or simply *neighbor* (N). Sometimes it is helpful to specify the direction of a neighboring tone by referring to it as an upper or a lower neighbor (UN or LN).

1-8

To see how passing and neighboring tones work in a musical composition, let's look again at bars 1-4 of the Mozart sonata. Example 1-9 quotes these bars with Mozart's accompaniment written as block chords (the tones have not been changed) and with a few purely decorative tones omitted from the melody.

1-9

Note that the chord in the first half of bar 2 consists, for the most part, of neighbors to $\hat{1}$ and $\hat{3}$. Both the B in the melody and the D in the lowest part participate in neighboring motions $\hat{8}$-$\hat{7}$-$\hat{8}$ and $\hat{1}$-$\hat{2}$-$\hat{1}$; the F functions as upper neighbor to E ($\hat{3}$-$\hat{4}$-$\hat{3}$). The high A in bar 3, right-hand part, comes from the G at the end of bar 1 and returns to the same tone; the A, therefore, is the upper neighbor of G. Note that the first G does not immediately move to A, its upper neighbor; the events of bar 2 separate the tones. But because of their closeness in pitch and because of the much lower pitch of the intervening tones, the ear easily connects the G and A. This sort of thing happens quite often; musical motions do not just proceed from one note to the next. (Just as in language, where a sentence is not organized on a word-by-word basis, we perceive the connection between the subject of a sentence and the verb even if there are many words in between.)

In addition to the neighbors, the Mozart excerpt features one prominent passing tone. The F in bar 4 (second beat, right-hand part) passes from G to E ($\hat{5}$-$\hat{4}$-$\hat{3}$).

10. Half steps as melodic intensifiers. When an active tone, P or N, lies a half step from the stable tone to which it is attracted, its motion to the goal tone has a particularly intense character. The closeness in pitch between the two tones draws the active tone into the gravitational field, as it were, of the stable one and enhances the attractional power of the latter. In major, therefore, $\hat{4}$ tends to move more readily to $\hat{3}$ than to $\hat{5}$, the other possible goal tone. And $\hat{7}$ is very strongly attracted to $\hat{8}$; in fact the term *leading tone* refers to the active way in which $\hat{7}$ "leads into" $\hat{8}$. The half steps are very well situated in major; the instability of $\hat{7}$ and $\hat{4}$ helps to strengthen $\hat{1}$ and $\hat{3}$ and leads to a clear definition of the key. Play the right-hand part of Example 1-9, extending the duration of B (bar 2) and F (bar 4). Notice how urgently the ear demands a continuation to C and E.

11. Incomplete neighbors; double neighbors. Sometimes a neighboring tone will connect with only one statement of the stable tone rather than two; it will move either to the stable tone or from it, but not both. In the melodic fragment shown in Example 1-10, the stable tones are A, C♯, and E ($\hat{1}$-$\hat{3}$-$\hat{5}$ of A major). The G♯, D, B, and F♯ are active tones that precede or follow (but not both) one of the main tones. We use the term *incomplete neighbor* (IN) to denote neighboring tones connected with one rather than two main tones.

1-10   Mozart, Piano Concerto, K. 488, I

Also derived from the neighbor is a four-note group consisting of stable tone, both the upper and the lower neighbor (in either order) and a return to the stable tone. Two neighbors occurring together are called a *double neighbor* (DN), as in Example 1-11.

1-11   Haydn, Symphony No. 98, II

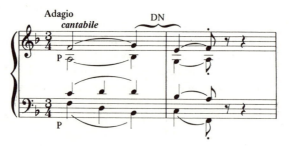

12. Transposition; key signatures. In bar 42 of the Mozart movement with which we began this unit, the opening idea returns; the technical name for such a return in a sonata movement is *recapitulation.* Usually a recapitulation is in the same key as the beginning of the movement, but most exceptionally, Mozart does not begin his recapitulation in C. Instead of C, F functions as the central tone; the music has moved to F major. Example 1-12 quotes the opening few bars of this F major recapitulation; observe that every time a B occurs, it is modified by a flat. A moment's reflection (and, perhaps, a glance at the keyboard) will show why the B♭ is needed. Without it, there would be a whole step between 3̂ and 4̂; the music would no longer be in major.

1-12   Mozart, Piano Sonata, K. 545, I

Putting a piece (or section) of music into another key is called *transposing* it. If we transpose a piece from C to any other major key, we have to use flats or sharps to preserve the half steps between 3̂ and 4̂ and 7̂ and 8̂. These sharps or flats are gathered together into a *key signature* that occurs at the beginning of each line of music. Sometimes a change of key within a piece is accompanied by a new key signature, but very often, as in the Mozart, the necessary flats, sharps, naturals, and so on, occur in the body of the music as *accidentals,* like the flats before the B's in Example 1-12.

Example 1-13 shows the signatures of the fifteen major keys. Note that the keys with sharps move *up* in 5ths; the tonic of each new key lies a 5th above the preceding tonic. And that the keys with flats do just the opposite—they move *down* in 5ths.

1-13   major key signatures

(b)

C   F   Bb   Eb   Ab   Db   Gb   Cb

If you have not already done so, memorize these key signatures *immediately*. Not doing so will cause you unnecessary difficulties in studying music theory. And, by the way, memorizing them means being able to recall them *instantly and automatically*.

13. Chromaticism; chromatic half steps. In the recapitulation of the Mozart, the use of an accidental—Bb—results from a change of key to F major. However accidentals do not always signal a change of key; most often, in fact, they do not do so. Very often they occur when a composer wishes to emphasize a scale degree by means of the melodically intense half-step progression. In Example 1-1, the F♯ in bar 10 (left hand, last tone) intensifies the G that follows. Example 1-14 shows the specific function of this F♯ by leaving out some of the less important tones and simplifying the use of registers. It reveals that the F♯ leads from the F♮ of bars 9 and 10 to the G of bar 11; it functions, therefore, as a kind of passing tone.

1-14

P

The use of tones that normally do not belong to a key is called *chromaticism*; Mozart's F♯, therefore, is a *chromatic passing tone*. Chromatic elements embellish a basically diatonic substructure; the term *chromatic* (Greek *chroma*, color) clearly conveys the decorative character of these tones. As Example 1-14 indicates, the use of chromatic tones creates the possibility for a new kind of half step, the *chromatic half step*. The half step F♮-F♯ involves two tones with the same letter name, whereas the *diatonic half step* (for example, B-C) involves two tones with adjacent letter names. Chromatic passing tones divide a whole step into a chromatic half step plus a diatonic one (F♮-F♯-G). The chromatic half step normally comes first; the chromatic passing tone uses the same letter name as the preceding diatonic tone. Thus a chromatic passing tone from A down to G would be Ab; the melodic progression, therefore, would be A♮-Ab-G.

Not every chromatic tone produces a chromatic half step. The C♯'s in bar 9 of Example 1-1 do not. They intensify the motion to D through the half-step progression, but they lie a whole step above the preceding tone, B.

MINOR KEYS; MODES; TONALITY

14. Minor keys. Example 1-15 is the beginning of a variation movement by Handel. The key signature contains two flats, but this composition is clearly not in Bb major. The lowest part begins and ends on G; the highest begins on D and ends on G; the opening chord contains the tones G, Bb, and D. All of this points to G as the tonic and to G-Bb-D as the tonic triad. And, in fact, the piece is in the key of G, but G *minor*, not G major.

1-15   **Handel, Passacaglia**

(from *Harpsichord Suite No. 7*)

Why this piece is in minor becomes very clear if we compare its tonic triad with the tonic triad of G major (Example 1-16).

Î and 5̂ are the same in both chords; only 3̂ varies. The Bb is closer to G than is the B♮; the 3rd G-Bb, therefore, is smaller than the 3rd G-B♮. *Minor* and *major* simply mean smaller and larger. A minor key is a key containing a small or minor 3rd between Î and 3̂; a major key is a key containing a large or major 3rd between Î and 3̂. There are other significant differences between major and minor, but the contrast in sound between the two kinds of 3rds marks the fundamental distinction between them.

1-16

15. The natural form of minor. Example 1-17a shows the beginning of a later variation from the Handel Passacaglia. The right-hand part contains descending scales that follow the key signature exactly; no chromatic alterations occur. Example 1-17b is a diagram of the scale Handel uses, showing its stable and active tones as well as the location of its two half steps. The scale in this diagram is the *natural* (or *pure*) *minor scale*.

1-17 (a) Handel, Passacaglia

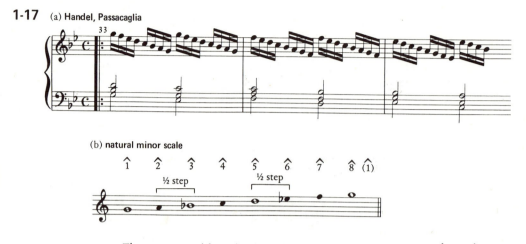

(b) natural minor scale

The contrast with major is striking. The minor 3rd between $\hat{1}$ and $\hat{3}$ lends its characteristic color to the scale. The half steps between $\hat{2}$ and $\hat{3}$ and $\hat{5}$ and $\hat{6}$ create an intensity in the motions from $\hat{2}$ to $\hat{3}$ and from $\hat{6}$ to $\hat{5}$ quite different from the corresponding progressions in major. Finally—and very significantly—the whole step between $\hat{7}$ and $\hat{8}$ fails to lead into the tonic with the same conviction as in major. For this reason, the term leading tone is not used to indicate the seventh degree of the minor scale in its natural form. We use the term *subtonic* instead.

When the minor scale descends (as in Example 1-17a), the lack of a leading tone does not present a problem, for $\hat{7}$ leads away from $\hat{8}$ rather than toward it. But when the scale ascends, the whole step between subtonic and tonic can constitute a real defect because $\hat{8}$ does not sound like a goal; its power to act as the central tone of the key is impaired. For this reason, $\hat{7}$ in minor must be raised to create the necessary half step whenever it moves to $\hat{8}$ as goal, or whenever the composer wishes to suggest such a motion, even if it is not immediately fulfilled. That is why Handel uses F♯ instead of F♮ in bars 3 and 4 of Example 1-15.

16. The harmonic form of minor. Raising the seventh degree but leaving the others unaltered produces the scale shown in Example 1-18. This scale is called the *harmonic minor,* for many important chord progressions use the tones it contains. However one characteristic of this scale makes it unsuitable for normal melodic progression. The interval between $\hat{6}$ and $\hat{7}$ is larger than a whole step; it is equivalent, in fact, to a step and a half. This larger interval creates a gap in the continuity of the scale that can be destructive of melodic flow. As Example 1-18 shows, the harmonic minor has three half steps: between $\hat{2}$ and $\hat{3}$, $\hat{5}$ and $\hat{6}$, and $\hat{7}$ and $\hat{8}$.

1-18 harmonic minor scale

17. The melodic form of minor. If we raise $\hat{6}$ as well as $\hat{7}$, we gain a leading tone, but without creating an awkwardly large interval between $\hat{6}$ and $\hat{7}$. In a melodic line in minor, therefore, if $\hat{6}$ comes before the leading tone (raised $\hat{7}$), it too will be raised. Note, for example, the E♮ in bar 4 of Example 1-14, used instead of the E♭ called for by the key signature.

    The minor scale that raises $\hat{6}$ and $\hat{7}$ ascending is called the *melodic minor scale* (Example 1-19a). Example 1-19b, still from the Handel Passacaglia, illustrates its use in a composition. Note that it contains two half steps, between $\hat{2}$ and $\hat{3}$ and $\hat{7}$ and $\hat{8}$.

1-19   (a) melodic minor scale

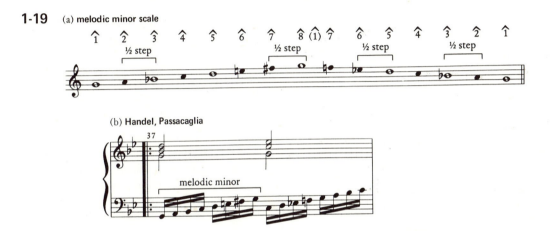

(b) **Handel, Passacaglia**

    Since $\hat{6}$ and $\hat{7}$ are raised in order to lead convincingly to $\hat{8}$, the raised forms of these degrees will normally occur only when the scale goes up. The descending form of the melodic minor, therefore, reverts to the natural form, with the accidentals for $\hat{6}$ and $\hat{7}$ canceled.

18. The three forms of minor. Beginning students sometimes have the misconception that the three forms of minor constitute three independent and unrelated scales. Actually, the harmonic and melodic forms are variants of the natural minor scale. The fact that the key signature *always* corresponds to the natural minor indicates that this is the basic form of the scale.

    Most compositions in minor will contain elements of all three forms of the scale. Some successions of chords will come from the natural form (Example 1-15, bars 1 and 2); others from the harmonic (Example 1-15, bars 3 and 4). Melodic lines that ascend $\hat{6}$-$\hat{7}$-$\hat{8}$ tend to use the ascending melodic scale; descending lines tend to use the descending melodic (or natural) form (Examples 1-17 and 1-19).

19. Key signatures in minor. Like C major, A minor has neither sharps nor flats. As we move up in 5ths from A, we must add one sharp each time to the key signature to preserve the correct pattern of whole steps and half steps. As we move down in 5ths, we add flats. Example 1-20 shows the signatures for the fifteen minor keys, which you should memorize.

1-20 minor key signatures

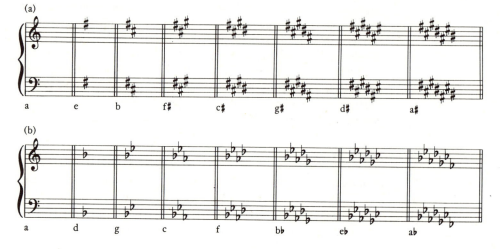

(a)

a   e   b   f#   c#   g#   d#   a#

(b)

a   d   g   c   f   b♭   e♭   a♭

20. Relative major and minor. The terms *relative major* and *relative minor* are often used to denote a major key with the same signature as a given minor one, and vice versa. Thus, C major would be the relative major of A minor, and D minor would be the relative minor of F major. These terms sometimes confuse students, who might think that F major and D minor, for instance, are the same key. Nothing could be more misleading; F major and D minor have different tonics; therefore they are different keys.

Knowing the relative major can help you learn the minor key signatures. Remember that the tonic of the minor key is $\hat{6}$ in the relative major. For example, the tonic of G♯ minor is $\hat{6}$ in B major; the key signature of G♯ minor, therefore, contains five sharps.

21. Parallel major and minor; mixture. Major and minor keys with different signatures but with the same tone as tonic are called *parallel.* G minor would be the parallel minor of G major. Actually, parallel major and minor keys are much more closely related than are relative majors and minors. In G minor as in G major, tonal activity is directed to the same goal, to G. In many compositions, elements from major and minor occur in very close proximity; in such cases we speak of a *mixture* of major and minor. Using raised $\hat{6}$ and $\hat{7}$ in minor constitutes one kind of mixture, for these tones are the same as the corresponding ones in the parallel major.

22. Modes; the diatonic order. Writers on music often refer to major and minor as *modes.* If we build scales starting on each of the white keys of the piano as a tonic, and using only white keys for the other tones, the result will be seven scales, each with a different pattern of five whole steps and two half steps within its octave. We will have created seven different tonal systems, for in each of these scales, the different arrangement of whole and half steps creates a different tonal structure.

The seven "white-key" scales constitute segments of the *diatonic order*, the pattern of whole and half steps that has given rise to most of the tonal systems of Western music. Like major and minor, these segments are known as *modes*. The seven patterns are shown in Example 1-21, together with their traditional names. Some of these modes had great importance in music before the eighteenth century, but some did not. The Locrian mode was scarcely more than a theoretical possibility, and the Lydian, at least in polyphonic music, made such regular use of B♮ as to be indistinguishable from Ionian (or major). Much great music was composed in the Dorian, Phrygian, and Mixolydian systems, and to understand early music, you must certainly investigate the way the modes were used. General information appears in any standard history of music and in some counterpoint texts. However the study of early music is still a fairly new discipline, and we are far from having a complete understanding of specific techniques of tonal organization in early music.

1-21    seven diatonic modes

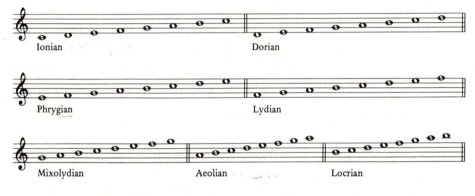

In the music we are dealing with in this book—the music from the Baroque through the Romantic periods—there are only two modes of any importance: major and minor. In this music, elements from some of the other modes—especially Phrygian—will sometimes appear. But they do so, for the most part, in a larger context of major or minor.

23. Tonality. Many musicians and writers use the term *tonal* to describe any piece or type of music organized around a central tone. And the principle of organization would be called *tonality*. Under these broad definitions of tonal and tonality, many—indeed, most—kinds of music would be tonal: music in major and minor keys, modal music, much non-Western music, and a good deal of twentieth-century music. The presence of a tonal center is an important common feature of these different kinds of music. But the ways in which the other tones function with respect to the central tone may vary considerably. Since the music we will deal with in this book is based, for the most part, on major and minor, the term *major-minor tonality* is the most accurate, though it is fairly unwieldy. So we will sometimes use the words "tonal" and "tonality" in a narrower sense as an abbreviated form of major-minor tonality.

24. The contrast between major and minor. Many people feel that music in a major key is "happy" and that music in minor is "sad." Sophisticated musicians often question this association, believing that it is a purely arbitrary one based on nothing except, perhaps, habit. And of course it is true that the emotional character of a piece depends on many factors in combination. Light and even comical pieces—some of Mendelssohn's Scherzos, for instance—are in minor. And some very solemn pieces are in major, for example the "Dead March" in Handel's *Saul.* But it is a mistake to ignore the likelihood that choice of mode is one of the factors that determine the character of a piece. And sometimes it may be the most important factor.

For one thing the association of mode and emotion is a very old one; it goes back at least 400 years. Writing in 1558, Gioseffo Zarlino, the greatest theorist of the late Renaissance, remarks that melodies (and modes) featuring a major 3rd above the central tone sound cheerful and that those with a minor 3rd sound sad.* Any cultural tradition that has persisted for so long takes on a certain importance even if it is based on nothing more than custom. That the great composers of the eighteenth and nineteenth centuries believed in this association is evident to anyone who studies their songs and other music they composed to texts. And (as you will see in Unit 2) there is a strong possibility that the emotional connotations of major and minor may reflect more than habit or conditioning—that they may arise out of qualities inherent in tonal relationships.

EXERCISES

1. Be able to write from memory and to recite fluently the fifteen major key signatures in the order shown in Example 1-13.
2. Be able to write from memory and to recite fluently the fifteen major key signatures in the following order: C, C♯, D♭, D, E♭, E, F, F♯, G♭, G, A♭, A, B♭, B, C♭.
3. Be able to write from memory and to recite fluently the fifteen minor key signatures in the order shown in Example 1-20.
4. Be able to write from memory and to recite fluently the fifteen minor key signatures in the following order: c, c♯, d, d♯, e♭, e, f, f♯, g, g♯, a♭, a, a♯, b♭, b.
5. Recite as quickly as possible the names of the major keys indicated by the key signatures in each numbered row (horizontal and vertical) in the diagram on page 17. Do not *write* the answers.

*Gioseffo Zarlino, *The Art of Counterpoint,* translated by Guy A. Marco and Claude V. Palisca (New Haven, Conn.: Yale University Press, 1968), pp. 21-23.

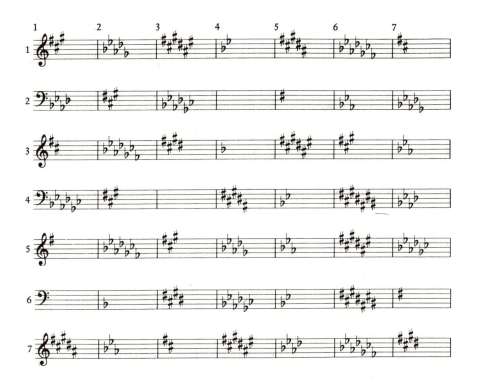

6. Using the same diagram, recite as quickly as possible the names of the minor keys indicated by the key signatures in each row. Do not write the answers.

7. Using the order of major keys in Exercise 2, name the relative minor of each of these keys.

8. Using the order of minor keys in Exercise 4, name the relative major of each of these keys.

9. Using the order of major keys in Exercise 2, name the key signature of the parallel minor of each of these keys. Which keys lack a parallel minor? Why?

TWO | INTERVALS

2-1 (a)

unison 2nd 3rd 4th 5th 6th 7th octave
or
prime

(b) Verdi, Recordare   (from the *Requiem,* Dies Irae)

(Adagio maestoso)
413

Re-de- mi - sti,   Re -   de - mi - sti   cru-cem pas -   sus;

intervals: d7 m6 m3 M2 m3   P5   m7 M6 m3 P5 M6 P4 m3   M3   m6 P4 M2   M3 P4 P5

translation: You have redeemed [me] through your suffering on the cross.

RECOGNIZING AND CONSTRUCTING INTERVALS

1. Numerical size; quality. As you'll remember from Unit 1 (section 6), the *numerical size* of an interval depends on the number of letter names the two tones span (Example 2-1a). But numerical size alone is not enough for the complete identification of an interval. For example, the intervals from C down to G♯, G♮, and G♭ are all 4ths, for they all have the same letter names. Yet the three intervals are different in size and *very* different in sound or *quality*. The complete identification of an interval, therefore, depends on both its numerical size and its quality.

Example 2-1b shows the intervals between two melodic lines labeled both by size and by quality. Intervals come in five qualities:

major (M)
minor (m)
perfect (P)
augmented (A)
diminished (d)

(Occasionally one encounters *doubly* augmented or *doubly* diminished intervals.)
    For purposes of classification, intervals may be divided into two groups:

Group 1: unisons, 4ths, 5ths, and octaves
Group 2: 2nds, 3rds, 6ths, and 7ths

The intervals belonging to the first group are basically *perfect*; they are never major or minor. The intervals belonging to the second group are basically *major* or *minor*; they are never perfect. Thus musicians never speak of a "major 5th" or a "perfect 6th." Intervals belonging to both groups are sometimes *augmented* or *diminished*.
    Group 1. If the upper tone of the interval belongs to the major scale of the lower tone, the interval is *perfect*. If the interval is a chromatic half step larger than perfect, it is *augmented*; if it is a chromatic half step smaller than perfect, it is *diminished* (Example 2-2).

2-2

Group 2. If the upper tone belongs to the major scale of the lower tone, the interval is *major*. If the interval is a chromatic half step larger than major, it is *augmented*. If it is a chromatic half step smaller than major, it is *minor*. And if it is a chromatic half step smaller than minor, it is *diminished* (Example 2-3).

2-3

Identifying and building intervals is easy if the lower tone normally begins a major scale and if the interval is built up from the lower tone. It is slightly more difficult if the lower tone is the tonic of an improbable major scale or if the interval must be built down from the upper tone. The two problems on page 20 show the way to proceed.

PROBLEM 1: IDENTIFY THE FOLLOWING INTERVAL.

Since few of us are familiar with the exotic key of B♯ major, we'll disregard the sharp for a moment. From B♮ to A is a minor 7th. (B to A♯ would be a major 7th, for A♯ belongs to the B major scale. B-A♮ is a chromatic half step smaller than major; therefore it is minor.) If B-A is a minor 7th, then B♯-A must be a *diminished* 7th, for raising the lower tone makes the interval a chromatic half step smaller than minor.

PROBLEM 2: WRITE AN AUGMENTED 6TH BELOW D.

To solve this problem we must first find the letter name of the lower tone. In this case, it is F, since F-D forms a 6th. From F♮ to D would be a major 6th, for D fits into the F major scale. An augmented 6th is a chromatic half step larger. Since we cannot change the given tone, D, we can enlarge the interval only by lowering the F. The correct answer, therefore, is F♭.

---

2. **Compound intervals.** *Compound intervals* are those larger than an octave. Owing to the principle of octave equivalence (see Unit 1, section 4), compound intervals are functionally the same as the corresponding simple ones. As Example 2-4 demonstrates, a *12th* is simply an expanded 5th, a *15th* an expanded octave, and so forth. And such intervals are almost always called 5ths and octaves rather than 12ths and 15ths. The only compound intervals whose names we need for our present purposes are the *9th* and the *10th*.

2-4   compound intervals

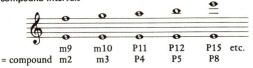

3. **Interval inversion.** We invert an interval of an octave or less by bringing the lower tone up an octave or the upper tone down an octave while leaving the other tone in place (Example 2-5); with compound intervals one of the tones would have to be displaced by two or more octaves. The numerical size of an interval plus that of its inversion adds up to 9. Thus the inversion of a unison is an octave (1 plus 8 equals 9), the inversion of a 3rd is a 6th (3 plus 6 equals 9), and so on.

2-5

The inversion of a perfect interval is also perfect. Inversion changes the other qualities to their opposites:

major	becomes	minor
minor	becomes	major
augmented	becomes	diminished
diminished	becomes	augmented

Because interval inversion results from the octave displacement of one of the interval's tones, an interval and its inversion form a related pair; this relationship is another consequence of octave equivalence.

THE OVERTONE SERIES

4. Composite sounds and overtones. Most musical tones are *composite sounds.* Their pitch results from the frequency with which the sounding body vibrates. (The sounding body may be a string, as on a violin; or an air column, as inside an oboe; and so forth.) As it vibrates, the sounding body divides itself into segments that vibrate independently. The vibration of the segments produces *overtones.* Normally we are not conscious of these overtones for they and the *fundamental tone* (the pitch we hear) blend into a single sound. But if you have a good musical ear you can easily train yourself to hear overtones, especially when the fundamental tone is in a low register. Overtones help to determine the *timbre* (or tone color) of the various instruments; they make possible the playing of harmonics on string instruments and the technique of overblowing on wind instruments.

The *intensity* (loudness) of the different overtones will vary depending on the instrument and on how it is played, but almost all musical sounds of any pitch contain the same group of overtones; we call this group the *overtone series.* Example 2-6 shows the series from Great C through the 16th tone (or *partial*). The series continues infinitely, the intervals between successive partials becoming smaller and smaller. But the higher partials are so weak as to lose any musical significance. Note that the partials are numbered from the fundamental, which is the first partial. All the other partials, or overtones, are literally "over" the fundamental.

2-6 the overtone series

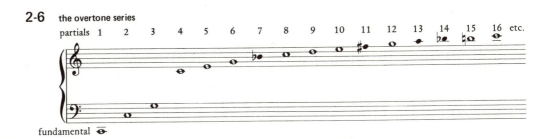

5. The overtone series and the tonal system. It is clear from Example 2-6 that the overtone series contains elements that coincide with some of the most important materials of the tonal system. Between the fundamental and its upper partials we find:

the perfect octave (partials 2, 4, 8, and 16)
the perfect 5th (partials 3, 6, and 12)
the major 3rd (partials 5 and 10)
the major triad (partials 1-6)

However the tonal system does not make use of all the sounds that occur in the overtone series. The partials shown by black noteheads in Example 2-6 (7, 11, 13, and 14) do not form part of major or minor scales, and their notation in the example is only an approximation of their true pitch. Furthermore, some of the important elements of tonal music—the minor triad, for example—do not relate directly to the overtone series.

The significance of the overtone series for the theory of tonal music is a matter of controversy. In the past, many theorists went to absurd extremes in their attempt to use the series as a "scientific" basis for music, contorting it in various ways to extract a minor triad from it and making it the basis for arbitrary "rules" of composition—rules that no great composer has ever followed. And even where the series and the tonal system correspond very closely—as with the major triad—there is no proof that the acoustical relationship causes the musical one.

Nowadays most musicians would maintain that the foundations for music theory should lie in the works of great composers, not in the laboratories of acousticians. But the following characteristics can be observed in the works of the great composers of tonal music:

1. The major triad functions as the most stable chord. From the Renaissance on, composers showed a marked preference for the major triad as final chord even in modes containing the minor 3rd. This tendency was strongest in the earlier stages of triadic music, but it never died out altogether.
2. In major-minor tonality, the major mode is normally the positive, happy, bright one, and the minor is the negative, sad, dark one. This again points to the greater stability of the major triad.
3. Two tones a 5th apart are in a particularly close relation.
4. The most stable intervals are the octave, 5th, and 3rd (the major 3rd more so than the minor).
5. A triad is generated from its root, or lowest tone, much as overtones are generated from the fundamental.

All these characteristics are at least compatible with the view that some of the most important features of tonality give expression to relationships that are inherent in a single musical tone. As noted before, it is impossible to demonstrate a causal connection between the overtone series and these aspects of tonal music. But if it is a coincidence, it is a most remarkable one.

CONSONANCE AND DISSONANCE

6. **Stable and unstable intervals.** Some intervals produce the impression of stability; others, the effect of activity or tension. We call the stable intervals *conso-*

nances or *consonant intervals*; the unstable ones are *dissonant.* The consonant intervals are:

> the perfect unison
> the perfect octave
> the perfect 5th
> the perfect 4th (sometimes)
> major and minor 3rds
> major and minor 6ths

The dissonant intervals are:

> all 2nds
> all 7ths
> all augmented and diminished intervals
> the perfect 4th (sometimes)

For the moment, in discussing consonance and dissonance, we will concentrate on vertical intervals, those whose tones sound simultaneously. Melodic intervals can also be characterized as consonant or dissonant, as we will discuss in later units.

7. The consonant intervals. In major-minor tonality, the consonant intervals are the unison and octave, plus all the intervals that make up major and minor triads. The most stable triadic intervals are those that lie between the lowest tone (root) of a triad and one of the upper tones; these are the perfect 5th, the major 3rd, and the minor 3rd. The remaining consonances—the major 6th, the minor 6th, and the perfect 4th—result from the inversion of the more stable ones. Example 2-7 illustrates the consonant intervals in an order that proceeds from the more to the less stable.

2-7

consonant intervals

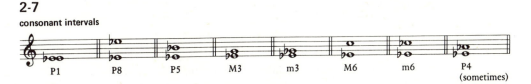

The unison and octave are the most stable of all the consonances; in the unison the two tones agree completely and in the octave they differ only in register. The lack of tension in these intervals is reflected in the tendency of composers to end pieces on unisons or octaves.

Next comes the perfect 5th. In music based on the triad, the 5th is uniquely important, for its upper tone defines the lower one as the root of a chord. Thus if we hear the bare 5th F-C, we understand F as the root, for F-C occurs in no triads except F major and F minor, in both of which F is the root. And since our feeling for key rests in part on the stability of the tones of the tonic triad, the 5th between $\hat{1}$ and $\hat{5}$ plays a most significant role in defining the key.

Composers have tended to treat the major triad as more stable than the minor. The major 3rd, therefore, which characterizes the major triad, is a more stable interval than the minor 3rd, which characterizes the minor triad. Both 3rds are more active intervals than the 5th.

Still more active are the major and minor 6ths, inversions of the 3rds. Differences in stability between the two kinds of 6th are not particularly significant. Their fluid character is reflected in the fact they are not used to end pieces except for special and unusual effects.

The perfect 4th—the only interval that is sometimes consonant and sometimes dissonant—is in a category of its own and will be discussed in section 11.

8. Perfect and imperfect consonances. We call unisons, octaves, and 5ths *perfect consonances*; we call major and minor 3rds and 6ths *imperfect consonances*. In two-part textures (music containing two melodic lines), composers prefer the more stable perfect consonances for important *points of articulation*—beginnings and endings of phrases, sections, or pieces. Because of their less stable, more fluid character, the imperfect consonances normally predominate in places where the music moves from one point of articulation to another. In textures of more than two parts, imperfect consonances tend to occur between the highest and the lowest parts (the most prominent lines), except at points of articulation.

9. The dissonant intervals. Unlike the consonances, all of which form part of major or minor triads and therefore function as chordal elements, dissonant intervals between two parts arise out of melodic activity in one or both of the parts. In Unit 1, section 9, we saw that *passing tones* move by step from one stable tone to another and that *neighboring tones* arise from the stepwise decoration of a single tone. In Example 2-8, the passing and neighboring tones in one part create dissonant intervals between the two parts.

2-8

All the dissonant intervals in Example 2-8 arise out of stepwise motion. This is a fundamental characteristic of dissonance treatment in tonal music. Approaching and leaving the dissonance by step ensures a close connection between it and the surrounding consonances. The stepwise connection channels the tension and energy of the dissonant intervals so that dissonance becomes a powerful force for musical direction. On the other hand, isolated dissonances—those without a close connection to consonances—run the risk of creating tensions that serve no musical purpose because they lead to no goals.

10. Dissonance and activity. In Unit 1, we saw that $\hat{2}$, $\hat{4}$, $\hat{6}$, and $\hat{7}$ function as active tones tending to move to $\hat{1}$, $\hat{3}$, and $\hat{5}$. The division of scale degrees into stable and active tones relates directly to the phenomenon of consonance and dissonance, for the active tones are those that form dissonances with one or more tones of the tonic chord, whereas $\hat{1}$, $\hat{3}$, and $\hat{5}$ (the tonic chord) are all consonant with each other. The simplest and most basic use of consonance and dissonance, therefore, would be $\hat{1}$, $\hat{3}$, and $\hat{5}$ as consonances and the other scale degrees as dissonances against the other part or parts (Example 2-9).

$\hat{4}$, $\hat{2}$, and $\hat{7}$ form dissonances

For composers to restrict themselves to the simplest possibilities, however, would be far too limiting. A most important compositional resource, therefore, is stabilizing the normally active tones by giving them the support of consonant intervals; at the same time, normally stable tones may become unstable by appearing as dissonances (Example 2-10). Note that $\hat{4}$, $\hat{2}$, and $\hat{7}$, the active tones stabilized by consonant support, do not altogether lose their active character, as we can ascertain by playing the example and stopping on one of those tones. The music does not sound at rest until it arrives at the final $\hat{1}$.

active $\hat{4}$, $\hat{2}$, and $\hat{7}$ given consonant support

11. The perfect 4th. In the early stages of medieval polyphony, the perfect consonances formed the basis for music composition. Not only unisons, octaves, and 5ths, but perfect 4ths as well, functioned as stable intervals.

Over the course of several centuries, composers experimented with the possibilities made available through the use of 3rds and 6ths; the most important of these possibilities were the complete triads, major and minor, that became the basis for later music. Using complete triads effected a fundamental change in musical structure; one consequence of this change threatened the consonant status of the 4th. Once the 3rd became a pervasive element in musical texture, many situations arose in which the 4th sounded less like an inversion of the 5th—and thus a more or less stable interval—than like an active interval gravitating to the 3rd. In such situations, the 4th takes on the character of a dissonance (Example 2-11).

dissonant 4ths

However if the 4th occurs in close proximity to the 5th of which it is an inversion, it sounds perfectly stable and consonant; it has no tendency to move to a 3rd. The same is true in situations where the 4th appears in the course of an arpeggiated triad. Example 2-12 illustrates the 4th as a stable, consonant interval.

2-12   consonant 4ths

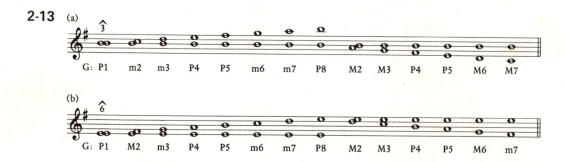

Unlike any other interval, therefore, the 4th is sometimes consonant, sometimes dissonant. It is consonant whenever the context shows it to function as an inverted 5th; otherwise it is dissonant. In simple textures, the 4th is mostly dissonant when it occurs in a two-part setting or between the lowest part and one of the upper ones in a setting of more than two parts.

INTERVALS IN A KEY

12. Intervals between scale degrees. Using the tones that belong to the major or the natural minor scales, we can produce the following intervals: perfect unisons and octaves, perfect and diminished 5ths, perfect and augmented 4ths, major and minor 3rds and 6ths, and major and minor 2nds and 7ths. No other intervals can be generated from these tones. Example 2-13a lists the intervals that contain $\hat{3}$ in G major, and 2-13b lists those that contain $\hat{6}$ in the same key. The two groups of intervals are almost the same, but not quite: $\hat{3}$ forms a minor 2nd and major 7th, whereas $\hat{6}$ does not. The fact is that every scale degree generates a unique collection of intervals; thus each tone of the diatonic scale has its own distinctive character.

2-13   (a)

| G: | P1 | m2 | m3 | P4 | P5 | m6 | m7 | P8 | M2 | M3 | P4 | P5 | M6 | M7 |

(b)

| G: | P1 | M2 | m3 | P4 | P5 | m6 | m7 | P8 | M2 | M3 | P4 | P5 | M6 | m7 |

13. The diminished 5th and augmented 4th in major. Among the intervals found in major and in natural minor are six perfect 5ths and six perfect 4ths (inversions of the 5ths). But there is only one diminished 5th and only one augmented 4th. In major, the diminished 5th occurs between $\hat{7}$ and $\hat{4}$; the augmented 4th, between $\hat{4}$ and $\hat{7}$. In Unit 1, we saw that $\hat{4}$ and $\hat{7}$ gravitate to the stable tones $\hat{3}$

and $\hat{1}$ owing to the particularly intense character of the half-step relationship. When $\hat{4}$ and $\hat{7}$ occur at the same time, their melodic tendencies remain; in fact, they are considerably enhanced by the tension of the dissonant interval they form. The motion of a dissonant interval to the consonance that acts as its goal is called a *resolution.* The diminished 5th resolves by moving in to a 3rd; the augmented 4th resolves by moving out to a 6th (Example 2-14).

2-14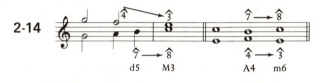

The resolution of the diminished 5th and augmented 4th to $\hat{1}$ and $\hat{3}$ creates a strong drive toward the tonic triad and helps to orient the listener as to the position of the tonic; for this reason we call it a *key-defining progression.* The key-defining function of these intervals is connected with the fact that any particular diminished 5th or augmented 4th occurs in only one major key. Thus, the minor 2nd E-F occurs in two major keys: C and F; the major 3rd C-E occurs in three: C, F, and G. But the diminished 5th B-F (and the augmented 4th F-B), unlike any other interval, occurs in one major key alone—the key of C.

Traditionally, the augmented 4th is called the *tritone,* which means three whole steps, thus: F-G, G-A, and A-B. (Strictly speaking, the diminished 5th is not a tritone, for it contains not three whole steps but a diatonic half step, two whole steps, and another diatonic half step: B-C, C-D, D-E, and E-F. However, for convenience, the term tritone is often used to mean the diminished 5th as well as the augmented 4th.)

14. The diminished 5th and augmented 4th in minor. In the natural minor, the diminished 5th lies between $\hat{2}$ and $\hat{6}$, the augmented 4th between $\hat{6}$ and $\hat{2}$. They resolve to $\hat{3}$ and $\hat{5}$, expressed as a 3rd (resolution of diminished 5th) or as a 6th (resolution of augmented 4th). Although $\hat{3}$ and $\hat{5}$ are members of the tonic triad, these resolutions do not define the key nearly as successfully as do the corresponding resolutions to $\hat{1}$ and $\hat{3}$ in major. When $\hat{3}$ and $\hat{5}$ are heard without $\hat{1}$, $\hat{3}$ tends to be heard as the root of a triad. Thus the progression shown in Example 2-15 suggests E♭ as tonic rather than C. It is partly because of this implication that the minor mode tends to gravitate to its mediant degree (or relative major).

2-15

does *not* define c

Raising $\hat{7}$ in the harmonic and melodic minor creates an "artificial" tritone between $\hat{4}$ and $\hat{7}$ that resolves to $\hat{1}$ and $\hat{3}$ as in major. The use of this tritone (or diminished 5th) lends to minor the clear definition of the key that occurs naturally in major (Example 2-16).

2-16

defines c

The raised $\hat{6}$ of the ascending melodic minor scale creates another tritone, in this case with $\hat{3}$. This tritone occurs much less often than the other two and has no significant influence on key definition.

15. The diminished 7th and augmented 2nd. The interval between raised $\hat{7}$ and natural $\hat{6}$ in the harmonic minor is a diminished 7th; inverted, it becomes an augmented 2nd. Like all diminished and augmented intervals, these are dissonant. As Example 2-17 indicates, they resolve to $\hat{1}$ and $\hat{5}$. The diminished 7th is the more useful of the two intervals, for it resolves to a 5th. The interval of the 4th, to which the augmented 2nd resolves, is itself often dissonant. Therefore the augmented 2nd cannot occur very freely; as a rule, it is used in those situations where the 4th to which it resolves is consonant.

2-17

This pair of dissonant intervals has a very strong key-defining power. The resolution to $\hat{1}$ and $\hat{5}$ unmistakably points out the location of the tonic. Furthermore, among the intervals in major and minor scales, the diminished 7th and augmented 2nd appear *only* between raised $\hat{7}$ and natural $\hat{6}$. Thus the diminished 7th C♯-B♭, for example, immediately points to D as tonic, for no other tonic can generate this particular interval. Because of its powers of key definition, the diminished 7th often appears in major as a consequence of mixture (see Unit 1, section 21). We can bring the diminished 7th C♯-B♭ into the key of D major by introducing B♭, $\hat{6}$ of the parallel minor (Example 2-17c).

16. The remaining intervals. We have already mentioned most of the intervals that are significant in the study of music theory. Of those not yet mentioned, one pair, the augmented 5th and diminished 4th, occurs in the inflected forms of minor; these intervals arise from the combination of $\hat{3}$ and raised $\hat{7}$ (Example 2-18).

2-18

Another pair, the diminished 3rd and augmented 6th, is the product of chromaticism. These intervals normally come about as a consequence of raising $\hat{4}$ in minor; the intervals between raised $\hat{4}$ and natural $\hat{6}$ are the diminished 3rd and augmented 6th. As Example 2-19 indicates, raised $\hat{4}$ functions as a lower neighbor to $\hat{5}$ or as a chromatic passing tone leading from $\hat{4}$ to $\hat{5}$.

Chromaticism sometimes produces other intervals, but they are of less significance. The diminished octave and augmented 3rd of Example 2-20 are formed by melodic ornamentation in one of the parts; the intervals are mere byproducts of this ornamentation.

17. Enharmonically equivalent intervals. On the piano, we depress the same key to produce C♯ and D♭, A♮ and B♭♭, and so on. In order to facilitate playing in all keys and to make possible an extensive use of chromaticism, keyboard instruments are tuned to the *equally tempered scale,* a scale that divides the octave into twelve equal semitones. Tempered tuning eliminates the minute differences in pitch between, say, G♯ and A♭ or B♯ and C♮. In tempered tuning, two tones that have the same pitch but that are notated differently are called *enharmonic equivalents.* The use of enharmonically equivalent tones makes it possible to construct two intervals of different size and quality, but whose tones have the same pitch in tempered tuning. Example 2-21a shows some of these enharmonically equivalent intervals. In isolation, an interval is indistinguishable from its enharmonic equivalent. In context, however, the two can sound very different indeed (2-21b).

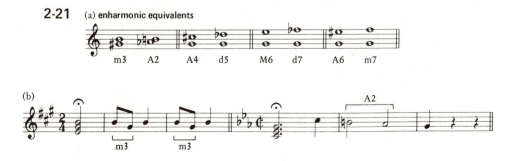

EXERCISES

1. Construct the following intervals above D: m2, M3, A4, d5, m6, M7, P8, m10, A2, P5. Do the same thing above F♯ and E♭.
2. Construct the following intervals below G: P4, A6, d7, A3, M2, m7, M6, m9, M10, m3. Do the same thing below C♯ and A♭.
3. Name the following intervals:

4. Name the inversions of the intervals in Exercise 3.
5. Name the major keys in which the following intervals would occur:

6. Name the minor keys in which the following intervals would occur:

7. The overtone series. Memorize the series starting on Great C at least as far as the 8th partial and preferably through the 16th. Then, write the series on other tones, as below. Proceed either by interval above the fundamental (P8, P5, P8, M3, P5, m7, and so on) or by melodic interval from one partial to the next (P8, P5, P4, M3, m3, m3, and so on). The method not initially chosen can be used to check your results.
   a. Write the series up through the 16th partial, starting on Contra G♭.
   b. Write the series of which g^1 is the 10th partial.
   c. Write the series of which ab^2 is the 12th partial.
   d. Write the series of which $c\sharp^2$ is the 5th partial.

THREE | RHYTHM AND METER

3-1   Mozart, Piano Concerto, K. 467, II

RHYTHMIC ORGANIZATION

1. The beat. Music moves in time; musical rhythm organizes the flow of time. This organization involves many factors, the most important being duration, accent, and grouping. The basic unit of duration is the pulse or *beat*. A beat is a span of time that recurs regularly; a succession of beats divides the flow of time into equal segments.*

We are aware of the beat even if it is not always expressed in the music. Thus, in the Mozart piano concerto passage of Example 3-1, the quarter note takes the beat. But the music does not move only—or even mainly—in quarter

---

*Actually, the segments are approximately, rather than strictly, equal, for in performance, slight deviations from exact measurement are the rule rather than the exception.

notes. Beats combine into half notes; they divide into eighths, triplets, and sixteenths; and additional time values are produced by dots, double dots, and ties. In the Mozart, we relate these other values to the quarter note as basic unit, so the beat persists as a background against which we hear the varied rhythms of the piece.

The simplest way both to divide and to combine beats is by twos (Example 3-2). Thus a quarter note divides into two eighths, an eighth into two sixteenths, a sixteenth into two thirty-seconds, and so on. Similarly, two quarters combine into a half note and two half notes into a whole note. The division and combination of rests follow exactly the same principle.

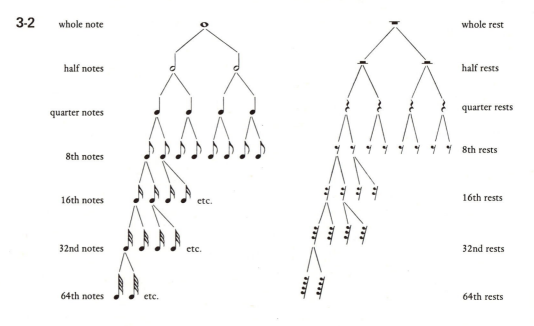

3-2

The use of dots permits more complex divisions and combinations (Example 3-3). A dot following a note or rest adds half its value to it; a second or third dot adds on half the value of the preceding dot.

3-3

A division of the beat into threes (*triplets*) is indicated by the numeral 3 above or below the notes. Other divisions can also be indicated through the use of the appropriate numerals. Example 3-4 shows some possibilities.

3-4

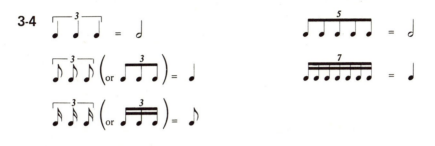

Using *ties* makes it possible to combine notes across a bar line and to create durations that cannot be achieved through note values or dots (Example 3-5). Sometimes two tied notes will replace a single dotted note to make for easier reading or a clearer expression of the rhythmic structure.

3-5   (a)   (b)

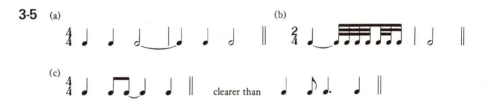

(c)

clearer than

2. Tempo. The musical term for the pace of a composition is *tempo* (Italian, time). In music whose rhythms are based on beats, the impression of a quick, moderate, or slow tempo comes from the pace of the beats, not from the speed of the quickest notes. A slow tempo such as an Adagio or Largo may contain passages in, say, 64th notes that move very quickly indeed. Yet we do not hear a change to a quicker tempo; as long as the beats move slowly, the tempo remains slow. The pace of the beats relates to tonal movement, to the frequency with which chords change, or to the rate of motion of the main tones of the melody.

The fact that music moves at different tempos relates to an important aspect of our notational system: note values indicate relative rather than absolute durations. A quarter note that occupies a beat in a Largo lasts much longer than a quarter note that gets the beat in a Presto. But no matter what the tempo, a quarter note equals two eighths or four sixteenths.

3. Accent. *Accent* means emphasis. A note that receives more emphasis than the ones surrounding it is heard as accented. Accents often arise in performance when a note is stressed by being played more loudly than those around it or when the performer emphasizes the beginning (attack) of the note. Other kinds of accents are, so to speak, built into the composition itself. In general, long notes attract accents, for their long duration creates an emphasis. Unusually high or low notes come across more strongly than those in a normal register. Dissonant or chromatic elements, because of the tensions they create, tend to sound accented compared to consonant or diatonic elements.

4. Meter and metrical accent. A repetitive pattern that combines accented and unaccented beats is called *meter.* Usually we speak of *strong beats* and *weak beats* to distinguish beats with and without accents. If the first of every two beats is strong, the meter is *duple*; if the first of every three is strong, the meter is *triple. Quadruple meter* (derived from duple) has a primary emphasis on the first beat and a weaker emphasis on the third beat of four. In normal musical notation, the bar line appears just before the strong beat; the accent that falls on the first beat of the bar is called the *metrical accent.*

Meters containing five or seven beats are frequent in twentieth-century music and occur occasionally in earlier music. Often these meters result from the combination of duple and triple meter. Changing meters (such as $\frac{2}{8}$, $\frac{3}{8}$, $\frac{3}{16}$, $\frac{5}{8}$, $\frac{4}{8}$, and so on) also occur in a good deal of twentieth-century music—much less often in music of the nineteenth century.

The inner organization of a divided beat mirrors in miniature the metrical organization of a measure. The beginning of a beat is stronger than the subdivisions that follow it. Within a divided quarter note, for example, the accent will fall on the first of two eighths, the first of three triplet eighths, or the first of four sixteenths. If the tempo is slow, the third of four sixteenths may get a subsidiary accent, just like the third beat in a bar of quadruple meter.

5. Time signatures. Composers indicate meter by means of *time signatures* placed at the beginning of a piece after the key signature and at any subsequent point where the meter changes. The time signature contains two numbers, one above the other. The lower number normally indicates the note value of the beat; the upper one indicates the number of beats per measure. Most often the quarter note gets the beat. Therefore duple, triple, and quadruple meter usually have the time signatures $\frac{2}{4}$, $\frac{3}{4}$, and $\frac{4}{4}$ (or its equivalent, **C**). However, composers can suggest the character and, sometimes, the tempo of a piece by using another note value, usually a half note or an eighth, for the beat. Time signatures like $\frac{2}{2}$ (**¢**), $\frac{2}{8}$, $\frac{3}{2}$, $\frac{3}{8}$, $\frac{4}{2}$, and $\frac{4}{8}$ occur frequently.

Some meters contain accentual patterning on more than one level. This is especially true of the so-called *compound meters,* those with beats grouped in multiples of three ($\frac{6}{8}$, $\frac{9}{8}$, $\frac{12}{8}$, $\frac{6}{4}$, and so on). In a bar of $\frac{6}{8}$ time, for instance, the first eighth note of each three receives an accent; the strong eighth notes, therefore, are the first and fourth. At the same time, a larger pattern of half bars is superimposed on this one; of the two dotted quarters in the bar, the first is the stronger. If the tempo is slow, we hear six beats in the bar arranged in two groups of three beats each; the beginning of the first group is stronger than the beginning of the second. If the tempo is quick, however, the $\frac{6}{8}$ has only two real beats; it sounds exactly like $\frac{2}{4}$ with triplet subdivisions.

6. Rhythmic accent versus metrical accent. Very often a composer underscores the metrical accent by making it coincide with some other kind of emphasis. In Example 3-1, long notes appear at the beginnings of bars 1, 2, 4, and 5. At these points, the rhythmic accents caused by longer note values coincide with the metrically strong beats. In general the simplest and most natural kinds of rhythm are those whose emphases fit into the metrical pattern.

Sometimes, however, a rhythmic emphasis contradicts the meter. The presence of a rhythmic accent at a metrically weak place is called *syncopation.* Syncopations arise in various ways; for our purposes the most important are those caused by a note that begins on a weak beat (or part of the beat) and is held through the next strong beat (or part). Since the beginning of a note is heard as stronger than its continuation, a note held from a weak through a strong beat conflicts—sometimes very strongly—with the meter. In Example 3-6 the syncopated notes are those tied over from the third to the first beat; the conflict between rhythmic emphasis and meter is evident.

3-6   Beethoven, Cello Sonata, Op. 69, II

Rhythmic emphases that contradict the meter sometimes set up such a consistent pattern of their own that we hear a temporary change of meter. A passage from Brahms's violin concerto sounds as if it is in $\frac{5}{4}$ time, though the composer continues to notate the section in the basic $\frac{3}{4}$ meter of the movement (Example 3-7).

3-7   Brahms, Violin Concerto, Op. 77, I

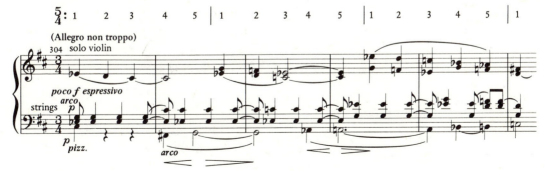

In triple and compound meters, shifted accents sometimes transform two groups of three beats into three groups of two beats. Such is the case in bars 8 and 9 of the Mozart sonata quoted in Example 3-8; the two bars of $\frac{3}{4}$ sound like a larger bar of $\frac{3}{2}$. The technical name for this rhythmic device is *hemiola*.

3-8 Mozart, Piano Sonata, K. 283, I

7. Rhythmic groups. Musical tones coalesce into small figures or *rhythmic groups*; such groups form an important element in the design of a composition. Sometimes, as in the opening melody of our Mozart C major sonata, rhythmic groups begin on a strong part of the measure (Example 3-9a). Often, however, they begin on an unaccented beat, as in the opening of another Mozart sonata (3-9b). Longer rhythmic groups are frequent, sometimes extending for more than a bar (Example 3-10). And one rhythmic group can merge into another; this happens when the last note of one also functions as the first note of the next. Such groups are said to *overlap* (Example 3-11).

3-9 (a) Mozart, K. 545, I

(b) Mozart, K. 283, I

3-10 Mozart, K. 545, II

3-11 Mendelssohn, Song Without Words, Op. 85/4

8. Measure groups and phrases. The principle of meter—regular and periodic groupings of weak and strong beats—often extends to groups of measures. Thus in a group of four measures, the first and third will normally be heard as strong compared to the second and fourth. The two excerpts shown in Example 3-9 can serve as illustrations. The normal organization of measure groups is duple; as in Examples 3-9 and 3-10, strong and weak measures alternate. However grouping in threes is also possible (Example 3-12).

3-12 Beethoven, Bagatelle, Op. 126/6

Very often the end of a group of measures coincides with a goal of tonal motion. In such cases the group is tonal as well as rhythmic, and we call it a *phrase*. In Example 3-13, the arrival at the tonic in the eighth bar signals the end of the phrase.

3-13 Beethoven, Piano Sonata, Op. 14/1, II

Phrases of eight bars, as in Example 3-13, are very common; so are four-bar phrases. But other groupings often occur, including asymmetrical ones of five or seven bars (Example 3-14).

3-14   **Schubert, Impromptu, Op. 90/1**

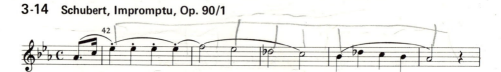

RHYTHM AND DISSONANCE TREATMENT

9. Dissonance, duration, and accent. The effective functioning of a dissonant element depends on its relation to the consonances surrounding it. We have already seen that dissonances normally arise out of stepwise motion; this rule governs the melodic aspect of dissonance treatment. There is a rhythmic aspect as well: dissonances tend to occur in notes of relatively brief duration and (with one important exception) in metrically unaccented places. This rhythmic aspect of dissonance treatment is of particular importance in the polyphonic music of the Renaissance, a period when composers subjected dissonance to stringent controls.

In and after the Baroque period, from about 1600 on, composers became more willing to extend the duration and highlight the prominence of dissonances. Nevertheless, brief duration and placement on unaccented beats remained the norm. Thus passing and neighboring tones—the types of dissonance we have already encountered—will normally appear on weak beats or weak parts of divided beats. When they appear in a strong metric position we call them *accented* passing or neighboring tones. Accented incomplete neighbors are frequently called *appoggiaturas*. Example 3-15 illustrates.

3-15

*accented passing tone   *accented neighbor   *appoggiaturas

10. Suspensions. One important type of dissonance, however, almost always appears in metrically accented positions; we call it the *suspension*. Suspensions originated as a consequence of syncopation. Tones in one part are shifted out of their normal rhythmic position with their beginning displaced from the strong beat to the following weak one; consequently they extend through the next strong beat. Example 3-16 shows how this process introduces dissonances (7ths) into a passage that consists, basically, of 6ths.

Suspensions also result from lengthening a tone so that it usurps part of the duration of the following tone (Example 3-17a). Or the suspended tone can be struck again rather than held over (3-17b). And in a texture of more than two parts, a suspension can delay the appearance of one of the tones belonging to a chord (Example 3-18).

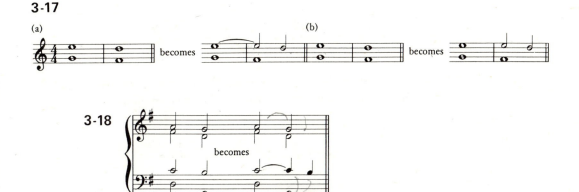

11. Anticipations. Syncopation can also give rise to unaccented dissonances. If a tone is shifted out of its normal rhythmic position by beginning *before* the strong beat, a dissonance can arise. We call such a tone an *anticipation* (Example 3-19). Anticipations are not always held over into the consonance that follows; often, the main tone is restruck. In textures of three and more parts, a chordal tone—most often in the highest part—can be anticipated. Example 3-20 shows both possibilities.

EXERCISES

1. Add bar lines to the following examples. None of the three begins with a complete measure; the final measure, also, may be incomplete.

(a)

(b)

(c)

2. Add rests to the following examples where indicated by x's. Some of the x's may indicate more than one rest. The final bar must be complete.

(a)

(b)

(c)

3. The following examples are melodic fragments from the literature. Supply time signatures and bar lines, bearing in mind that neither the opening nor the final measures are necessarily complete. Finally, supply a tempo you consider appropriate.

(a) Beethoven

(b) Haydn

(c) Mozart

(d) Mendelssohn

FOUR | TRIADS AND SEVENTH CHORDS

4-1   Clementi, Piano Sonatina, Op. 36/2, I

(a)

(b) **reduction**

TRIADS

1. The triad as basic chord. Example 4-1 shows a phrase from a sonatina by Clementi. Under the music is a *reduction* (simplification) of its contents, with the left-hand part written in block chords and only the most essential tones of the melody shown. The purpose of this reduction is to help us concentrate on the chords that occur in this phrase. As Example 4-2 shows, the chords are of three types, which are determined by the intervals between the lowest tone and the upper ones. Omitting octaves (which merely duplicate one of the other tones) we find the following intervals:

1. 5th and 3rd
2. 6th and 3rd
3. 6th and 4th

The arabic numerals written under the chords refer to these intervals.

4-2

Only the first of these types is a triad as defined in Unit 1: a three-tone chord consisting of a 5th and 3rd above the lowest tone. But the other two types are derived from triads. In this unit we will discuss how the triad—the basic chord of tonal music—generates other consonant and dissonant chords.

2. Triad qualities. As we know, triads consist of two intervals—a *5th* and a *3rd*—above the lowest tone (the *root*). Since there are different kinds—or qualities—of 5ths and 3rds, there are different qualities of triads. Example 4-3 shows the four types of triads, which are followed by a summary of their qualities.

4-3   **triad types**

(a)	(b)	(c)	(d)
P5 M3	P5 m3	d5 m3	A5 M3
major	minor	diminished	augmented

<table>
<tr><td colspan="3" align="center">TRIADS</td></tr>
<tr><td>triad quality</td><td>5th quality</td><td>3rd quality</td></tr>
<tr><td>major</td><td>perfect</td><td>major</td></tr>
<tr><td>minor</td><td>perfect</td><td>minor</td></tr>
<tr><td>diminished</td><td>diminished</td><td>minor</td></tr>
<tr><td>augmented</td><td>augmented</td><td>major</td></tr>
</table>

Of the four qualities, the major and minor are by far the most important; because they contain only consonant intervals (perfect 5ths, major and minor 3rds), they are consonant chords. Diminished and augmented triads are dissonant because each contains a dissonant interval—a diminished or augmented 5th. Of the two dissonant triads only the diminished has any importance for the beginning stages of music theory.

3. The use of roman numerals. The chordal vocabulary of tonal music has as its basis a group of seven triads, each constructed on a different degree of the diatonic scale. Example 4-4 shows this group of triads in the key of C major. Note that the group contains three major triads, three minor triads, and one diminished triad.

4-4   triads in major

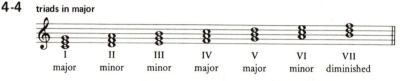

As we saw in Unit 1, the major triad is the most stable of all chords. If music were merely a succession of stable, well-balanced chords, it might well contain nothing but major triads. But such a procedure would contradict the unity and continuity that form an essential aspect of musical composition. In D major, for example, if the chords on F♯ and B were expressed as major triads, they would contain the tones A♯ and D♯, tones that do not belong to the D major scale and that would conflict with the D♮ and A♮ of the tonic triad. In order to avoid such contradictions, the basic chordal vocabulary of tonal music confines itself to diatonic elements—those belonging to the scale.

The roman numerals under the chords in Example 4-4 designate the scale degrees on which the triads are built. These scale degrees are the roots or fundamental tones of the triads. (Remember that the roman numerals refer to scale degrees only as the roots of chords, not as elements in a melodic line; for the latter purpose we use the capped arabic numerals.

Here are the seven major-scale triads grouped in terms of qualities:

major triads	I, IV, and V
minor triads	II, III, and VI
diminished triad	VII

4. Triads in natural minor. Example 4-5 shows the triads on the degrees of the C minor scale. Note that each triad's quality differs from that of the corresponding triad in major.

4-5   triads in natural minor

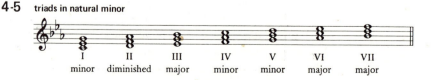

Here are the minor-scale triads grouped in terms of qualities:

minor triads	I, IV, and V
major triads	III, VI, and VII
diminished triad	II

Note that I, IV, and V are major triads in the major mode and minor triads in the minor mode. The characteristic color of each mode comes not only from the quality of the tonic triad—though that is the most important factor—but also from the fact that IV and V, the other major triads in the major mode, are minor triads in the minor mode.

5. Triads in the inflected forms of minor. The lack of a leading tone in the natural minor makes it necessary to raise $\hat{7}$ whenever a motion to $\hat{1}$ is expected; the raising of $\hat{7}$ frequently necessitates raising $\hat{6}$ to avoid the awkward melodic interval of an augmented 2nd (see Unit 1, sections 15-17). When $\hat{7}$ and $\hat{6}$ occur as members of chords, raising them changes the quality of the chords. Example 4-6 shows the three chords containing $\hat{7}$ in its raised form. The qualities of these chords are: *harmonic minor*

III	augmented
V	major
VII	diminished

4-6   triads with raised $\hat{7}$

c: III   V   VII
augmented   major   diminished

Note that V and VII become just the same as in the parallel major key, reinforcing the idea that the inflected forms of minor result from mixture with major. As an augmented triad, III is more visible in harmony books than audible in real music. The basic form of III as it occurs in composition—a major rather than an augmented triad—is the one derived from the natural form of minor. On the other hand, V and VII occur frequently in both forms; in fact they occur more frequently with raised than with natural $\hat{7}$.

Example 4-7 illustrates what happens to II, IV, and VI when $\hat{6}$ is raised. The chords become: *melodic minor*

II	minor
IV	major
VI	diminished

4-7   triads with raised $\hat{6}$

c: II   IV   VI
minor   major   diminished

II, IV, and VI with raised $\hat{6}$ occasionally make a fleeting appearance in musical compositions. But the characteristic form of these chords is the one with natural $\hat{6}$. The following summary shows the qualities of triads in minor and indicates the typical usage of each.

		TRIADS IN MINOR	
	in natural minor		*other quality*
I	minor		none
II	diminished		minor (with raised $\hat{6}$)—infrequent
III	major		augmented (with raised $\hat{7}$)—infrequent
IV	minor		major (with raised $\hat{6}$)—infrequent
V	minor		major (with raised $\hat{7}$)—very frequent
VI	major		diminished (with raised $\hat{6}$)—infrequent
VII	major		diminished (with raised $\hat{7}$)—very frequent

The problematic character of minor compared with major is reflected in the presence of these alternative forms of triads—especially of V and VII. Only as we begin to work with these chords will we be able to learn how to use the two forms of V and VII. But the basic principle is simple: a motion to $\hat{1}$, or the expectation of such a motion, requires the raising of $\hat{7}$ and the accompanying change in the quality of V and VII.

6. Triads in inversion. The normal position of the triad, with the root as the lowest tone, is called the *root position.* Like intervals, however, triads can be *inverted.* A triad is in inversion when a tone other than the root is the lowest. If the 3rd of the triad is the lowest tone, the triad is in *first inversion*; if the 5th is the lowest tone, the triad is in *second inversion.* Whether a triad is in root position or one of the inversions depends solely on which tone is the lowest; the upper tones can be in any position (Example 4-8).

4-8   triad inversions

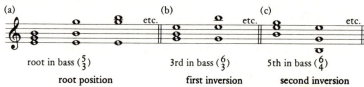

root in bass ($\frac{5}{3}$)   3rd in bass ($\frac{6}{3}$)   5th in bass ($\frac{6}{4}$)

root position   first inversion   second inversion

Just as the 3rd G-B and its inversion, the 6th B-G, form a pair of related intervals, so do the triad G-B-D and its inversions, B-D-G and D-G-B, form a group of related chords. And just as a 3rd and a 6th, though related, are not completely equivalent (the 6th is less stable), so, too, a root-position triad and its inversions are by no means completely equivalent. Learning to distinguish their various functions will form a significant part of later units.

7. $\frac{5}{3}$, $\frac{6}{3}$, and $\frac{6}{4}$ chords; figured bass. We know that the intervals between the lowest and the upper tones of a root-position triad are a 5th and 3rd. As Example 4-8

shows, the intervals between lowest and upper tones in a first-inversion triad are a 6th and a 3rd; in a second-inversion triad, they are a 6th and a 4th. Musicians frequently use the term *five-three chord* (written $\frac{5}{3}$) when referring to a triad in root position. The terms *six-three chord* ($\frac{6}{3}$) and *six-four chord* ($\frac{6}{4}$) denote triads in first and second inversion.

This terminology comes from the old practice of *figured bass,* sometimes called *thorough bass.* During the Baroque period, composers did not normally write out the accompaniments to solos and ensemble music, but indicated them instead in a kind of musical shorthand. The accompanist (usually a keyboard player) would play from a part containing the bass line of the composition; the bass line was supplemented by numbers (or figures, hence figured bass). The numbers denote intervals above the bass that indicate the chords the accompanist must play. Thus the sign $\frac{6}{4}$ indicates that the bass tone and a 6th and 4th above it are to be played at the same time. The resulting chord would be a $\frac{6}{4}$ chord. Often the figures are abbreviated. Triads in root position occur so frequently that the symbol $\frac{5}{3}$ is usually omitted; the omission also reflects the fact that a bass tone, heard alone, tends to sound like a root. If the lowest tone of a chord is not figured, therefore, the chord is a $\frac{5}{3}$. Also the symbol $\frac{6}{3}$ is frequently shortened to 6. Sometimes other symbols—sharps or flats, for example—modify the figures.

By means of the figured bass the composer indicated the essentials of the accompaniment, but in the execution (or "realization"), many of the details were left to the accompanist, who would sometimes contribute extensive improvised elaborations. People trained to play from a figured bass, therefore, received an excellent preparation for improvisation and for composition. And long after composers stopped including figured-bass accompaniments (or *continuo* parts) in their compositions, they used the figured bass in their preliminary sketches. Indeed, realizing figured basses both on paper and at the keyboard is an incomparably useful and convenient way to master the basic materials and procedures of tonal music.

Example 4-9 shows the basic figured-bass symbols for $\frac{5}{3}$, $\frac{6}{3}$, and $\frac{6}{4}$ chords. During the time that figured bass was an essential part of musical performance, a variety of symbols were used at different times and places or by different composers.* The procedures we follow in this book are fairly standard:

1. Key signatures apply to figures as well as to notes.
2. Modifications of key signatures (accidentals) are indicated by the appropriate sign ($\flat$, $\natural$, $\sharp$, $\flat\flat$, and so on) next to the figure.
3. An accidental standing alone (not next to a figure) always affects the third above the bass.
4. Sometimes the raising of a tone is indicated by a slash through the figure ($\cancel{6}$) or a little vertical line (4, 2, or 5) rather than by a $\sharp$ or $\natural$.
5. Figures do not specify the arrangement of the upper voices. Thus a $\frac{6}{4}$ chord can be played with either the 6th or the 4th on top; the choice is the accompanist's.

*For an exhaustive account of figured-bass practice see one of the standard works dealing specifically with figured bass. An excellent source is F. T. Arnold, *The Art of Accompaniment from a Thorough-Bass* (Oxford: Oxford University Press, 1931), reprinted in two volumes (New York: Dover, 1965).

4-9   **figured-bass symbols**

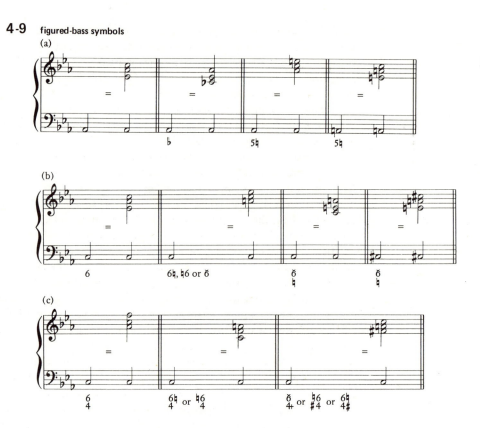

8. $\frac{6}{3}$ and $\frac{6}{4}$ chords as products of melodic motion. It is convenient to think of $\frac{6}{3}$ and $\frac{6}{4}$ chords as inversions of root-position triads. Quite often, however, the context in which these chords occur makes another explanation far more musically convincing. Look at Example 4-10, the first two bars of the slow movement from a Schubert piano sonata. The movement is in D major, and D is the first bass tone we hear. Since this tone happens to be the tonic, it would make little sense to understand the opening chord as an inversion of a B minor triad. Instead one hears the B of the melody as a tone that ornaments and delays A, the 5th of the tonic triad. In this situation, therefore, the $\frac{6}{3}$ chord D-F♯-B results from melodic activity in one of the parts rather than from chord inversion.

4-10   **Schubert, Piano Sonata, D. 664, II**

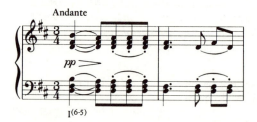

I(6-5)

What the Schubert excerpt indicates is that $\frac{6}{3}$ chords—and the same is true of $\frac{6}{4}$'s—can derive from $\frac{5}{3}$'s through melodic motion above a stationary bass as well as through inversion. Example 4-11 shows these two contrasting possibilities. It also shows how such melodic motions are indicated in figured bass: by figures placed next to each other horizontally above a stationary bass tone. Such figures (5-6, 6-5, $\frac{5}{3}$-$\frac{6}{4}$-$\frac{5}{3}$) are normally executed by keeping the melodic motions in the same voice or pair of voices.

4-11   (a)   (b)

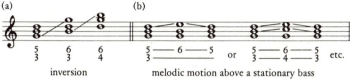

$\begin{matrix} 5 \\ 3 \end{matrix}$ $\begin{matrix} 6 \\ 3 \end{matrix}$ $\begin{matrix} 6 \\ 4 \end{matrix}$ $\frac{5}{3}$ —— 6 —— 5   or $\frac{5}{3}$ —— $\frac{6}{4}$ —— $\frac{5}{3}$ etc.

        inversion   melodic motion above a stationary bass

9. Harmonic analysis. Chordal analysis by roman numerals or the system of figured bass follows different principles. Roman numerals indicate the *roots* of chords and the scale degrees on which they fall. Figured-bass symbols are calculated from the *bass tones,* not the roots, so that we do not need to think of the chord roots in order to realize a figured bass. But it is possible to combine elements from both approaches; the roots can be indicated by means of roman numerals, and the inversions, if any, by figured-bass symbols. Thus, E-G-C in C major would be I⁶—I because the root is C and 6 because the chord is in $\frac{6}{3}$ position. Example 4-12 consists of a short chord progression in C major; underneath the progression is a *harmonic analysis* that combines roman numerals and figured-bass symbols.

4-12

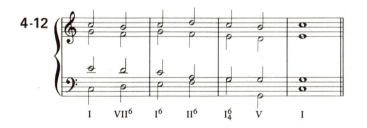

    I   VII⁶   I⁶   II⁶   I$_4^6$ V   I

This kind of harmonic analysis is the usual one, and it is useful up to a point. However, such an analysis has serious limitations, one of which we can already perceive. Placing a roman numeral under each chord implies that all the $\frac{6}{3}$ and $\frac{6}{4}$ chords are the products of inversion. But we have already seen that some of these chords arise from melodic motion over a stationary bass. In such cases—and they are very frequent—a harmonic analysis like the one shown in Example 4-12 can be misleading, for it ignores the origin, behavior, and function of some of the chords. In general, the further you advance in the study of theory, the less need you will find for analysis by roman numeral.

Theorists follow two different approaches in naming the tones of inverted chords; Example 4-13 illustrates these approaches. In discussing a $\frac{6}{3}$ chord, for instance, some refer to the tones as "3rd, 5th, and root," just as if the chord were in root position (4-13a). Others, following a figured-bass approach, name the tones from the bass and call them "bass, 3rd, and 6th" (4-13b). In general, we follow the second approach. Our reason is the fact—already familiar—that F is the "root" of A-C-F only when that chord is the product of inversion, not when it comes from melodic activity. When the chord clearly functions as an inversion, however, it is sometimes necessary to refer to its "root" or "5th." One can always avoid confusion by specifying "3rd above the bass" or "5th of the root position," and so on.

4-13

10. An easy way to remember triads. In music theory, it is vital to be able to recognize and construct triads instantly and to relate them to major and minor keys. In this connection it helps to remember that only seven combinations of letter names form the intervals of a 5th and a 3rd; only these seven groups, therefore, form triads. They are:

C-E-G   D-F-A   E-G-B   F-A-C   G-B-D   A-C-E   B-D-F

Thus the first sonority shown in Example 4-14 is not a triadic chord, for it cannot be reduced to one of the seven groups. The second one is, however; it can be reduced to B-D♯-F♯ or, without the sharps, to B-D-F.

4-14

SEVENTH CHORDS

11. The melodic origin of seventh chords. All the consonant chords of tonal music are triads in root position or inversion (though not all triads are consonant—diminished and augmented ones are not). Most of the dissonant chords used in tonal music belong to the category of *seventh chords*. The name reflects the fact that all these chords contain the interval of a 7th above the root.

Example 4-15 shows how seventh chords originated. In 4-15a, the 7th is formed by a passing tone that leads down from an octave to the 3rd of the following chord. The figured-bass sign 8-7 symbolizes this motion from the octave through the passing 7th to the following consonance. Around the beginning of the Baroque period, composers began to intensify the effect of the dissonance by omitting the octave and allowing the 7th to occupy the full duration of the chord, a process called *contraction* or *elision*. That the dissonant 7th still represents a passing tone is indicated by the basic rule governing the use of seventh chords: the dissonance moves down by step to resolve (4-15b), just as it would if it were a normal passing tone.

4-15

Every seventh chord consists of a triad plus the interval of a 7th. The triad —especially if it is a major or minor one—is the stable part of the chord. The 7th is the active, unstable, dissonant element that must resolve by stepwise descent.

12. Qualities of seventh chords. The quality of a seventh chord depends on the qualities of the triad and 7th it comprises. And since all seventh chords are unstable and all follow the same basic rule of resolution (the 7th moves down by step), the quality of a seventh chord has less influence on its function than is the case with triads. Example 4-16 lists the most important types of seventh chords; using the names by which they are usually called. The term *dominant seventh* reflects the fact that this chord appears on the 5th degree (dominant) of the major and inflected minor scales; it is the most important of all the seventh chords. A summary of seventh-chord qualities follows the example.

4-16

seventh-chord types

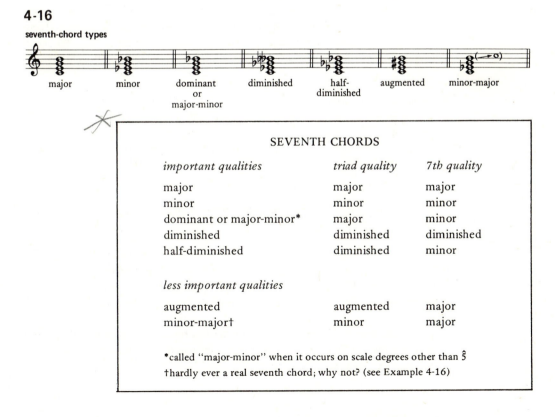

SEVENTH CHORDS

important qualities	triad quality	7th quality
major	major	major
minor	minor	minor
dominant or major-minor*	major	minor
diminished	diminished	diminished
half-diminished	diminished	minor
less important qualities		
augmented	augmented	major
minor-major†	minor	major

*called "major-minor" when it occurs on scale degrees other than $\hat{5}$

†hardly ever a real seventh chord; why not? (see Example 4-16)

13. Seventh chords on scale degrees. Seventh chords, like triads, appear on all degrees of the major and minor scales. Like triads, they are identified by roman numerals (showing roots), but with an arabic 7 added. Thus a seventh chord built on the subdominant would be called IV^7. Example 4-17 shows the seventh chords on the degrees of the E major and C# minor scales. The alternative forms of minor make possible a bewildering array of qualities; we have indicated only the most important possibilities.

4-17

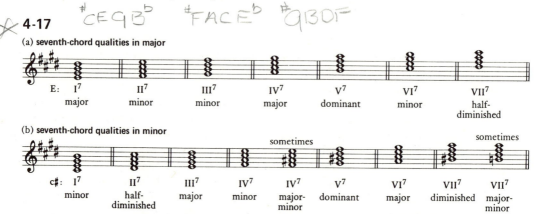

(a) seventh-chord qualities in major

E: I^7 — major II^7 — minor III^7 — minor IV^7 — major V^7 — dominant VI^7 — minor VII^7 — half-diminished

(b) seventh-chord qualities in minor

c#: I^7 — minor II^7 — half-diminished III^7 — major IV^7 — minor IV^7 — major-minor (sometimes) V^7 — dominant VI^7 — major VII^7 — diminished VII^7 — major-minor (sometimes)

14. Inversions of seventh chords. Since seventh chords contain four tones—root, 3rd, 5th, and 7th—they occur in three inversions as well as in root position (Example 4-18). In the first inversion, the 3rd appears as the lowest tone; in the second inversion, the 5th is the lowest tone; in the third inversion, the 7th is lowest.

4-18   seventh-chord inversions

7 — root in bass — root position $^6_5$ — 3rd in bass — first inversion $^4_3$ — 5th in bass — second inversion $^4_2$ — 7th in bass — third inversion

15. Figured-bass symbols for seventh chords. The complete figures for a seventh chord and its inversions are $^7_5{}_3$, $^6_5{}_3$, $^6_4{}_3$, and $^6_4{}_2$. Usually these figures are abbreviated to 7 (sometimes $^7_5$ or $^7_3$), $^6_5$, $^4_3$, and $^4_2$ (or 2). It is easiest to memorize the figures as "seven, six-five, four-three, two," but $^4_2$ is used more frequently than 2 to indicate the third inversion. Sometimes the figure appears in complete rather than abbreviated form—for example, if one of the numbers is modified by a sharp or flat.

Just as with triads, one can indicate the roots of seventh chords by using roman numerals and the root position or inversion by figured-bass symbols. Example 4-19 illustrates.

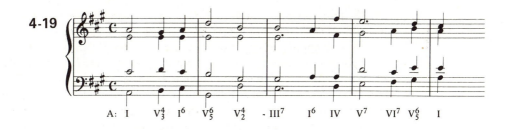

4-19

A: I V$\frac{4}{3}$ I^6 V$\frac{6}{5}$ V$\frac{4}{2}$ - III^7 I^6 IV V^7 VI^7 V$\frac{6}{5}$ I

16. Remembering the seventh chords. Again, as with the triads, only seven combinations of letter names form seventh chords. They are:

C-E-G-B   D-F-A-C   E-G-B-D   F-A-C-E   G-B-D-F   A-C-E-G   B-D-F-A

Note that the first three letters of these groups correspond to the seven triads.

TEXTURE AND STRUCTURE

17. Note-against-note and figurated textures. Music in a simple chordal style usually proceeds in a *note-against-note* texture; all the voices or parts maintain the same rhythm. In the simplest form of this style, only tones that are chord members will appear. Example 4-20 illustrates such a texture. Real music, however, seldom maintains this kind of simplicity for long. More often, the texture will be enlivened by *figuration,* quicker notes in one or more of the parts. These quicker notes sometimes arpeggiate the chord that is sounding at the time; that is, they leap from one chord tone to another. At other times, the play of figuration introduces tones that do not form part of the chord against which they sound. The most important of these figuration tones are the passing tone, neighboring tone (complete and incomplete), suspension, anticipation, and appoggiatura, all of which were discussed in Unit 1 and all of which will frequently appear in the examples of later units. The progression shown in Example 4-21 is the same as the one in 4-20, but the texture is figurated.

4-20 note-against-note texture

4-21 figurated texture

18. The progression of chords. The material in this unit will enable you to recognize and label all the chords that appear frequently in tonal music, except those modified by chromatic alteration. The ability to identify and construct chords is an important and necessary step toward the goal of musical understanding; but by itself it does not guarantee such understanding. Far more important is learning—with both ear and mind—how these chords function, how they relate to each other, how they interact to create musical motion. The principles that regulate the progression of chords form a large part of the subject matter of this book, and they do not lend themselves to quick summary. However, two of these principles—*harmony* and *voice leading*—are sufficiently general and broad in their application to be mentioned appropriately at this point.

By harmony we mean that aspect of music concerned with relationships among chords. By voice leading we mean that aspect of music concerned with the simultaneous motion of two or more parts. The unit of harmony is the chord; the unit of voice leading is the melodic line. However, the simultaneous motion of several lines necessarily creates chords. And it is hard to conceive a progression of chords without the explicit or implicit presence of melodic lines. In practice, therefore, the two principles interact with and influence each other.

19. Harmony; the 5th relationship; tonic and dominant. In tonal music, harmonic progression is organized by the *5th relationship*. We have already mentioned the close affinity that exists between two tones pitched a perfect 5th apart. The 5th is the first "new" tone in the overtone series; in triadic music the 5th is uniquely able to define the root or fundamental tone of a triad. The 5th forms the basis of organization not only of elements within a single chord but of movement from one chord to another. That the interval of the 5th dominates harmonic progression is reflected in the use of the term *dominant* to denote the scale degree a 5th above the tonic and the chords built on that degree. Since relationships in tonal music are organized around the tonic, the basic harmonic relationship is that between tonic and dominant—between the chord built on the central tone and the one built on its upper 5th.

This relationship controls not only many immediate successions from one chord to the next, but large-scale connections as well. In the Mozart C major sonata (Example 1-1), for instance, the opening theme moves from the tonic to the dominant of bars 11 and 12; the tonic begins the motion and the dominant is its goal. The large-scale progression from I to V forms the framework within which the numerous details are organized. And at the end of the piece (Example 1-3), V—this time as a seventh chord (V^7)—precedes the final tonic (bar 70). Beginning in Unit 6, you will have many opportunities to observe the overriding importance of the 5th relationship and, in particular, of the connection between tonic and dominant harmonies.

20. Voice leading. Many chord progressions of tonal music arise out of voice leading or counterpoint—that is, the chords result from the simultaneous motion of several melodic lines. This principle of organization is older than harmony; composers became aware of the possibility of relating chords to each other after centuries of contrapuntal music in which the chords arose as byproducts of the voice leading. Just as the basis of harmonic progression is motion by 5th, so the basis of melodic progression is motion by step. In successions of chords controlled by voice leading (*contrapuntal progressions*), stepwise motion predominates.

You will begin to understand the manifold elaborations of harmony and voice leading and the countless ways in which they join forces to create musical textures when you study the basic techniques of four-part writing in Unit 5.

EXERCISES

1. On E build major, minor, augmented, and diminished triads in root position. Do the same on B♭, G♯, and A♭.

2. Major key and roman numeral given. Write root-position triads as indicated.

B:	II	F♯:	VII
G:	VI	E♭:	III
A♭:	IV		

3. Minor key given. Write root-position triads as indicated, using natural form.

f:	III	d♯:	VI
c♯:	IV	e♭:	VII

4. On E build major, minor, augmented, and diminished $^6_3$ chords.
5. On B♭ build major, minor, augmented, and diminished $^6_4$ chords.
6. On G♯ build all four qualities of $^6_3$ chords.

    On A♭ build all four qualities of $^6_4$ chords.

7. Major key and roman numeral given. Write triads as indicated.

E:	IV^6	G:	III$^6_4$
B♭:	II^6	C♯:	I$^6_4$
F:	VII^6	A♭:	VI$^5_3$
B:	V^6	D:	IV$^6_4$
G♭:	III^6	A:	II$^6_4$

8. Minor key given. Write triads as indicated, using natural form.

c:	VII$^6_4$	e♭:	VI^6
f♯:	V$^6_4$	a:	IV$^5_3$
c♯:	III^6	e:	II$^6_4$
g:	I^6	b♭:	VII$^5_3$
d:	VI$^6_4$	f:	V^6

9. On F♯ build all qualities of root-position seventh chords. Label each chord, using the following symbols:

major	M	diminished	o
minor	m	half-diminished	∅
dominant	X	augmented	A

10. Do the same on A$\flat$.

11. Major key and roman numeral given. Write root-position seventh chords as indicated, labeling each chord with the symbols given in Exercise 9.

E$\flat$: IV^7	C: V^7
A: VI^7	F$\sharp$: VII^7
B: II^7	A$\flat$: III^7
F: IV^7	C$\sharp$: V^7
E: VI^7	D: I^7

12. Minor key given. Write root-position seventh chords as indicated, using harmonic form.

g: VII^7	g$\sharp$: V^7
a: VII^7	b$\flat$: V^7
b$\flat$: VII^7	b: V^7

13. Major key and roman numeral given. Write inverted seventh chords as indicated and label the quality of each.

A: II$^6_5$	B: VII$^4_3$
D$\flat$: VI$^4_2$	E$\flat$: V^7
F: IV$^6_5$	G: III$^4_3$
A$\flat$: II$^4_2$	B$\flat$: I^7
C: VII$^6_5$	

14. Minor key given. Write inverted seventh chords as indicated, using natural form.

d: VI$^4_3$	e: IV$^4_2$
f$\sharp$: III^7	g$\sharp$: II$^6_5$
b$\flat$: I$^4_3$	c: VII$^4_2$
c$\sharp$: VI^7	d$\sharp$: IV$^6_5$

15. Minor key given. Write inverted seventh chords as indicated, using harmonic form.

f: V$^6_5$	g: V$^4_3$
a: V$^4_2$	b: V^7
c: VII^7	d: VII$^6_5$
e$\flat$: VII$^4_3$	f$\sharp$: VII$^4_2$

I–V–I
AND ITS
ELABORATIONS

FIVE | PROCEDURES OF FOUR-PART WRITING

5-1   Bach, Chorale 293, phrase 1

CHORD CONSTRUCTION

1. Four-part vocal texture. To study harmony and voice leading is to study how chords and lines interact—chord with chord, line with line, and line with chord. For you to concentrate on these essentials, particularly in written exercises, the simplest rhythm and texture is the most desirable. In this respect four-part vocal writing—the traditional medium for harmony exercises—has many advantages. By its very nature, vocal music is simpler than instrumental: many complexities of rhythm, extremes of range, and changes in register that are easy on an instrument are difficult or even impossible for voice. At the same time, a setting in four parts, using the natural combination of high and low men's voices plus high and low women's or children's voices, provides a texture in which complete chords occur easily. Indeed, since the sixteenth century the four-part texture has come to represent the norm, especially in vocal music.

Four-part vocal writing is an ideal medium for the study of harmony not only because of its simplicity, but because of its applicability to music of greater complexity. Much instrumental music—though often more elaborate on the surface—is based on a framework of four voices. Example 5-1, a phrase from J. S. Bach's Chorale 293, illustrates certain principles of chord construction. Bach's 371 chorales are universally acknowledged to be among the masterpieces of four-part choral writing. Although they are in many ways complicated little pieces, their complexities are not those of rhythm, texture, and register, all of which remain relatively simple. For this reason the chorales have served as models for generations of music students, from Bach's day to yours.

As with nearly all the 371 chorales, Example 5-1 is set for four voices:

soprano—high women's or children's voices
alto—low women's or children's voices
tenor—high men's voices
bass—low men's voices

When notated on two staves, as in the example, the two upper voices (soprano and alto) are written on the treble staff and the two lower ones (tenor and bass) on the bass staff.* The stems of the soprano and tenor voices always point up; those of the alto and bass always point down. The soprano and bass are referred to as *outer voices*; the alto and tenor, *inner voices*.

2. Vocal range. In simple four-part vocal writing, each voice is set in a range that it can sing without strain. The usual ranges are shown by the whole notes of Example 5-2; the smaller noteheads represent allowable extensions. The greater part of each line will normally lie within the middle of the range rather than at the extremes.

5-2 vocal ranges

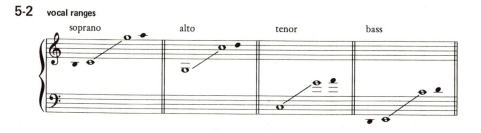

3. Doubling. In Example 5-1, all but one of the chords—the V^7 just before the fermata—are triads. Since a triad consists of only three notes, one of its tones must appear twice—that is, it must be doubled. Example 5-3 indicates the doublings that occur in the first phrase of Chorale 293. Note that doublings can occur at the unison as well as at the octave or multiple octave.

*Bach himself notated his chorales in an open score of four staves, using soprano, alto, tenor, and bass clefs. If you are familiar with these clefs, you will find it valuable to write some of your exercises in open score.

5-3   Bach, Chorale 293

brackets indicate doubled tones

"Rules" for doubling are formulated on the basis of an ideal vertical sonority. In practice, however, doublings are very much influenced by the way the voices move. Therefore most of the rules of doubling depend on other factors; violations, however, should always occur for a reason, not arbitrarily. One rule must be regarded as virtually absolute: the leading tone, because of its active tendency toward $\hat{1}$, should never be doubled when it is part of V or VII or their inversions. Thus, to construct the third chord of Chorale 293 in the way shown in Example 5-4 would be wrong.

5-4

wrong (doubled
leading tone)

With root-position chords the tendency is to double the more stable parts of the triad; thus with major and minor triads, the root is most often doubled, as in the excerpt from Chorale 293. The root of a final tonic chord is virtually always doubled. Seventh chords, since they already contain four tones, contain no doublings if they are complete chords (Example 5-3, V^7 just before fermata). Sometimes the root is doubled and the 5th omitted. Since the chord 7th always forms a dissonance, it must never be doubled.

4. Complete and incomplete chords. The best vertical sonority is achieved when, as in our opening example, all the tones of a triad are present in the chord. The 5th of a major or minor root-position triad, however, may be omitted without confusing the identity of the chord. Owing to the strength of the second overtone, the ear assumes a 5th above the bass unless there is some other interval present that contradicts the 5th. Most often when the 5th is omitted the root is tripled and the chord 3rd not doubled. Example 5-5 illustrates. Because of the empty sound and the lack of major or minor quality, the 3rd of the triad is never omitted except for special effects. Triads in inversion are usually complete. Root-position seventh chords frequently omit the chord 5th and double the root. Inversions of seventh chords are usually complete, exceptions occuring even less often than with inversions of triads.

5-5   Bach, Chorale 250

*incomplete chords

5. Spacing. Except for special effects, the voices of a multivoiced texture should blend. Too great a distance between the soprano and alto or the alto and tenor, especially if continued beyond one or two chords, may create an impression of thinness. Normally, adjacent upper voices should not be more than an octave apart, as in both the Bach excerpts (Examples 5-1 and 5-5). However, it is perfectly acceptable for the tenor to be separated from the bass by as much as two octaves. The resulting high tenor register gives a particularly intense choral sound. On the other hand, to have the alto and tenor in a low register and separated from the soprano often produces muddiness. Play the three "rewritten" versions of Chorale 293 (Example 5-6) and compare their effect with each other and with the original.

5-6   (a)   (b)

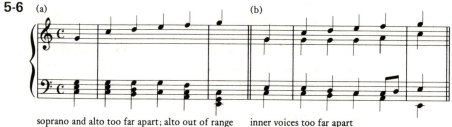

soprano and alto too far apart; alto out of range   inner voices too far apart

(c)

possible in keyboard style (why not for voices?)

6. Open position and close position. Strict observance of the rule of spacing still leaves room for considerable variety in the construction of a chord. Of the many "correct" possibilities, two general types are commonly distinguished: *open position* and *close position* (Example 5-7). Close position occurs when the three upper voices are as close together as possible—no additional chord tone can be inserted between adjacent voices. In open position, the upper voices are separated so that a chord tone could be inserted between either alto and soprano, or tenor and alto, or both pairs of voices, as in Example 5-7b. Open position tends to give a full but clear and well-balanced sound. Both open and close position can be used within a single phrase, as in Example 5-1, where the first two chords are in close position and the rest are in open position. Changing from close to open position, or the reverse, is often necessary for good voice leading; the change can also give a welcome variety of sound.

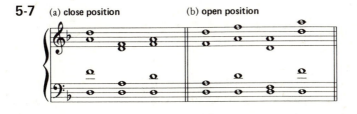

5-7   (a) close position   (b) open position

7. Keyboard style. As far back as the late seventeenth century, a figured bass was normally realized at the keyboard with the right hand playing the three upper parts and the left hand playing the bass only. This would mean that the distance between soprano and tenor could not exceed an octave, a comfortable stretch for most hands. Except for its notation, then, keyboard style is similar to close position. In this instrumental style, the limitations of vocal range need not be followed strictly. The tenor, in particular, tends to move higher than would be practical for voices.

Example 5-8 illustrates two conventional notations for keyboard style. In both notations the bass is alone on the lower staff with the stems pointing up or down depending on whether the note is above or below the third line. In 5-8a, the three right-hand parts are stemmed together. The direction of the stems is determined by whether the majority of tones are above or below the third line. In 5-8b, all the soprano tones are stemmed up, while a stem pointing down connects the inner voices.

5-8   keyboard style

(a)   (b)

8. Unusual spacing. Like the rules for doubling, the rule of spacing refers to a norm and is therefore not absolutely binding. Even in chorale style, Bach's settings clearly show that melodic considerations and motivic development may make a departure from the rule logical or even necessary. In a chorale, exceptional spacing is of brief duration, most often just a chord or two, as in the second phrase of Chorale 293 (Example 5-9) where the stepwise descent in the alto causes a gap between it and the soprano. In the even simpler texture of written exercises, such spacings are best avoided.

5-9   Bach, Chorale 293, phrase 2

 At the same time it is important to realize that, particularly in solo instrumental compositions, extremes of spacing and register can be a most important expressive factor. In the beginning of the Arietta from Beethoven's Piano Sonata, Op. 111 (Example 5-10), the left hand is written an octave below its normal register so that the inner parts are separated by as much as two octaves. The great distance between the upper and the lower parts suggests an immensity of space that could not be achieved otherwise. And the extreme register of the lower parts gives by contrast an ethereal quality to the upper parts, which are written in a normal register.

5-10   Beethoven, Piano Sonata, Op. 111, II

VOICE LEADING

Voice leading, unlike chord construction, involves motion—the motion of each of the four voices considered individually and the sense of progression created by their combination. First, we will discuss the melodic motion of the single voice and then proceed to the consideration of several voices moving simultaneously.

9. Melodic motion. In addition to sustaining or repeating a tone, a line may move by step (*conjunct* motion) or by skip or leap (*disjunct* motion). The proportion of conjunct to disjunct motion varies according to the function of the line. In a simple four-part setting, such as the first two phrases of Chorale 293 (Examples 5-1 and 5-9), we can distinguish three types of function: that of the top voice (soprano), of the bass voice, and of the inner voices.

As the highest, and therefore most exposed, voice, the soprano carries the main melodic line. Most good soprano lines contain a preponderance of conjunct motion, but the inclusion of one or two leaps will help greatly in adding interest and variety to the line. On the other hand, too much disjunct motion may keep the line from holding together and may make it difficult to sing. The first two phrases of Chorale 293 illustrate a good balance of conjunct and disjunct motion within a simple vocal melody. Note that this soprano line has no repeated tones. In general, excessive repetition of a single tone can result in a static melodic line, but an occasional repetition can create a good effect, especially if the other voices move.

Because the lowest tone is the crucial member of the chord, the bass voice has the special function of regulating the succession of chords. Bass and soprano lines are interdependent. The bass must make explicit the harmonic meaning of the soprano. For example, in the opening of Chorale 293, the soprano D could stand for the root of V, the 3rd of III, or the 5th of I. The bass G shows that the soprano D means the 5th of I. For its part, the top voice must move in such a way as to allow logical harmonic direction in the bass. Bass lines are often quite disjunct, particularly at the ends of phrases, as Example 5-1 illustrates, but stepwise motion, such as at the beginning of the second phrase of the same chorale, can give a welcome melodic quality to the line.

Inner voices sometimes have a melodic interest of their own, particularly in places where the soprano does not move very much. Their main function, however, is to complete the tones of the chord framed by the bass and soprano. The position of the outer voices may limit the melodic possibilities of the inner voices, so that extensive repetition of one or two tones may be unavoidable. Such repetition is not injurious to the total effect if the bass and soprano are good. In general, the inner voices will have a less distinct profile than the soprano and bass. Smooth voice-leading connections make likely a preponderance of conjunct motion, as in the tenor voice of Chorale 293, but the alto voice of the same two phrases shows that skips are also a possibility, if they occur for a valid reason.

10. Treatment of leaps. Disjunct motion gives variety and tension to a melodic line, but can be disruptive if used carelessly. The effect a leap produces depends largely on its size and on whether it is consonant or dissonant. (In context, other factors may be of importance, for instance whether or not there is a chord change.)

Consonant leaps—upward or downward—occur fairly frequently even in the simplest vocal textures (Example 5-11). The smaller the leap, the less it tends to disrupt the continuity of the line. Thus a leap of a major or minor 3rd interferes least with melodic continuity, especially where it is preceded or followed by stepwise motion (5-11a). A leap of a 6th or octave, on the other hand, generates considerable tension, and should usually be followed by a change of direction, preferably by step (5-11b). Leaps larger than an octave are not permitted. Large leaps must be used sparingly in a short harmony exercise; although their occasional use creates interest and variety, too many will create a disconnected, meaningless line. The melodic perfect 5th and perfect 4th (as a melodic interval the perfect 4th is always consonant) are more moderate in their effect than the octave or 6th but far more noticeable than the leap of a 3rd. It is best often to change direction after such a leap, but stepwise motion in the same direction, as in the opening of Chorale 293 (soprano), is a good possibility (5-11c).

Two or more leaps in a row and in the same direction are usually avoided except when a 3rd combines with another 3rd or with a 4th to arpeggiate a chord (Example 5-12). The sparing use of arpeggiation, within a limited range, is a good source of variety in vocal music, but excessive use will destroy the vocal character.

Dissonant leaps represent a more advanced stage of complexity than consonant ones; consequently they are excluded entirely from the simplest vocal styles. In a four-voice chordal setting, certain types of chords—particularly the dominant seventh—and certain harmonic progressions make dissonant leaps logical and attractive, and we will discuss their use in a later unit. The augmented 2nd, an interval traditionally excluded from four-part chorale settings and figured-bass realizations, should not be used.

11. Simultaneous motion. The motion of one voice relates to the motion of another in one of the four following ways:

Parallel motion: Both voices move in the same direction and maintain the same numerical interval (Example 5-13).

Similar motion: Both voices move in the same direction but the interval between them changes (Example 5-14).

Oblique motion: One voice remains stationary while the other moves (Example 5-15).

Contrary motion: Both voices move in opposite directions (Example 5-16).

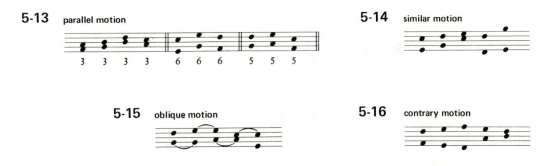

Contrary motion creates the greatest contrast between the two voices and helps to give each an individual contour. Each voice is independent of the other in a way that adds to the listener's interest. Of the remaining types, oblique motion is the next most independent, similar motion less so, and parallel motion least of all. Since there are only two directions, up and down, all four voices cannot be going in contrary motion to each other; thus the other types of motion are not only permissible but necessary and desirable. In particular, parallel motion in 3rds, 6ths, and 10ths can be among the most useful types of voice leading.

12. Forbidden parallel motion. In any multivoiced setting, the voices must join forces to create an overall sense of movement and direction. Within this unified web of sound, however, each voice must maintain its own individuality as much as possible. Certain types of parallel motion interfere either with the individuality of parts or with the forward momentum of the voice leading. Consequently, the following types of parallel motion are forbidden:

Parallel unisons: Here individuality does not exist, since the one part merely duplicates the pitch, register, and motion of the other (Example 5-17).

Parallel octaves: Here one part duplicates the pitch and motion of the other in a different register; this provides some contrast but not enough to give the feeling of two individual voices (Example 5-18).

Parallel perfect 5ths: The perfect 5th is unique in that it is the only interval that can define a triadic root (see Unit 2, section 7). This quality gives the interval a very strong stability and resistance to forward momentum. Composers from the fifteenth through the nineteenth centuries have excluded parallel 5ths from their writings, as well as unisons and octaves (Example 5-19).

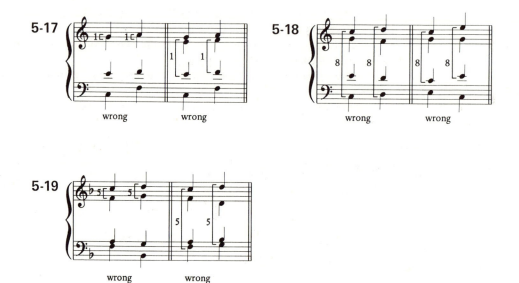

Motion from a perfect 5th to a diminished 5th is acceptable. Motion from a diminished 5th to a perfect 5th does not constitute parallel 5ths but is normally avoided since the dissonant interval does not resolve (Example 5-20).

The prohibition of parallel unisons, 5ths, and octaves refers only to motion within the *same* pair of voices. Example 5-21 shows two chords, one with an octave between bass and alto, the other with an octave between bass and soprano. Progressions like this do *not* contain parallel octaves.

The exact repetition of a unison, octave, or perfect 5th does not create motion and is therefore not a case of forbidden parallels (Example 5-22).

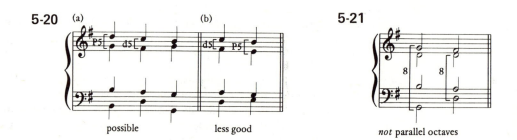

5-22 (a)   (b)

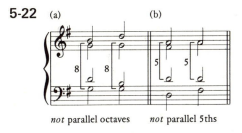

not parallel octaves   *not* parallel 5ths

13. Doubling in free textures. In instrumental pieces, in which the number of parts will change from time to time, doublings at the octave may occur, usually in order to obtain variety of sound or for emphasis. Such doublings are *not* parallel octaves. Example 5-23, an excerpt from a piano piece of Brahms, illustrates octave doubling. The reduction shows that the piece begins with three real parts; at the repetition of the theme, the texture changes to four parts and contrasts with the first statement by the absence of doublings, the change of register, and the different harmonization.

5-23   **Brahms, Intermezzo, Op. 76/7**

Doublings at the unison occur frequently in chamber and orchestral music. This is shown in the Schumann passage in Example 5-24. Where the number of voices must remain the same, as in a chorale or harmony exercise, such doublings should be strictly avoided.

5-24 Schumann, Trio, Op. 63, I

14. 5ths and octaves by contrary motion. Consecutive 5ths and octaves by contrary motion (Example 5-25) are not, strictly speaking, illegal, although they are best avoided in most cases, since the succession of two perfect intervals in the same pair of voices tends to cause unwanted accents. (The same applies to motion between a unison and an octave.) In compositions—usually those with a free texture—octaves in the outer voices may occur at the end of a phrase for purposes of emphasis (5-25a). 5ths in the outer voices are less frequent (5-25b), but sometimes occur between an outer and an inner voice, as in 5-25c.

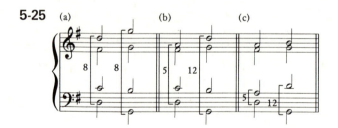

15. Hidden 5ths and octaves. 5ths or octaves approached by similar motion are called *hidden* (or *direct*) 5ths or octaves. The term hidden reflects the old theoretical idea that hidden 5ths or octaves conceal actual parallels that would occur if the intervals were filled in (Example 5-26).

Hidden 5ths and octaves are far less drastic in their effect than parallels, and theorists disagree about their effect in four-part writing. In this respect, keep the following in mind:

1. The fewer the voices, the stronger and more problematic the effect. (Thus hidden 5ths and octaves are forbidden entirely in two-part writing.)
2. The more complex the texture, the weaker, and therefore less problematic, the effect.
3. The greater the concentration of dissonance, the weaker the effect.
4. Hidden octaves tend to be more obtrusive than hidden 5ths.
5. Hidden octaves and 5ths are most noticeable in outer voices, least so in inner voices.
6. They are most noticeable where there is no common tone between the two chords, least so where they occur within a single chord.
7. Skips in both voices emphasize hidden 5ths and octaves; stepwise motion in the upper voice minimizes their effect.
8. And most important: Bach, in his chorales, avoids hidden octaves in the outer voices except where the soprano moves by step (Example 5-27a). Follow this practice, use your ear in doubtful cases, and otherwise don't worry.

5-27 (a)   (b)

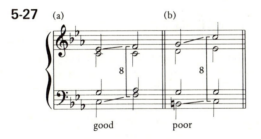

good   poor

16. Voice crossing. If two voices exchange position—if the alto moves below the tenor, for instance—the voices are said to cross (Example 5-28). Voice crossing occurs for a variety of reasons; it is least problematic when it involves only inner voices, and it is best when of very brief duration. A soprano or bass line may become obscured if crossed by an inner voice; you should therefore avoid such crossings.

5-28   voice crossing

(a)   (b)   in soprano   (c)
                                        and alto

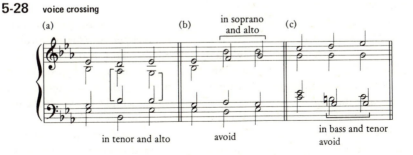

in tenor and alto   avoid   in bass and tenor
                                                avoid

17. Overlapping. Example 5-29 illustrates overlapping. Here the two voices do not cross, but the lower voice moves above the former position of the upper voice or vice versa. Such voice leadings may be confusing, particularly if a melodic stepwise connection can be made between the two voices. In the interest of clarity, overlaps, while not strictly forbidden, should be avoided wherever possible in four-part vocal style. They occur more appropriately in keyboard style; indeed, they are unavoidable if the soprano leaps any great distance.

5-29 voice overlapping

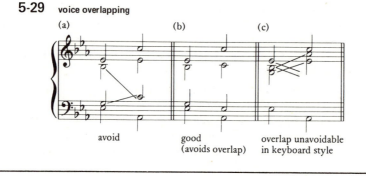

(a)   (b)   (c)

avoid   good   overlap unavoidable
(avoids overlap)   in keyboard style

POINTS FOR REVIEW

1. The ranges of the four vocal parts are: soprano—c^1 to g^2; alto—g to c^2; tenor—c to g^1; bass—E to c^1. (See example 5-2 for possible extensions.)

2. The soprano and alto are notated on the upper staff with treble clef; the tenor and bass are notated on the lower staff with bass clef. The soprano and tenor stems always point up; the alto and bass stems always point down.

3. It is usually best to double the most stable tone(s) of a chord. Therefore, the leading tone in V or VII and the 7th of seventh chords should not be doubled.

4. Complete chords create the best sonority. The 5th of major or minor root-position triads may be omitted, but *not* the 3rd. If the 5th is omitted, the root is often tripled. Similarly, the 5th may be omitted from root-position seventh chords and the root doubled.

5. Except for bass and tenor, the distance between adjacent voices should not exceed an octave. In close position, the upper three voices are as close together as possible. In open position, the upper voices are separated so that a chord tone could be inserted between alto and soprano or alto and tenor. In keyboard style, the distance between soprano and tenor is an octave or less and vocal ranges—particularly in the tenor—need not be strictly observed. (See Example 5-8 for notation.)

6. There are two types of melodic motion: conjunct and disjunct. In disjunct motion the augmented 2nd is forbidden, as is a leap larger than an octave. After any large leap, it is best to change direction.

7. There are four types of simultaneous motion: parallel, similar, oblique, and contrary.

8. Parallel unisons, parallel octaves, and parallel perfect 5ths are forbidden.

9. Hidden 5ths or octaves occur where the 5th or octave is approached by similar motion. Hidden octaves in the outer voices should be avoided unless the soprano moves by step.

10. Voice crossing (Example 5-28) is best avoided where it involves an outer voice. Overlap (Example 5-29) is also best avoided except in keyboard style.

EXERCISES

1. Write at least five different versions of each of the following chords. Vary the spacing, the doubling, and the position of the soprano. Name the major key to which (e), (f), and (g) belong; name the minor key to which (h) belongs.

    a. F major $\frac{5}{3}$
    b. C♯ minor $\frac{5}{3}$
    c. F♯ diminished $\frac{6}{3}$
    d. A♭ major $\frac{6}{4}$
    e. D dominant 7th
    f. E dominant $\frac{6}{5}$
    g. B♭ dominant $\frac{4}{2}$
    h. A♯ diminished 7th
    i. D♯ half-diminished $\frac{6}{5}$
    j. D♭ major 7th

2. There are many mistakes of voice leading and chord construction in the following example. Indicate each one you can find.

6-1 **Kuhnau, Biblical Sonata No. 5**

Gideon incoraggia i suoi soldati

TONIC AND DOMINANT

1. I-V-I. Example 6-1 is a rather special piece. It is from the fifth of a set of six Biblical Sonatas for keyboard composed by Bach's predecessor in Leipzig, Johann Kuhnau (1660-1722). This sonata is entitled "The Savior of Israel: Gideon," and the Italian subtitle at the beginning of the movement means "Gideon encourages his soldiers." Kuhnau may have wanted to indicate that Gideon was a man of few words, for in all its 33 measures the piece uses only two chords, a curious and unusual procedure. The two chords are I and V, and the choice is not an accident; it would be scarcely possible to compose a coherent piece of tonal music with any other combination of two chords. Only the V chord can contrast with the tonic and, at the same time, lead to and affirm it so convincingly.

V leads to I by both *harmonic* and *contrapuntal* motion. The harmonic motion is that of the descending 5th (or its inversion, the ascending 4th), discussed in Unit 4. At the same time the 5th and 3rd of V, $\hat{2}$ and $\hat{7}$, stand in a stepwise *contrapuntal* relation to $\hat{1}$. The progression V-I, therefore, combines the strongest possible harmonic motion (in the bass) with the strongest possible melodic motion (Example 6-2). The progression from an opening tonic through a dominant to a closing tonic constitutes the harmonic nucleus of many phrases, sections, and, as with the Kuhnau, complete pieces. It is *the* basic progression of Western music.

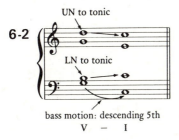

2. Expanding I and V. Obviously if I-V-I is to become the basis for an entire piece, the progression must somehow be expanded. To begin to understand this process, look at bars 7 (beat 3)-14 of the Kuhnau. The bass repeats the tonic once every measure, while for about four measures the tones of the upper voices—imitating trumpet calls—simply change position within the chord; then beginning with the last eighth note of bar 11, passing tones in the upper voices fill in the 3rds between chord tones. What happens in the preceding eight bars is similar, if slightly more complicated. In bars 3 (beat 3)-7, the melody is in the left hand. Its tones do not actually function as the bass of the chord, which is sustained by implication from the C of bar 2. Beginning with bar 14, the dominant is expanded in an almost identical way but with the opening melody inverted. Tonic harmony returns in bar 28 and continues to the end except for the V of bar 31, which we will discuss in the next section. The Kuhnau piece demonstrates one of the simplest ways of expanding a chord: arpeggiating above a sustained bass, with or without figuration. In later units we will discuss more complex techniques.

3. Cadences. Music has its punctuations and groupings, roughly comparable to the sentences and paragraphs of language. In bar 15 of the Kuhnau, the impact of the change of harmony, the slower rhythm, and the stepwise descent of the melodic line from G to D make us hear the arrival of V as a goal and mark the end of an important group. But there is still more to follow: we have reached the end of a sentence, so to speak, not a paragraph. Having reached V and $\hat{2}$, we feel the need to continue to I and $\hat{1}$. This doesn't happen right away. After the double bar, dominant harmony continues, and the rhythmic activity increases again. The tonic returns in bar 28, but without a feeling of repose: the melody is on $\hat{3}$, and the rhythm becomes more active, as it did in bars 12-13. V and $\hat{2}$ are once more reached in bar 31, beat 2, but this time the motion continues to the final goal: tonic chord and $\hat{1}$.

We call a succession of chords that marks the end of a musical phrase or section, as in bars 14-15 and 31-32 of the Kuhnau, a *cadence* (Latin *cadere,* to fall). Because it creates a halt in the musical motion, a cadence is a rhythmic as well as a tonal event. Many cadences, as in the Kuhnau, show a broadening of time values; in most the final chord falls on a strong beat. The Kuhnau piece illustrates the two most important types of cadence: the *authentic cadence* (V-I) in bars 31-32, and the *semicadence,* or *half cadence* (ends on V), in bars 14-15. Example 6-3 illustrates typical cadential patterns in four voices.

6-3   cadential patterns

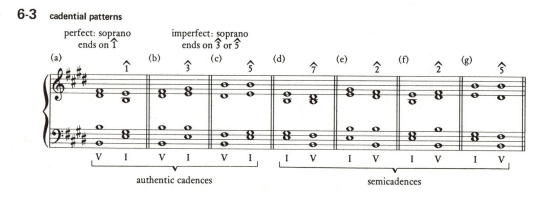

Authentic cadences (6-3 a-c): 6-3a is the most final sounding and is often called a *perfect* authentic cadence. This cadence is used mostly at the end of a piece, but it is possible earlier. 6-3b and c are *imperfect* authentic cadences; that is, they are less final sounding than 6-3a. Of the two, 6-3b occurs much more frequently than 6-3c.

Semicadences (6-3 d-g): 6-3g occurs somewhat less frequently than 6-3d, e, and f because of lack of melodic activity in the soprano.

4. Different functions of I and V. Chords derive their meaning—as opposed to their label—from the way they function. In the Kuhnau, the tonic functions first as an *opening tonic,* establishing the tonality and serving as a point of departure. At the end it is a goal of motion, thus a *closing tonic.* The V has three different functions in this piece. In bars 15-16, V is the goal chord of the cadential progression I-V (semicadence) and articulates the close of the first section. In bars 17-28, V is expanded so that it becomes a significant portion of the piece; V thus helps to shape the form. And in bar 31, V functions as part of an authentic cadence leading to the final tonic and thus identifying it as goal. Finally, the Kuhnau illustrates an important fact about harmonic progression—namely, that it operates over both large and small spans. As Example 6-4 illustrates, the expanded I and V chords create a large-scale harmonic progression, whereas the quicker successions of chords at the cadences mark important points of arrival.

6-4

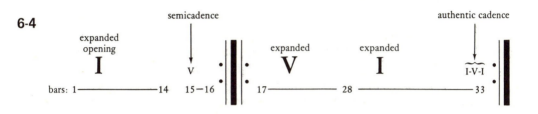

5. Doublings. (For doublings of I and V, review Unit 5, section 3.) Most often the root is doubled both in I and in V, but the 5th and 3rd of I and the 5th of V are also possibilities. *Never* double the leading tone (3rd of V)!

6. I-V-I in four parts. (Review Unit 1, sections 9-10.) The progression I-V-I makes possible many important melodic and voice-leading techniques. In Unit 1 you learned that $\hat{2}$ and $\hat{7}$ can function as neighbors to $\hat{3}$ or $\hat{1}$ and that $\hat{2}$ can function as a passing tone between $\hat{1}$ and $\hat{3}$. All these melodic figures frequently occur harmonized by I-V-I. Writing the progression with these different possibilities in the soprano voice can provide valuable practice. Don't feel obliged to memorize every detail of voice leading shown in the following examples, but do refer to them from time to time, especially when working out the exercises. What you *must* remember is that I supports $\hat{1}$, $\hat{3}$, and $\hat{5}$; V supports $\hat{5}$, $\hat{7}$, and $\hat{2}$.

Lower-neighbor figures (Example 6-5): These figures occur frequently and present no voice-leading problems. The common tone $\hat{5}$ is kept in the same voice; other voices move to the nearest position.

6-5   lower-neighbor figures

(a) $\hat{1}$ in soprano

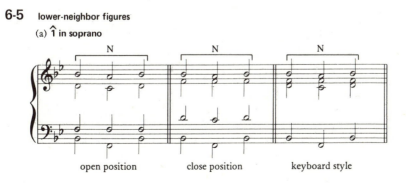

open position   close position   keyboard style

(b) $\hat{3}$ in soprano

(c) $\hat{5}$ in soprano

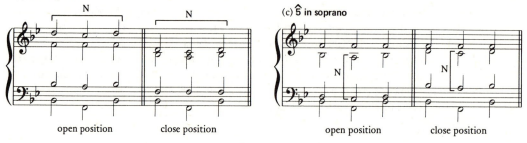

open position   close position   open position   close position

Descending passing motion (Example 6-6): The very important melodic progression $\hat{3}$-$\hat{2}$-$\hat{1}$ often supports the cadential progression I-V-I, as at the end of Example 6-1. $\hat{3}$ and $\hat{1}$ are stable tones belonging to the tonic triad; $\hat{2}$ is a passing tone, dissonant against the tonic triad. The V provides consonant support for this passing tone. With this soprano line the common tone does not always remain in the same voice. In 6-6a the 5th of the final tonic chord is omitted in order to allow the leading tone (in the tenor) to move to the tonic. In 6-6b the leading tone descends to the 5th of I in order to make possible a complete chord. In 6-6c the common tone $\hat{5}$ is kept in the alto throughout. The tenor leaps from the leading tone to the 3rd of the tonic chord.

6-6   descending passing tones

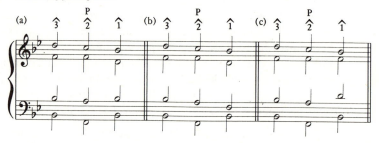

Upper-neighbor figures (Example 6-7): Compare the voice leading here with that of Example 6-5.

6-7   upper-neighbor figures

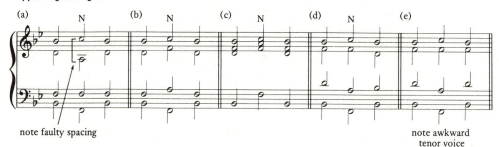

note faulty spacing   note awkward tenor voice

Other figures (Example 6-8).

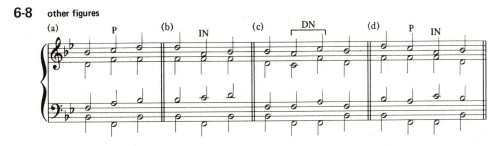

7. I-V-I in minor. (Review Unit 4, section 5.) In any progression where V goes to I, or creates the expectation of such a motion, $\hat{7}$ must be raised to form a leading tone, so that V becomes a major triad as in Examples 6-9b and c; the progression shown in 6-9a is *wrong*. It will be good practice for you to rewrite Examples 6-5 through 6-8 in various minor keys. Only one detail of voice leading requires comment: the progression shown in Example 6-9c will contain a diminished 4th in the tenor voice. Although melodic dissonances are generally to be avoided in the inner voices, this progression, which occurs frequently in the Bach chorales, is permissible.

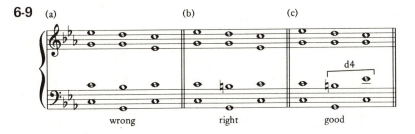

8. Expanding I and V in four parts. In the Kuhnau we saw how I and V were expanded by changing the position of all the upper voices, so that when the soprano moved, the alto and tenor followed in parallel or similar motion. The inner voices need not always follow the soprano, however; sometimes considerations of vocal range make it better for one or both of them not to. In moving from one chord position to another it is not necessary to keep the chord complete: the 5th may be omitted, but take care not to omit the 3rd (Example 6-10).

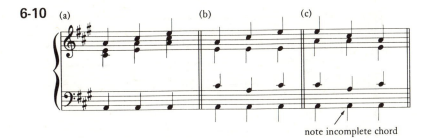

THE DOMINANT SEVENTH

9. V⁷ as dissonant chord. Example 6-11, the beginning of the trio from a minuet by Haydn, provides an excellent introduction to the use of V⁷. In bars 3-5, and in bar 7, $\hat{5}$ is in the bass, but the chord contains a 7th above the bass as well as a 3rd and a 5th. Because of the 7th, V⁷, unlike V⁵₃, is a *dissonant* chord; the 7th,

6-11   Haydn, Symphony No. 97, III

which represents a descending passing tone, must therefore resolve (review Unit 4, section 11). Thus, in the Haydn, the $\hat{4}$ (7th of V^7) of bars 3-5 resolves to $\hat{3}$ in bar 6; likewise the inner-voice $\hat{4}$ of bar 7 (second violin) moves to $\hat{3}$ in bar 8. V^7 has the same harmonic meaning as V, but the dissonance (a contrapuntal factor) intensifies its drive to the tonic. V^7 is therefore often part of an authentic cadence, as in bars 7-8 of the Haydn.

10. **V^7 and the soprano voice.** (Review Unit 1, sections 9-11, especially in reference to uses of $\hat{4}$.) One very important function of V^7 is to support $\hat{4}$ in the soprano. In bars 3-5 of the Haydn, $\hat{4}$ is part of a somewhat elaborated stepwise descending line—in other words $\hat{4}$ functions as a passing tone; Example 6-12a shows this in reduced form. $\hat{4}$ supported by V^7 can also appear as a neighbor, either complete (6-12b) or incomplete (6-12c).

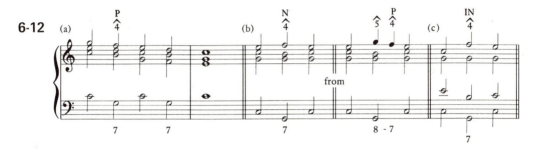

V^7, like V^5_3, can also support $\hat{7}$, $\hat{2}$, and $\hat{5}$ in the soprano. If $\hat{5}$ is in the soprano, the V^7 will be incomplete, as in Example 6-13c. Sometimes, however, V^5_3 is a better choice for supporting these tones. If the melodic line comes to rest on $\hat{7}$, $\hat{2}$, or $\hat{5}$, V will generally produce a better effect than V^7, which conveys an inappropriate feeling of activity. For this reason, V^7 is rarely used in a semicadence.

11. **V^7 in four voices: doubling.** In four parts, V^7 may appear as a complete chord ($^7_5_3$), in which case there is no doubling, or as an incomplete chord with root doubled and fifth omitted ($^8_7_3$). Example 6-14 illustrates. In this example the figures represent *all* the intervals above the bass. In actual figured basses of the Baroque period incomplete chords are not necessarily indicated by special symbols.

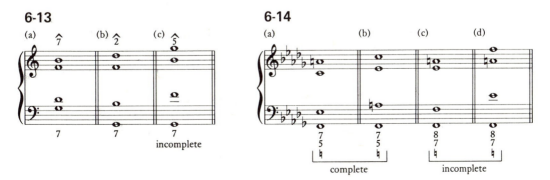

12. **V⁷-I: voice-leading techniques.** V⁷ contains two "tendency" tones: $\hat{4}$ and $\hat{7}$, the scale degrees that form a tritone in major and in the inflected forms of minor. (Like V_3^5, V⁷ in minor must always contain a leading tone.) As we have seen, $\hat{4}$, which forms a dissonance with the bass, *must* move down by step to $\hat{3}$. $\hat{7}$ tends strongly to move to $\hat{8}$, and if it appears in the soprano voice (an exposed position), it must do so. Where both these tendency tones resolve, one of the chords in the progression V⁷-I will be incomplete. In Example 6-15a, for instance, where the V⁷ is complete, the I will be incomplete; in 6-15b, where the V⁷ is incomplete, the I will be complete. However, since $\hat{7}$ is consonant with the bass, it may move to $\hat{5}$ if it is an inner voice; this procedure makes it possible for both V⁷ and I to be complete chords (6-15c). The last is the voice leading preferred by Bach in his chorale settings, especially at cadences, but all three possibilities are good.

6-15

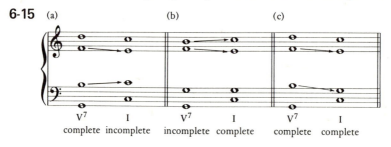

Normal resolution of the 7th combined with the melodic motion $\hat{2}$-$\hat{3}$ will result in a tonic with a *doubled 3rd,* as shown in Example 6-16.

Sometimes a melodic interpolation decorates the resolution; this occurs most frequently in the soprano voice (Example 6-17).

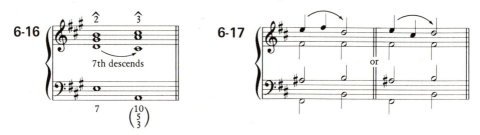

13. **V⁸⁻⁷.** Dominant harmony is often extended and intensified by moving from $_3^5$ to 7, as shown in Example 6-18. This happens frequently in an authentic cadence, where the introduction of the 7th can be emphasized by a downward leap of an octave in the bass. Note that the 7th sometimes comes from $\hat{5}$ rather than $\hat{8}$.

6-18

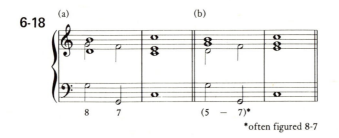

*often figured 8-7

14. Expanding V⁷. Like I and V$\frac{5}{3}$, V^7 may be expanded by changing the positions of the upper voices. This may result in a *transfer* of the dissonant 7th from one voice to another; the 7th will resolve in the last voice in which it occurs, as in Example 6-19.

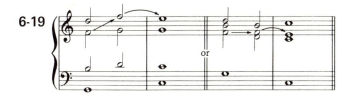

Extending V^7 creates the possibility of dissonant melodic leaps of the 7th, diminished 5th, and augmented 4th, which we will discuss in Unit 8.

15. Harmony and rhythm. (Review Unit 3, sections 6-7.) Patterns of chord change create groupings and accents, and consequently exert a strong influence on our impression of rhythm. Especially in simple styles with more or less uniform note values and few changes in texture, the succession of chords can be the most important factor in defining the rhythm. In general, repeating a chord attracts very little accent. Because there is minimal contrast, the ear tends to hear the repeated chord as an extension of the preceding one. Changing a chord, on the other hand, tends to attract an accent; a "new" chord, therefore, tends to sound rhythmically stronger than a repeated one.

Although conflict between rhythm and meter is a very important compositional resource, it is one that demands a good deal of skill and experience. For the time being, therefore, try to organize your written work so that the changes of chord support the meter. Avoid repeating a chord from a weak to a strong beat, for this contradicts the meter (Example 6-20). Repeating a chord from a strong beat to a weak beat is permissible, and repetition from a strong beat, through a weak beat, to the next strong beat is also possible. Weak-strong repetition of an *initial* tonic emphasizes the tonality and is therefore justifiable.

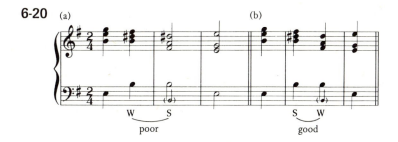

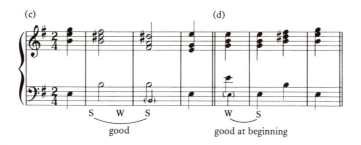

good   good at beginning

Sometimes the segmentation of a musical idea into rhythmic groups creates patterns that also justify weak-strong repetition; in such cases we hear the weak beat as the end of one pattern rather than as an upbeat to the next (Example 6-21).

6-21

good

POINTS FOR REVIEW

1. I-V-I is the basic harmonic progression. V leads to I by harmonic motion in the bass and by contrapuntal motion in the upper voices.

2. I and V (and every other major or minor root-position triad) can be expanded by changing the position of the upper voices over a sustained bass.

3. I supports $\hat{1}$, $\hat{3}$, and $\hat{5}$. V supports $\hat{5}$, $\hat{7}$, and $\hat{2}$.

4. V-I at the end of a phrase is an authentic cadence; if the soprano leads to $\hat{1}$, the result is a *perfect* authentic cadence. I-V is a semicadence.

5. In doubling I or V, the root is best; next best is the 5th; the 3rd of I is possible. The leading tone (the 3rd of V) must not be doubled.

6. In minor, the 3rd of V must be raised to form a leading tone.

7. V⁷ is V$_3^5$ plus a 7th above the bass. This 7th is dissonant and must resolve downward by step ($\hat{4}$-$\hat{3}$).

8. V⁷, which supports $\hat{4}$, $\hat{5}$, $\hat{7}$, and $\hat{2}$, intensifies motion to I. V⁷-I is therefore good at an authentic cadence, but V⁷ is not normally the goal of a semicadence.

9. V⁷ may be complete, with no tone doubled, or the 5th may be omitted and the root doubled.

10. V⁸⁻⁷ is a common way of expanding V at authentic cadences. If the 7th of V⁷ is transferred from one upper voice to another, it must resolve in the last voice.

11. When repeating a chord, strong-weak repetition is good; weak-strong repetition is poor; strong-(weak)-strong repetition is good.

EXERCISES

NOTE. Beginning in this unit, avoid chords and techniques in your written work that have not yet been explained in the text.

  Learn to *hear* what you write. Sing the given melody or bass so that you know what it sounds like; sing the individual lines of your harmonizations, and play your completed exercises at the piano. When you check for errors in voice leading, be sure to test all six combinations of voices: bass-tenor, bass-alto, bass-soprano, tenor-alto, tenor-soprano, and alto-soprano.

REALIZING FIGURED BASSES. First make sure you know what chords are de-manded by the figures. Next give your attention to the soprano; try to invent a top voice that is interesting and, if possible, beautiful—one with a good balance between stepwise motion and leaps.

HARMONIZING MELODIES. Remember that $\hat{5}$ belongs both to I and $V^{(7)}$. In deciding which to use, remember to avoid weak-strong repetitions of the same chord.

  We do not recommend the addition of passing tones, neighboring tones, suspensions, and the like, until the subject of figuration is dealt with in the begin-ning of Volume 2.

1. Preliminaries. Complete the following melodic fragments and set for four voices in note-against-note texture, so that each melody tone gets a chord.

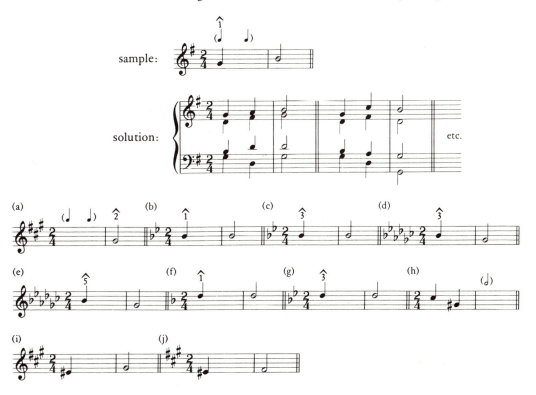

2. Figured bass with some melody tones. Complete the soprano and add inner voices.

3. Melody. Set for four voices; harmonize each tone of the melody.

4. Melody.

SEVEN | I⁶, V⁶, AND VII⁶

7-1

(a) Chorale melody, Das neugeborne Kindelein

(b) Bach, Chorale 178

I⁶ AND V⁶

1. New possibilities for the bass line. Example 7-1 shows two settings of the first phrase of a chorale melody. The first setting, done by us for purposes of illustration, uses only I, V, and V⁷, the chords discussed in Unit 6. The second, a harmonization by Bach, adds three important $\frac{6}{3}$ chords: I⁶, V⁶, and VII⁶. There is a considerable difference, to put it mildly, in the effect of the two bass lines. The first is rather primitive. Confined to two tones, it can provide only the minimal harmonies implied by the melody. On the other hand, Bach's bass with its three new scale degrees ($\hat{3}$, $\hat{7}$, and $\hat{2}$) is far more sophisticated. Here the listener can sense a distinction between goals of motion and intermediate steps. In addition, the bass has a partly melodic or contrapuntal character arising out of the stepwise line (review Unit 4, section 20). Both these characteristics relate directly to the use of $^6_3$ chords.

2. I⁶ and V⁶ expanding I and V. In Example 6-1 we saw how chords can be extended by changing tones in the soprano line. However useful that possibility is, musical composition would not have evolved very far if composers had not learned to extend a chord by changing its bass tone. Perhaps the most frequent and important way of expanding *any* major or minor triad is by moving the bass between the root and 3rd of the chord (Example 7-2). This, of course, changes the position of the chord from $^5_3$ to $^6_3$ (or the reverse). In this context $^6_3$ functions as an inversion of $^5_3$. Such a procedure creates a melodic activity in the bass which makes it possible to continue the same harmony without monotony. Thus in bar 1 of the Bach excerpt the initial tonic is expanded by a motion in the bass from $\hat{1}$ to $\hat{3}$ and back, producing the succession $^5_3$-$^6_3$-$^5_3$. The two eighth notes in the bass are passing tones and do not affect the harmony. (Note the imitation in the alto of the bass figure G-A-B♭, which causes the two upper parts to cross.) At the beginning of a Handel variation (Example 7-3a), both I and V are expanded. Here the $^6_3$ chords come first, producing a pattern of descending 3rds (7-3b and c).

7-2
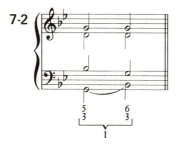

7-3   (a) **Handel, Double IV**   (from *Harpsichord Suite No. 5*)

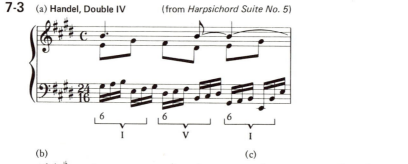

3. $\frac{6}{3}$ expanding $\frac{5}{3}$. Example 7-4 shows the most important possibilities for the soprano over the bass progression I-I⁶ (which could also be V-V⁶, and so on). Particularly important, because of their far-reaching compositional applications, are parallel 10ths between the outer voices (7-4a) and voice exchange (interchanging two tones between two voices, as in 7-4c). Example 7-5 shows characteristic voice leadings in four parts.

7-4   I-I⁶ and soprano

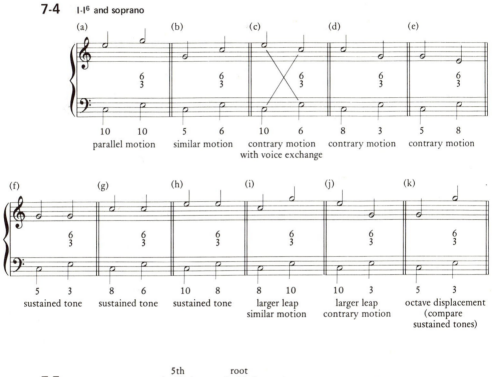

7-5   (a)

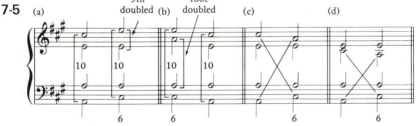

4. $\frac{6}{3}$ substituting for $\frac{5}{3}$. I⁶ and V⁶ can support the same melody tones as I and V; they imply the same harmonic function, though less strongly. They can, therefore, substitute for $\frac{5}{3}$ in some circumstances. For example, I⁶ may replace I where the greater stability of the root position chord is not needed, as in Example 7-6, a fragment from Schumann's *Papillons*.

7-6   Schumann, Papillons, Op. 2, Finale

However the two positions are by no means completely interchangeable. $\frac{6}{3}$ chords attract less accent than their root-position equivalents and give a more flowing effect; their use imparts a melodic character to the bass line. This is largely because the 6th, the most characteristic interval of the $\frac{6}{3}$ chord, is a much less stable consonance than the 5th, which occurs in root position. Therefore, where stability is needed, as in most beginnings and virtually all endings, $\frac{6}{3}$ is *not* a satisfactory substitute for $\frac{5}{3}$.

A further limitation on the use of I⁶: avoid the progression V⁷-I⁶ where the soprano moves $\hat{4}$-$\hat{3}$, since the similar motion of the outer voices into $\hat{3}$ will cause a bad set of hidden octaves, particularly if I⁶ is in a rhythmically strong position (Example 7-7).

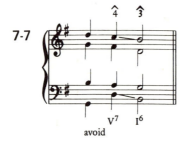

7-7

5. V⁶ within expanded tonic. Using V⁶ between two root-position tonics produces the stepwise bass line $\hat{8}$-$\hat{7}$-$\hat{8}$ and make possible a contrapuntal expansion of tonic harmony. Here the specific function of V⁶ is that of a neighboring chord. Where a clear expression of the harmonic 5th relationship is needed (as in most cadences), root-position V should appear; but in other situations, especially near the beginning or the middle of phrases, V⁶ often functions more effectively. Compare bars 1-2 of the two chorale settings shown in Example 7-1.

Example 7-8 shows three characteristic uses of V⁶ within an expanded tonic. In 7-8a V⁶ supports $\hat{2}$ in a rising soprano line, the kind that frequently occurs at the beginning of a phrase. In 7-8b V⁶ forms an effective support for $\hat{5}$; the stepwise bass balances the disjunct soprano. The same is true of 7-8c where the melodic progression would be virtually impossible with root-position I-V-I, because of the consecutive octaves.

7-8 **V^6 within an expanded tonic**

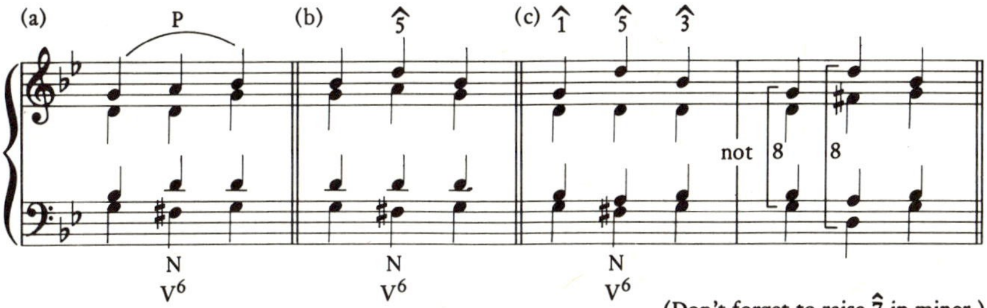

(Don't forget to raise $\hat{7}$ in minor.)

I^6 can replace the initial tonic in the progression I-V^6-I (Example 7-9). Here the bass of V^6 functions as an incomplete neighbor to I. In minor, the progression produces a perfectly allowable diminished 4th in the bass line (compare Example 6-9c, tenor). Because $\hat{7}$ is active in the direction of $\hat{8}$, V^6 normally continues on to I^5_3, not I^6.

7-9 **I^6 replacing I^5_3**

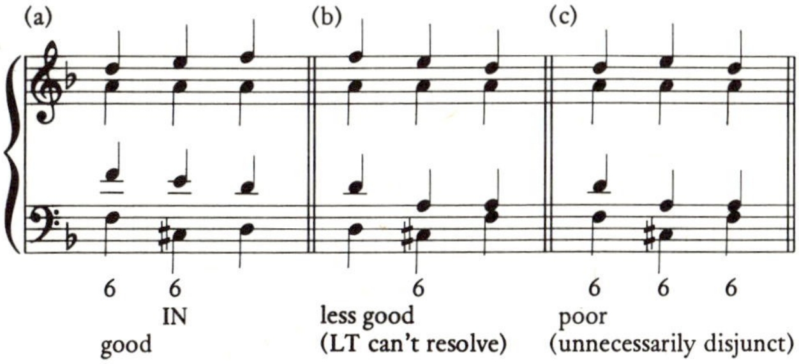

6. **$^5_3$ expanding $^6_3$.** In most cases where the $^6_3$ and $^5_3$ positions of a chord appear together or in close conjunction, $^5_3$ is the principal chord, owing to the stability of its perfect 5th. However rhythmic and melodic factors may cause the reverse to be true. In an excerpt from Handel's G minor Oboe Concerto (Example 7-10), both the strong rhythmic position of the first F♯ and its stepwise connection to the tonic, G, make the V^5_3 chord subordinate to its first inversion. (Note that the incomplete chords in this example would be filled in by the continuo player.)

7-10 **Handel, G Minor Oboe Concerto, IV**

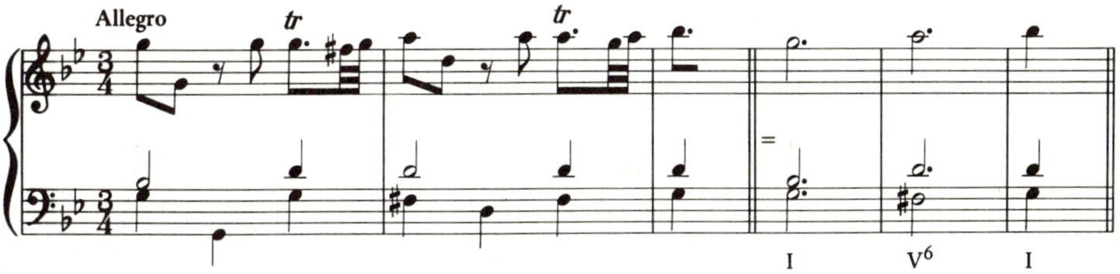

Brief expansions of $\frac{6}{3}$ chords occur fairly often; however, for large-scale expansions where the chord becomes the basis of an entire section (like the V in Example 6-1, bars 17-27), the stable sonority of the root position is necessary.

7. Doubling I⁶ and V⁶. Any tone of I⁶ may be doubled; doubling the soprano often gives a good sonority. In V⁶ the leading tone must *never* be doubled. Both the remaining tones of V⁶ ($\hat{2}$ and $\hat{5}$) are possible choices.

VII⁶ (LEADING-TONE TRIAD)

8. $\hat{2}$ in the bass line. VII⁶, like V, contains the two scale degrees adjacent to the tonic. To them it adds a 3rd above the bass. It contains the three upper tones of V⁷ and, like it, can support $\hat{7}$, $\hat{2}$, and $\hat{4}$. Compared with V$^5_3$ or V⁷, however, VII⁶ is a contrapuntal (passing or neighboring) rather than a harmonic chord and most typically serves as a passing chord filling in the 3rd between I and I⁶ or, as in bar 3 of the Bach chorale (Example 7-1b), between I⁶ and I. Very often, as with the progression I-I⁶ (or I⁶-I), the soprano will either move in parallel 10ths with the bass (Examples 7-11a and 7-1b, bar 3) or form a voice exchange with the bass (7-11b). 7-11c and d show some other outer-voice possibilities; you should work out further combinations. Another function of VII⁶ is as a neighboring chord to I or I⁶ (Example 7-12).

7-11 passing VII⁶ and soprano

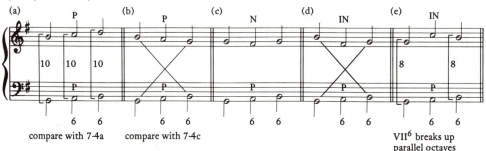

compare with 7-4a   compare with 7-4c

VII⁶ breaks up
parallel octaves

7-12 neighboring VII⁶ and soprano

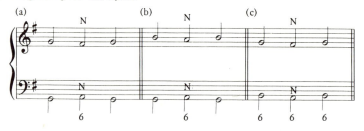

9. Doubling VII⁶. It is usually best to double the bass tone, $\hat{2}$, since this is not part of the tritone; however, voice-leading considerations may make doubling $\hat{4}$ preferable. The leading tone must never be doubled.

10. Resolution of tritone. VII⁶ contains an augmented 4th or diminished 5th in the upper voices. Because the bass of VII⁶ is consonant with both the other tones, the effect of the dissonance is considerably softened. Very frequently the tendency of the tritone to resolve regularly ($\hat{7}$ to $\hat{8}$ and $\hat{4}$ to $\hat{3}$) is offset by other considerations such as achieving a complete tonic chord or stepwise voice leading. Example 7-13, taken from Bach chorales, illustrates some typical voice leadings, and you will find it useful to consult it when doing your written work. The resolution of the tritone can lead to an incomplete I with doubled 3rd (7-13a), if all the voices proceed by step. Only if one of the inner voices leaps can a complete chord be gained (7-13b). However, if the tritone is expressed as an augmented 4th, Bach will sometimes let it move to a perfect 4th, $\hat{4}$ moving up to $\hat{5}$, thus producing a complete chord and stepwise voice leading (7-13c and d). If the tritone is a diminished 5th, Bach tends to resolve it normally (7-13a), for the progression diminished 5th-perfect 5th creates hidden 5ths. As part of the diminished 5th, $\hat{4}$ will move up to $\hat{5}$ only if the bass moves up to $\hat{3}$ in parallel 10ths, thereby bringing in the tone of resolution in another voice but very prominently (7-13e). This voice leading, incidentally, occurs very frequently. Quite often Bach doubles $\hat{4}$, a strategy that permits resolution of the tritone, stepwise voice leading, and a complete chord (7-13f and g). If $\hat{4}$ is doubled at the octave, both a diminished 5th and an augmented 4th may result. In such a case, resolve the diminished 5th as in 7-13f.

7-13   VII⁶: resolution of tritone

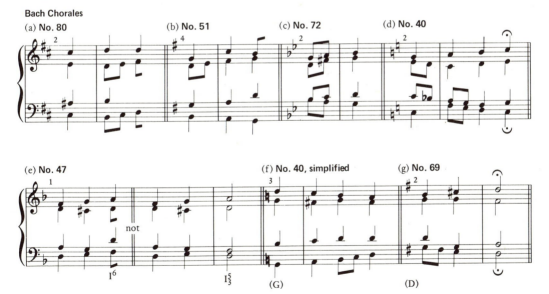

VII⁵₃ occurs much less frequently than VII⁶ owing to the dissonance (diminished 5th) involving the bass. Its use will be explained in Unit 15; until then avoid it.

11. New cadential possibilities. (Review Unit 6, section 3.) Example 7-14a demonstrates how I^6 may be used to precede V. Often the bass arpeggiates $I-I^6-V$ ($\hat{1}-\hat{3}-\hat{5}$), as in 7-14b.

VII^6 and V^6 make possible two contrapuntal cadences leading to I—contrapuntal because they are based on stepwise motion rather than on a leap of a 5th or 4th in the bass. These do not produce as strong an articulation as root-position $V^{(7)}$-I, but are sometimes used to end a phrase or a group of measures within a larger phrase, where stronger cadences are not needed. They are virtually *never* used to end a piece (or exercise). Example 7-15 illustrates.

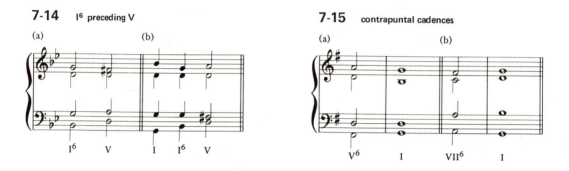

7-14 I^6 preceding V

(a)   (b)

I^6 V   I I^6 V

7-15 contrapuntal cadences

(a)   (b)

V^6 I VII^6 I

12. Avoiding unwanted cadential effect. In a chorale, the unvarying rhythmic pulse (and to some extent the shortness and irregularity of the phrase lengths) often makes the progression $V^{(7)}$-I undesirable except at cadential points, especially if the soprano moves to $\hat{1}$. For the moment, most of your exercises will be chorale-like in rhythm and texture, so you should generally seek alternative progressions except where a cadence is needed. Using VII^6 or V^6 instead of root-position V, or using I^6 instead of $I\frac{5}{3}$, will also help you become more familiar with these new chords.

13. Expanding I. As we saw in the preceding unit, the basic harmonic progression is a motion from an initial tonic through a dominant to a closing tonic. Sometimes the progression occurs in incomplete form, as in the Bach chorale phrase of Example 7-1b, which leads to V. One of the most important of the many ways of expanding this progression is to extend the initial tonic of a phrase or section and move from it to a cadence. This provides a strong point of departure for the subsequent tonal motion. In addition, many important motivic ideas grow out of elements of tonic harmony; prolonging the tonic therefore provides an opportunity for working out the motivic design of a piece. In Example 7-1, for instance, the tune begins with three G's followed by two statements of a descending 3rd, D-C-B♭. The melody, therefore, moves from $\hat{1}$ to $\hat{5}$ to $\hat{3}$—all elements of tonic harmony—before closing on $\hat{2}$.

In dealing with VII^6 and V^6 we saw that these chords can fulfill contrapuntal functions—neighboring or passing—within an expanded tonic. In Bach's setting (7-1b), such functions are clearly evident. The V^6 of bar 2 is a neighboring chord (bass motion $\hat{1}$-$\hat{7}$-$\hat{1}$) and the VII^6 of bar 3, a passing chord (bass $\hat{3}$-$\hat{2}$-$\hat{1}$). It would be a great mistake to regard V^6 and VII^6 as identical in function with V or V^7. In listening to the Bach phrase, we don't hear a harmonic cadence until the root-position V arrives in bar 4. The technique discussed here—expanding an initial tonic before leading to a cadence—is one that occurs at some point in virtually every piece of tonal music, and one we will be discussing from different perspectives throughout this book.

POINTS FOR REVIEW

1. I^6 and V^6 expand root-position I and V. Important voice leadings in the progression I-I^6 or V-V^6 are parallel 10ths in the outer voices or voice exchange in the outer voices.

2. I^6 and V^6 may substitute for I and V where the stability of the root-position chord is not needed. V^6 functions as a neighboring chord (N) within an expanded tonic (bass: $\hat{8}$-$\hat{7}$-$\hat{8}$) or as an incomplete neighbor (IN) in the progression I^6-V^6-I.

3. Any tone of I^6 and V^6 may be doubled *except* the leading tone of V^6.

4. VII^6 functions as a passing chord between I and I^6 or as a neighboring chord to I or I^6.

5. In VII^6, either $\hat{2}$ or $\hat{4}$ may be doubled, but never $\hat{7}$ (the leading tone).

6. The tritone in VII^6 often resolves normally ($\hat{7}$-$\hat{8}$ and $\hat{4}$-$\hat{3}$), with all voices tending to move by step. $\hat{7}$ virtually *always* moves to $\hat{8}$, but $\hat{4}$ may move to $\hat{5}$ in an inner voice. In the soprano, $\hat{4}$ may move to $\hat{5}$ *only* if the bass moves to I^6 ($\hat{3}$). (See Example 7-12.)

7. Avoid VII$^{\frac{5}{3}}$ for the time being.

8. New cadential possibilities include I^6-V at a semicadence. VII^6 and V^6 may occasionally be used to approach I in a contrapuntal cadence, but not where a strong close is required.

9. To avoid an unwanted cadential effect, it is usually best not to use V$^{(7)}$-I in the middle of a phrase. Use VII^6 or V^6 instead of root-position V$^{(7)}$, and use I^6 instead of I.

EXERCISES

NOTE. Beginning in this unit, the soprano and bass lines in the exercises frequently include idiomatic figures associated with chord progressions discussed in the unit. You will find it helpful, therefore, to review the musical examples in the text before and while you work on the exercises.

With the new chords in this unit, you can now make a distinction between cadential and noncadential functions. Therefore, in harmonizing a bass—figured or unfigured—look for indications of cadences and direct the soprano line to points of repose at these cadences. To prevent the bass from creating an unwanted cadential effect, lead the soprano to $\hat{3}$ or $\hat{5}$ in preference to $\hat{1}$.

In harmonizing a given soprano, also look for melodic halts that might indicate a cadential progression.

1. Preliminaries. Using a different major or minor key for each, write short progressions (no more than six chords) that end with an authentic cadence and show the following chord combinations:

a. tonic expanded by $\frac{6}{3}$; outer voices in parallel 10ths

b. tonic expanded by $\frac{6}{3}$; outer voices exchange

c. V expanded by $\frac{6}{3}$; outer voices in parallel 10ths

d. V⁶ as neighbor to I

e. V⁶ as incomplete neighbor to I

f. VII⁶ passing between I and I⁶ with voice exchange

g. VII⁶ passing between I and I⁶ with parallel 10ths

h. VII⁶ passing between I and I⁶ with soprano $\hat{7}$ as IN

i. VII⁶ passing between I⁶ and I with soprano $\hat{4}$ as IN

2. Outer voices given. Add alto and tenor.

3. Figured bass given. Add three upper voices.

4. Melody given. Add three lower voices.

EIGHT | INVERSIONS OF V⁷

8-1   Schubert, Impromptu, D. 935

V⁶₅, V⁴₃, AND V⁴₂

1. New ways to expand I. It is hard to imagine a better introductory illustration of the inversions of V^7 than the opening eight bars of Schubert's Impromptu in A♭, D. 935 (Example 8-1). This eight-bar phrase contains only tonic chords (in $\frac{5}{3}$ and $\frac{6}{3}$ position) and dominant chords in inversion; all the dominant chords except the last are inversions of V^7. The phrase unmistakably expands an underlying tonic; the important stable tones of the melody and bass, for example, are A♭ and C, both elements of the tonic triad. A sense of movement is contributed by the active outer-voice tones G, B♭, and D♭. In the bass, B♭ (bar 2) is a passing tone between A♭ and C; G (bar 3) forms an incomplete neighbor to the following A♭, and D♭ (bar 6) is an incomplete neighbor leading to C. These three active tones support the three inversions of V^7 in the order in which they appear in the Schubert—$\frac{4}{3}$, $\frac{6}{5}$, and $\frac{4}{2}$. Like V^6 and VII^6, the inversions of V^7 serve to prolong an underlying tonic through melodic-contrapuntal activity. Their bass tones function as neighbors (complete or incomplete) to the bass tones of I or I^6 or as passing tones leading from one to the other. Compared to V^6 and VII^6, the inversions of V⁷ have a much stronger urgency to move to the tonic. This is because of the dissonances—2nd or 7th (as well as tritone)—that they contain. Starting with the late Baroque period these are among the most frequently used of all chords. They fulfill several important compositional functions. In this unit we will concentrate on the most characteristic of these: to create movement within an extended tonic harmony, often (as in the Schubert example) the opening tonic of a large-scale harmonic progression.

2. Descending resolution of 4̂. In the inversions of V⁷, as in the root position, the contrapuntal function of the chord 7th (4̂) imposes a descending stepwise resolution to 3̂. As in the root position, the 7th can appear as a descending passing tone, an upper neighbor, or an upper incomplete neighbor entering by leap (Example 8-2). The one frequent exception to the normal descending resolution of the 7th will be discussed below.

8-2

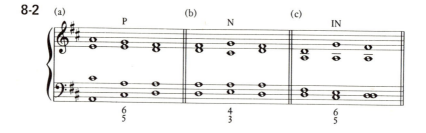

3. V⁶₅. V⁶₅, like V⁶, has the leading tone as its bass and functions similarly as a neighboring chord to I (Example 8-3a). Any of the remaining chordal tones can appear in the soprano; perhaps the most characteristic soprano progression is 4̂-3̂, as in the Beethoven excerpt (8-3b). Bar 3 of the Schubert Impromptu shows another characteristic function: there the bass of V⁶₅ forms an incomplete neighbor leading from I⁶ to I. The bass of V⁶₅ is involved in a dissonant relationship (diminished 5th) with 4̂ in one of the upper parts. Because the diminished 5th involves the bass it must resolve according to rule. Consequently the bass of V⁶₅ always ascends to 1̂ except in those cases where it forms part of an expansion of V⁷. V⁶₅ can be used in the contrapuntal cadence shown in Example 7-14a. (Compare Example 1-1, bar 4, where V⁶₅-I ends a group within a larger phrase.)

8-3   (a) V⁶₅ as N to I

(b) Beethoven, Piano Sonata, Op. 2/1, I

4. V^4_3. Like VII^6, V^4_3 has $\hat{2}$ as its bass. V^4_3, in fact, resembles VII^6 so closely that they are almost interchangeable chords. The bass of V^4_3 is a more neutral tone than that of V^6_5 (or, as you will see, V^4_2) and can move convincingly either to $\hat{1}$ or to $\hat{3}$. Consequently V^4_3, like VII^6, forms a natural connection between I and I^6 and appears very frequently as a passing chord within an extended tonic, as in bars 1-3 of the Schubert example—bars that illustrate a most important detail of voice leading: the D♭ of bar 2 (right-hand part) moves up to E♭ in bar 3 rather than down to C. In other words, $\hat{4}$—the 7th of the root position—moves up to $\hat{5}$ rather than down to $\hat{3}$. This is by no means an unusual case. Very frequently when V^4_3 leads from I up to I^6 with parallel 10ths (less often 3rds) above the bass, $\hat{4}$ ascends in order to complete this motion. In the Schubert, the 10ths above the bass lie in an inner part. More often, as in Example 8-4, they occur in the soprano. This usage of V^4_3 corresponds to the usage of VII^6 shown in Example 7-12g. Note that other uses of V^4_3 require the normal descending resolution—for example, its function as a neighbor of I, or (very frequent) as a passing chord leading down from I^6 to I (Example 8-5).

8-4 Mozart, Non ti fidar   (from *Don Giovanni*, K. 527)

translation: O miserable one, don't trust that villainous heart.

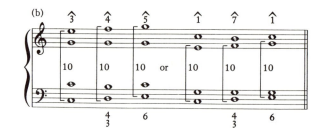

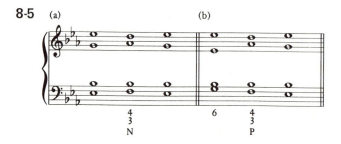

Like VII^6, V$_3^4$ most often occurs in a stepwise bass line. It can, however, form part of a double-neighbor figure, together with V^6 or V$_5^6$, as in Example 8-6.

8-6 (a)

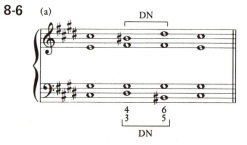

(b) Beethoven, String Quartet, Op. 131, IV

(c) **reduction**

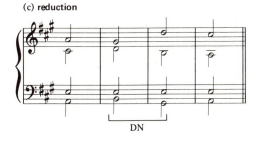

V_3^4 can occur in place of VII^6 in the contrapuntal cadence shown in Example 7-14b.

5. V_2^4. V_5^6 and V_3^4 resemble chords we already know: V^6 and VII^6. V_2^4, however, functions differently from any chord we have previously encountered. Since $\hat{4}$ is its bass tone, V_2^4 must move to a chord whose bass tone is $\hat{3}$ in order to resolve the dissonance by stepwise descent. For the present the only possibility is a progression to I^6. But even later when other chords become available the progression V_2^4-I^6 will remain by far the most frequent one. The bass of V_2^4 has two characteristic functions: descending passing motion from V to I^6 and upper neighbor—complete or incomplete—to I^6. These are shown in the chord progressions and the Bach chorale excerpt of Example 8-7. Very characteristic: the soprano leaps up a 4th from $\hat{5}$ to $\hat{8}$ or—more frequently—from $\hat{2}$ to $\hat{5}$.

8-7   functions of V_2^4

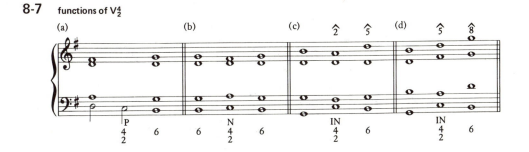

(e) **Bach, Chorale 67**

V_2^4 occasionally passes from V^7 (rather than V_3^5) to I^6. The 7th of V^7 transfers from one of the upper voices to the bass of V_2^4 and, of course, resolves in the bass. This provides a convenient way of moving from V^7 to I^6 (review Unit 7, section 4). Example 8-8 (including the excerpt from a Mozart quartet) illustrates this possibility.

8-8

(a)

(b) Mozart, String Quartet, K. 428, IV

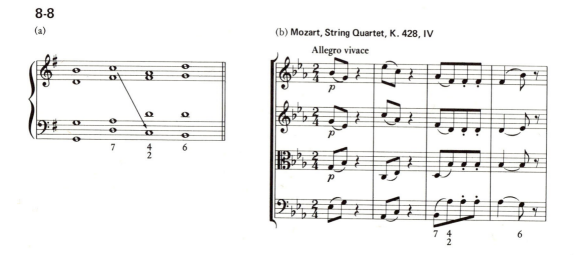

6. Double-neighbor and passing figures. As we saw in Examples 8-6 and 8-8, double-neighbor and passing figures in the bass create opportunities for moving from V^7 to an inversion or from one inversion to another. Such progressions occur frequently. The chordal 7th ($\hat{4}$) will resolve in the last voice in which it appears (see Example 6-19).

7. Incomplete chords. In Example 8-1, bar 6 contains an incomplete V_2^4. The special texture that Schubert creates here—in particular the E♭ sustained in both hands and in the octave doubling of the soprano line—makes it impossible to introduce the missing G gracefully. In general, however, inversions of V^7 almost always appear, as complete chords unless there are fewer than four parts; incomplete chords are seldom necessary or desirable.

8. Common tones. In the inversion of V^7, $\hat{5}$ appears in one of the upper parts and is available as a common tone (with I). Repeating this common tone in the same voice produces a smooth connection with I and helps to reduce voice-leading hazards (review Examples 8-1 through 8-7). (If the soprano line demands the skip $\hat{5}$-$\hat{8}$, as in 8-7e, repeating the common tone becomes impossible unless the inversion of V^7 is incomplete.) One caution: do not proceed in similar motion to $\hat{3}$ doubled at the octave or unison; the interval successions 2-1 and 9-8 usually produce awkward voice leading in moving from an inversion of V^7 to I (Example 8-9).

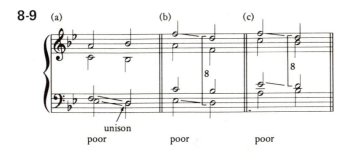

unison

poor   poor   poor

CONTRAPUNTAL EXPANSIONS OF TONIC AND DOMINANT

9. Typical figures for bass and soprano. Examples 8-10 through 8-13 illustrate some of the most important possibilities for expanding tonic harmony through the use of V^6, V^7 and its inversions, and VII^6. In a sense these examples summarize the contents of this unit and the preceding one. They are grouped according to typical bass-line figures. The possibilities shown for the soprano are by no means the only ones, but they are among the most important; notice the great number of different soprano figures possible over the same bass. The more familiar you are with these progressions, the easier it will be for you to harmonize melodies, realize basses, and write phrases. Work with them, try to understand the principles they exemplify, and refer to them when you do your written work. Playing them at the keyboard (and supplying the inner voices) is also of great value, but trying to memorize them is not necessary.

Passing chords: VII^6 and V_3^4 are often used as passing chords between I and I^6 (Example 8-10).

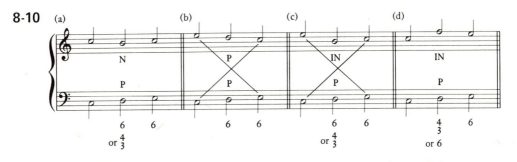

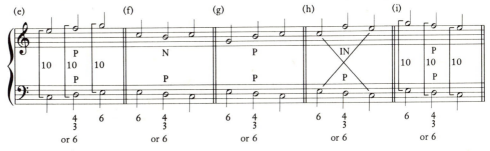

Neighbor chords: V⁶ or V⁶₅ can be used as LN to I⁵₃; V⁴₃ and VII⁶ as UN to I⁵₃ as well as LN to I⁶; V⁴₂ as UN to I⁶ (Example 8-11).

8-11

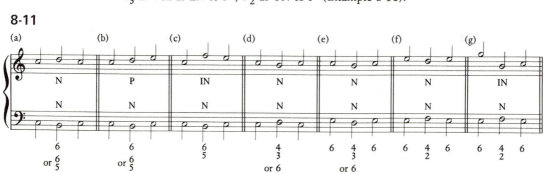

Incomplete-neighbor chords: V⁶₅ and V⁴₂ can be approached by leap as long as they resolve correctly. This produces the incomplete-neighbor figure in the bass (Example 8-12).

8-12

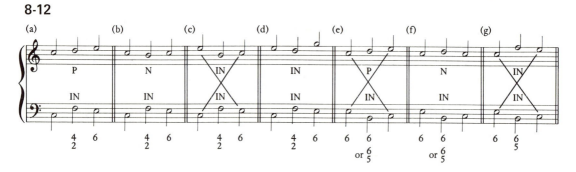

More elaborate figures: These involve leaps from one inversion of V⁷ to another (Example 8-13).

8-13

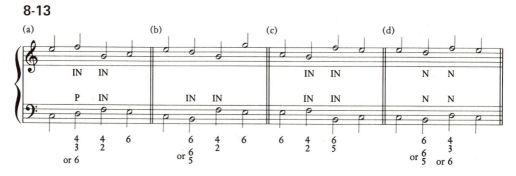

10. "I" as a neighboring or passing chord. We have seen that 1̂, 3̂, and 5̂—normally the stable degrees of the scale—can become active tones if the context makes them dissonant (review Unit 2, section 10). In a similar fashion, the triad formed by these three tones—normally the most stable of all triads—can function as a passing or neighboring chord subordinate to another chord. Example 8-14 shows the end of the opening theme from the first movement of Mozart's "Jupiter" Symphony. It closes with a half cadence and reaches the goal, V, in bar 19. Since the dominant is clearly the goal, the "I" chords that appear in bars 19-21 do not demonstrate the typical tonic function of beginning or ending harmonic progressions; rather they serve to extend and intensify dominant harmony. Since they support a neighboring tone in the soprano, their specific meaning is that of neighboring chords.

8-14   Mozart, "Jupiter" Symphony, K. 551, I

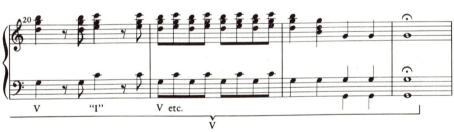

Example 8-15 shows "I" as a passing chord between V_3^4 and V^6. Compare the effect of the F minor chord in bar 3 with the one in bar 4. Melodic and rhythmic factors make it impossible to hear the first one as a goal; the same factors make it impossible to hear the second as anything else.

8-15   Beethoven, Piano Sonata, Op. 2/1, III

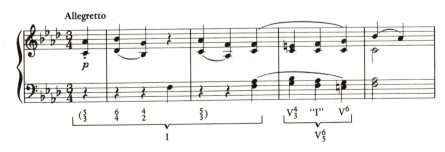

11. Melodic dissonance. The use of V^7 and its inversions presents a number of possibilities for the effective use of melodic dissonance (Example 8-16). In using such dissonances remember that changing direction after a leap—especially one that creates tension—helps to produce a satisfactory melodic line (see Unit 5, section 10).

8-16 melodic dissonance

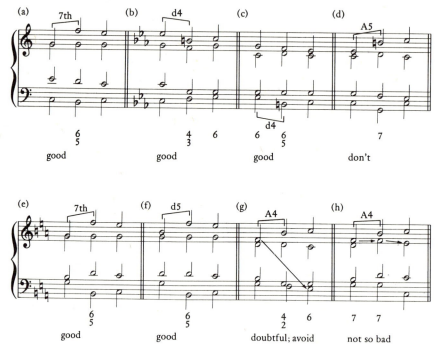

Leaps from I to V⁷: 8-16a shows the leap of an ascending 7th in the soprano. Note that resolving the 7th of V^7 produces a desirable change of direction after the leap. 8-16b and c show the diminished 4th that occurs in minor with a downward leap from $\hat{3}$ to raised $\hat{7}$. The inversion of the diminished 4th—the augmented 5th—creates an unbalanced effect (8-16d); the tone following the leap does not change the direction.

Leaps within V⁷: 8-16e shows a leap from the root of V^7 to its 7th. Best in the soprano voice, but possible in the bass. As in 8-16f, the leap of a diminished 5th will work well in bass or soprano as long as the 7th resolves. The augmented 4th (8-16g and h) is unsatisfactory because the tone following the leap does not change direction. Of the two progressions 8-16h is better because the soprano F is taken over *in the same register* by the alto and resolves as expected.

Leaps in inner voices: At present they should be avoided, with the exception of diminished 4ths between I and V in minor (Example 6-9c).

POINTS FOR REVIEW

1. In moving from an inversion of V^7 to I (or I^6), $\hat{4}$ descends to $\hat{3}$; in inversions, the 7th resolves in the same way it does in root position.

2. The three inversions of V^7 function as follows:

    V^6_5. Resolves to I; its bass functions as a neighbor to 1, either complete (I-V^6_5-I) or incomplete (at present I^6-V^6_5-I; other possibilities in later units).

    V^4_3. Functions as a passing chord between I and I^6, or I^6 and I. A less frequent function is as a neighboring chord to I or I^6. In the progression I-V^4_3-I^6 with parallel 10ths (3rds) above the bass, $\hat{4}$ ascends to $\hat{5}$; otherwise the normal descending resolution occurs.

    V^4_2. Moves to I^6 to resolve $\hat{4}$. Functions as a passing chord between V and I^6 and as an upper neighbor to I^6.

3. Inversions of V^7 are almost always complete chords.

4. "I" can function as a passing or neighboring chord subordinate to V, V^7, or their inversions.

5. In moving from I to V^7 or within V^7 the following dissonant leaps in the bass or soprano are allowable: minor 7th, diminished 4th, and diminished 5th.

EXERCISES

NOTE. With the chords presently available, you will sometimes find it impossible to avoid the frequent repetition of $\hat{5}$ in one of the inner voices. Don't worry about this; to try to achieve active inner voices often creates unnecessary problems in voice leading and may make it impossible to get a good soprano or bass line.

In moving to I, $\hat{5}$ should be kept as a common tone wherever possible. Avoid similar motion to $\hat{3}$ doubled at the octave or unison.

1. Preliminaries. Write short progressions (three or four chords each) showing characteristic uses of VII^6, V^6, V^6_5, V^4_3, and V^4_2. Each progression should begin and end with some form of the tonic and should be written in a different major key and in its parallel minor.

2. Write two 4-measure phrases, one in major, the other in minor. In both, expand an initial tonic contrapuntally by V^6, VII^6, and/or the inversions of V^7. Do not use root-position V or V^7 End each phrase with an authentic cadence.

3. Melody.

4. Unfigured bass.

5. Melody.

6. Unfigured bass.

NINE | LEADING TO V: IV, II, AND II⁶

9-1 Schubert, Impromptu, D. 899

INTERMEDIATE HARMONIES

1. Moving to V and V⁷. Compare the opening phrase of Schubert's Impromptu in E♭ (Example 9-1) with the Schubert excerpt that begins Unit 8. Although they could hardly differ more in texture and in the way the piano is used, the two phrases are partly very similar in tonal design. Both begin with contrapuntal motion through an expanded tonic harmony; the first five bass tones are identical (compare bars 1-4 of Example 8-1 with bars 1-5 of Example 9-1). In one important respect, however, our present example differs from any of the previous ones. The harmony that fills bar 6 is a II in $\frac{6}{3}$ position; its function is to lead from the extended tonic of bars 1-5 to the cadential dominant of bar 7 and to intensify the latter chord. Because it connects the initial I and the V of the basic I-V-I progression, we call such a chord an *intermediate harmony*. Intermediate harmonies occur very frequently and can assume great significance in the structure of tonal music.

Although a number of different chords can function as intermediate harmonies, IV, II, and their derivatives form the most important possibilities. They are particularly well suited to lead into and intensify dominant harmony. Neither contains $\hat{5}$ or $\hat{7}$; therefore they contrast with and highlight the V. In moving from IV or II to V we can easily use a descending soprano line, so often appropriate at cadences. IV stands on the scale step just below V and leads into it by stepwise bass motion. II is the upper 5th of V and moves to it through the fundamental harmonic progression of the falling 5th (or rising 4th). Remember that the function of these intermediate harmonies is to lead *toward* V, not away from it. Thus: I-IV-V-I or I-II-V-I but *not* I-V-IV-I or I-V-II-I.

2. Cadential uses. IV and II can move either to a cadential V or to a noncadential V. In the former case they typically appear shortly before (often, as with the II⁶ in the Schubert Impromptu, *immediately* before) the cadential V, so that they form part of the cadence. Using them makes available to us the expanded cadences of Example 9-2.

9-2 cadences with IV, II, and II⁶

3. Subdominant harmony (IV). IV lies a 4th above or a 5th below the tonic; the progression I-IV is analogous to V-I (falling 5th), the I moving easily and naturally to IV. IV lies a step below V; there is a strong *melodic* connection between the two chord roots. Two triads with roots a 2nd apart share no common tones; in moving from IV to V, therefore, all four voices must proceed to a new tone. If you're not careful, you will soon find that the absence of common tones makes it dangerously easy to produce parallel 5ths and octaves; to avoid them, lead the upper voices in contrary motion to the bass, as in Example 9-3. As with most $\frac{5}{3}$ chords, the root is usually the best tone to double.

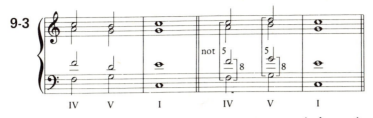

9-3

IV   V   I   IV   V   I

Any of the three tones that belong to IV ($\hat{4}$, $\hat{6}$, and $\hat{1}$) can appear in the soprano. At cadences $\hat{4}$ (moving to $\hat{2}$ over dominant harmony) and $\hat{1}$ (moving to $\hat{7}$) are the most usable. The same melodic tones can occur when IV moves to a noncadential V. In addition—and very characteristically—IV supports $\hat{6}$ as upper neighbor to $\hat{5}$ in the progression I-IV-V. Example 9-4, from Brahms's Third Symphony, shows this very frequent and important usage. The repetition (I-IV-I-IV) emphasizes the neighboring figure.

9-4   **Brahms, Symphony No. 3, Op. 90, II**

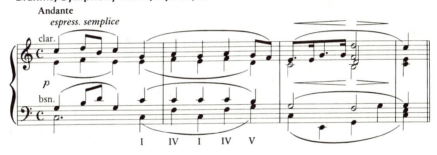

Andante
espress. semplice

I   IV   I   IV   V

4. Supertonic harmony (II). II lies a 5th above V and a step above I. Thus its connection with V is a harmonic one (similar to V-I); its relation to I is melodic (similar to IV-V). I and II, like IV and V, have no tones in common. To avoid parallels, lead the upper voices in contrary motion to the bass—just as with IV-V. II and V share $\hat{2}$ as a common tone. We can repeat the common tone in the same voice; the remaining two voices will normally move up by step (Example 9-5a). Very frequently, however, the upper voices will all descend (much as with IV-V). This allows $\hat{1}$ to be preceded by both its adjacent tones, $\hat{2}$ and $\hat{7}$.

9-5   (a)   (b)

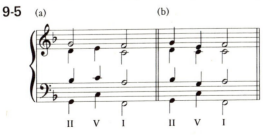

II   V   I   II   V   I

II tends to support $\hat{2}$ or $\hat{4}$ in the soprano more often than $\hat{6}$. At cadences the typical possibilities are $\hat{2}$-$\hat{7}$, $\hat{2}$-$\hat{2}$, and $\hat{4}$-$\hat{2}$, all over II-V. Unlike I-IV-V, I-II-V cannot harmonize the neighboring motion $\hat{5}$-$\hat{6}$-$\hat{5}$ because of the 5ths that would occur between I and II.

In minor, II is a diminished triad. Because of its unsatisfactory quality—at once harsh and thin—in root position, the $\frac{6}{3}$ position is generally used instead. However, circumstances sometimes justify the use of II$\frac{5}{3}$ in minor, as we will see in section 10 of this unit (see also Example 16-9).

In major, II presents no problems of doubling. In minor, doubling the 3rd of II$\frac{5}{3}$ improves its sonority, as the 3rd is the only tone that does not form a dissonance with one of the other chord members. However, if the soprano contains $\hat{2}$ the doubled root is obviously the only possibility.

5. II⁶. II⁶ leads very convincingly to V, occurring particularly often at cadences. As a cadential chord it is especially characteristic of the music of Mozart, Haydn, and Beethoven. Besides its obvious relation to II, II⁶ is also closely related to IV. The progression II⁶-V combines features of II-V and IV-V. It embodies the root progressions by falling 5th of II-V, though expressed less strongly, the root of II not being in the bass. And it has the stepwise bass line of IV-V.

In minor, II⁶ can occur freely; as with VII in major the diminished triad sounds much less harsh in $\frac{6}{3}$ position.

In II⁶-V, the upper voices usually descend, $\hat{2}$ moving to $\hat{7}$. Very often the progression $\hat{2}$-$\hat{7}$ occurs in the soprano, as in Example 9-6a and c. The descending upper voices are almost mandatory in minor because of the augmented 2nd between $\hat{6}$ and raised $\hat{7}$ that would otherwise occur. In moving from II⁶ (or II) to V in minor, the diminished 5th or augmented 4th between $\hat{2}$ and $\hat{6}$ *cannot* resolve normally. $\hat{6}$ can (and usually should) descend to $\hat{5}$, but $\hat{2}$ cannot ascend to $\hat{3}$, for the V chord does not contain that tone. However the harmonic force of the progression is sufficiently strong to offset the melodic irregularity.

9-6 (a)   (b)

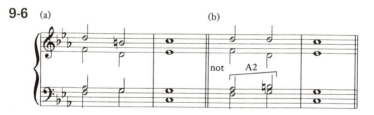

(c) Haydn, Piano Sonata, Hob. XVI/35, I

F:

The bass of II⁶ is very frequently doubled, both in major and—especially—in minor. In major, the doubling of $\hat{2}$ is also quite frequent. The doubling of $\hat{6}$ is less frequent—particularly in minor where it will probably produce a melodic augmented 2nd. Example 9-7 illustrates.

9-7

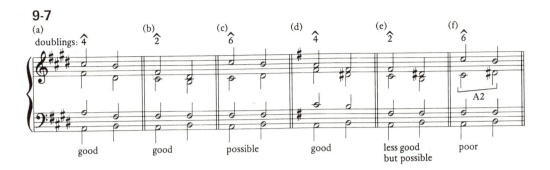

6. Moving to V⁷. IV, II, and II⁶ all lead very easily into V⁷. All contain $\hat{4}$; at the change of harmony, this tone becomes the 7th of V⁷. If we keep $\hat{4}$ in the same voice, first as a consonance, then as the dissonant 7th of V⁷, the dissonance is said to be *prepared*. Preparing the dissonance allows it to enter in a smooth and unobtrusive manner; if the prepared 7th is metrically strong, it functions as a suspension. The good effect of preparing the 7th justifies irregular doubling, especially where the soprano moves away from $\hat{4}$ and cannot keep it as a common tone (Example 9-8d and e). Especially in free, instrumental textures, but often in four-part vocal style as well, the 7th of V⁷ can enter by leap, the preparation occurring in another voice (Example 9-9).

9-8   approaching V⁷

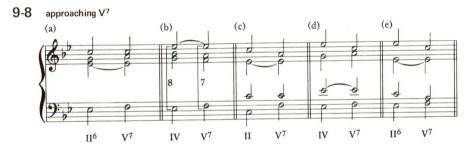

9-9   Beethoven, Bagatelle, Op. 33/1

*7th prepared in another voice

Note in 9-8a how V^7 eliminates the octaves that could occur with II^6-V. In 9-8b the incomplete V^7 is the best way to avoid parallel 5ths between bass and alto.

The melodic leap of a diminished 5th from $\hat{4}$ down to $\hat{7}$ (normally moving on to $\hat{1}$) can create a beautiful soprano for the progression from IV or II$^{(6)}$ to V^7 (Example 9-10).

9-10 Schumann, Fantasy, Op. 17, III

7. Connecting I and V by stepwise bass. A bass rising by step from I to V is a natural and beautiful way to connect the initial tonic of a phrase with the cadential dominant. Using II^6 and IV (both with $\hat{4}$ in the bass) makes it possible to do this. In Example 9-11, notice the accelerating rate of chord change, which intensifies the drive toward the dominant.

9-11 Beethoven, Piano Sonata, Op. 2/1, I

stepwise bass

In general II^6 lends itself to this progression more readily than IV; there are more good possibilities for the soprano and fewer voice-leading difficulties. But IV is also usable as is shown by Example 9-12 (and Example 10-1). Be careful about parallel octaves when moving from I^6 to IV!

9-12 II and IV in stepwise bass

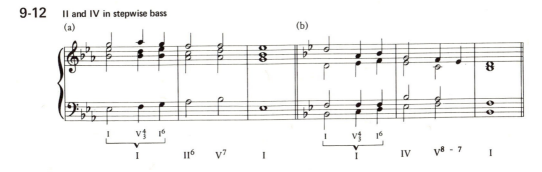

8. Expanding supertonic harmony. Supertonic harmony is often expanded by moving from II to II⁶, or the reverse, in a manner exactly analogous to the expansions of I and V by I⁶ and V⁶ discussed in Unit 7. A passing "I⁶" often appears between II and II⁶ as in the Mozart excerpt of Example 9-13a. Such a chord is a "tonic" in appearance only—not in function. It is neither the beginning nor the goal of a harmonic motion, but rather a detail within the unfolding of the II chord: Example 9-13b and c, shows two possible applications to four-part writing.

9-13

(a) Mozart, Piano Concerto, K. 271, II

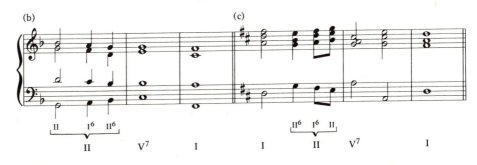

Passing from II to II⁶ gives us another possibility for a rising stepwise bass from I to V (Example 9-14).

9. **IV-II⁶: the 5-6 technique.** IV and II share two common tones and are thus closely associated. The basis of this association is contrapuntal: a melodic motion above a sustained bass as discussed in Unit 4, section 8. If we start with a IV chord and move its 5th up to a 6th (thus: F-A-C to F-A-D), we produce a II chord in $\frac{6}{3}$ position, a procedure called the *5-6 technique*; this process occurs very often in composition and can fulfill a variety of functions (for example, breaking up parallel 5ths). In Example 9-15, a 5-6 progression transforms the IV into a II⁶; the II⁶ is then expanded by its own root position before moving on to V. It is not immediately apparent, but there would be 5ths between the two lowest parts in the progression from IV to V were it not for the change to II⁶.

9-15   Mozart, String Quartet, K. 387, III

Sometimes the bass will leap down a 3rd at the same time that the 5th of IV moves up to a 6th; this produces the succession IV-II. In Example 9-16 the basic progression is IV-V; the II results from a 5-6 motion together with a leap in the bass to the root of II.

10. **II$\frac{5}{3}$ in minor.** We mentioned in section 4 of this unit that II$\frac{5}{3}$ seldom occurs in minor because of the harsh quality of the diminished triad in root position. If it follows II⁶ or IV and occurs without rhythmic stress, the chord loses much of its unpleasant quality, as in Example 9-17.

9-16 Beethoven, Piano Concerto, Op. 58, III

(a)

(b) **reduction**

bars 1-4   bar 5

etc. | from

IV   (II)   IV⁵ — 6

9-17 Schubert, Piano Sonata, D. 279, Menuetto

(Allegro vivace)

II⁶   (⁵₃)   II⁶   (⁵₃)

IV AND II IN CONTRAPUNTAL PROGRESSIONS

11. Moving to VII⁶, V⁶, and to inversions of V⁷. We have learned that VII⁶, V⁶, and the inversions of V⁷ can function as melodic, contrapuntal equivalents to root-position V and that these inverted chords are particularly useful in avoiding an unwanted cadential effect. IV, II, and II⁶ can move to any of these chords. One of the most useful possibilities is IV or II⁶ moving over a stationary bass to V$\frac{4}{2}$, as in Example 9-18.

9-18 Mozart, Piano Sonata, K. 310, I

Moving from II to V$\frac{6}{5}$ produces a particularly smooth bass line (Example 9-19a). Compare it to the much sharper effect of leading IV or II⁶ to V⁶ or V$\frac{6}{5}$ (9-19b). These latter progressions necessarily result in a dissonant leap. Of the two possibilities (augmented 4th or diminished 5th) the diminished 5th is almost always better because the subsequent motion to I changes direction and produces a more flowing bass line.

12. The melodic progression $\hat{5}$-$\hat{6}$-$\hat{7}$-$\hat{8}$. At the beginning or in the middle of a phrase (less often at the end) we might encounter a melodic progression ascending by step from $\hat{5}$ to $\hat{8}$. What might seem the most likely harmonization—I-IV-V-I—is difficult to achieve without parallels (Example 9-20a). One way of averting them is to use descending leaps in both the inner voices (9-20b), a solution that produces correct voice leading but not a very flowing effect unless there is a passing tone (9-20c).

9-19 (a) Chopin, Nocturne, Op. 62/2

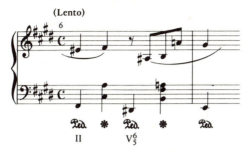

(b) Haydn, String Quartet, Op. 76/3, III

9-20

(c) Bach, Chorale 26

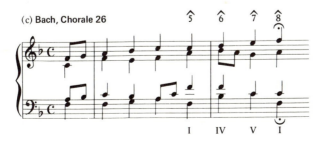

However if we replace V by VII⁶ (or its equivalent, V⁴₃) all difficulties of voice leading disappear. And since the line $\hat{5}$-$\hat{6}$-$\hat{7}$-$\hat{8}$ usually occurs in places where a strong cadence is not needed (or might even be inappropriate) the absence of a root-position V is frequently an advantage (Example 9-21).

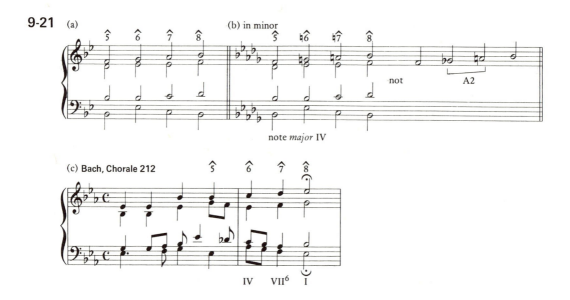

As we mentioned in section 4 of this unit, II tends to support $\hat{2}$ or $\hat{4}$ in the soprano more than $\hat{6}$. II or II⁶ will seldom support $\hat{6}$ in a melodic progression rising from $\hat{5}$ to $\hat{8}$; it is difficult (sometimes impossible) to avoid 5ths in moving from I. However the succession I-IV-II⁽⁶⁾-V⁽⁷⁾-I works well if the rhythm of the melodic line allows it—that is, if $\hat{6}$ lasts long enough to serve as the top-voice tone of both IV and II (Example 9-22; also Example 16-7).

SOME NEW WRITING TECHNIQUES

13. Chord progression and rhythm. In Unit 6, section 15, we saw that repeating a chord from a weak to a strong beat tends to neutralize the metrical accent. The following procedures can also cause contradiction of the meter:

1. Moving between root position and inversion or between the different inversions of the same chord from a weak to a strong beat. (V and V⁷ count as the same chord.)
2. Repeating a bass tone, while changing the chord it supports (as in IV-II⁶ or II⁶-IV), from a weak to a strong beat.

Thus in each of the first progressions of Example 9-23a, b, and c, maintaining the same chord or bass tone across the bar line creates an unintended syncopation; the weak beat (new chord or bass tone) actually sounds stronger than the following strong beat (same chord or bass tone). Awareness of these rhythmic implications of chord progression is of great importance for harmonizing melodies, setting unfigured basses, and writing phrases. This is especially true in simple textures where there are no quickly moving passing or neighboring tones to enliven the rhythm and to produce a contrast in sonority lacking in the progression of the main tones.

The progressions shown in 9-23d and e demonstrate two situations where moving within the same chord or repeating a bass tone from a weak to a strong beat are good. In 9-23d, the repeated motive in the soprano creates enough emphasis on the downbeat to offset the lack of chord change. In 9-23e, the $\frac{4}{2}$ chord arises from a dissonant suspension (ninth against the alto) in the bass. Suspensions, by definition, are held over or repeated from a weak to a strong beat; the dissonance produces enough contrast to give an accented quality to the downbeat despite the static bass. (In this connection review Example 9-18b.)

9-23 chord progression and rhythm

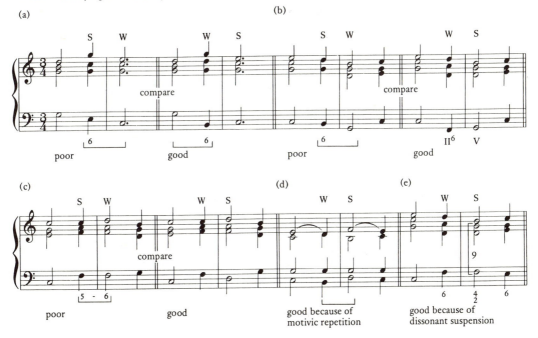

As with repeating a chord, repeating a bass tone or changing the position of the bass within the same chord are problematic *only* from a weak to the following strong beat. They are good if they occur from a strong to a weak beat or from a strong (through one or more weak beats) to another strong beat.

14. Subordinate and incomplete progressions. The chords in this unit will enable you to write more varied and interesting musical phrases, and will enhance your understanding of the techniques found in the works of great composers. One new possibility is to extend the initial tonic of a phrase through IV, II, or II⁶ moving to a noncadential $V^{(7)}$. In Example 9-24 the first four chords constitute a harmonic progression clearly subordinate to the larger I-II⁶-V⁷-I; we therefore refer to the first succession of chords as a *subordinate harmonic progression* (Example 9-24; compare Example 9-4).

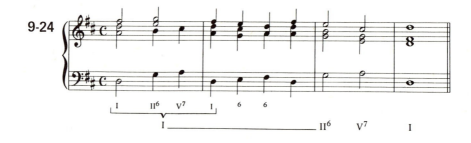

9-24

If the subordinate progression threatens to produce an inappropriate cadential effect, I⁶ can be used in place of the final I, or an inversion of $V^{(7)}$ or VII⁶ in place of the V, or both (see again Example 9-18).

Sometimes IV, II, or II⁶ will begin a phrase—or even, as in Example 9-25, a piece. Here the opening progression is II⁶-V⁷-I. Because it lacks an initial tonic we call such a chord succession an *incomplete harmonic progression.* (Compare with Example 9-16, which also contains an incomplete progression.) Regardless of the actual metrics, phrases like that of Example 9-25 often produce the effect of beginning with an upbeat; the lack of a tonic can weaken the rhythmic stress of the first downbeat.

9-25 Schumann, Davidsbündlertänze, Op. 6/5

POINTS FOR REVIEW

1. The intermediate harmonies IV, II, and II⁶ lead from I to V—*not* from V to I. They can appear immediately before a cadential dominant, forming part of the cadence.

2. In IV-V or I-II, lead the upper voices in contrary motion to the bass to avoid parallel 5ths and octaves.

3. In general, IV is better than II or II⁶ as support for $\hat{6}$.

4. Avoid II⁵₃ in minor except on a weak beat following II⁶ or IV.

5. The best doubling of IV and of II (in major) is the root; of II in minor (if used), the 3rd; of II⁶, the bass or root. *Warning:* Be careful of parallel octaves in II⁶-V if the bass of II⁶ is doubled.

6. IV, II, and II⁶ allow the 7th of V⁷ to be prepared as a common tone; they also make possible a stepwise bass ascent from I to V.

7. The following expanded usages can precede V; II-II⁶ or II⁶-II, possibly connected by a passing "I⁶"; IV-II⁶, or IV-II.

8. As alternatives to root-position V or V⁷, the following are possible: VII⁶ or V⁴₃, especially with melodic line $\hat{5}$-$\hat{6}$-$\hat{7}$-$\hat{8}$; V⁴₂; V⁶ or V⁶₅.

9. Avoid the following types of progression, which can cause a contradiction of the meter: a weak-strong progression within the same chord, such as II-II⁶; a weak-strong bass repetition, such as IV-II⁶ (exception: IV or II⁶ to V⁴₂ is good).

EXERCISES

NOTE. With the expanded chord vocabulary now available to you, you will often have to decide what chord a given scale degree might belong to—for example, $\hat{1}$ in the soprano could indicate I or IV; $\hat{2}$ in the bass could indicate II or VII⁶ or V⁴₃. Of the various possibilities, make the best choice by relating the tone both to its immediate context and to the direction of the phrase as a whole. First, determine the cadential points; then, decide provisionally all the places where tonic harmony might occur. This will make it easier to complete the outer voices, then the entire exercise.

1. Preliminaries.
    a. Write a phrase that begins with a contrapuntal expansion of I (omitting root-position V); lead it to a cadence that includes IV, II, or II⁶.
    b. Write a phrase that begins with a subordinate harmonic progression ending on I⁶; lead it to a cadence that includes IV, II, or II⁶.

2. Melody

(I⁶)

3. Figured bass.

4. Melody.

bass: whole note

5. Unfigured bass.

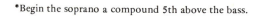

*Begin the soprano a compound 5th above the bass.

THE TEN CADENTIAL 6/4

10-1 Beethoven, String Quartet, Op. 18/3, I

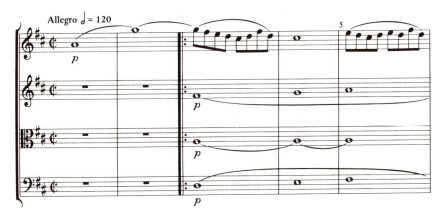

AN INTENSIFICATION OF V

1. Non-tonic function. Example 10-1 begins with a bass that rises by step from I to V in a manner familiar to us from the preceding unit. When the bass arrives at the goal tone, A, in bar 7, however, the upper parts do not play a dominant chord. Instead they sound the tones D, F♯, and A, thus producing a $\frac{6}{4}$ chord above the bass. In the next bar the bass leaps down an octave, and the upper voices move to a cadential dominant. The $\frac{6}{4}$ chord of bar 7 contains the same tones as the tonic triad; for this reason most harmony books label such chords "I$\frac{6}{4}$." This label may be helpful for purposes of identification but it contradicts the meaning and function of a $\frac{6}{4}$ chord used in this way. The chord does not act as an inversion of I$\frac{5}{3}$; it serves neither to extend it nor to substitute for it (play the Beethoven with a D in the bass in bar 7 and hear how different the chord sounds). The purpose of this $\frac{6}{4}$ is to embellish and intensify the dominant; therefore we shall use the notation V$\frac{6\text{-}5}{4\text{-}3}$ or, when appropriate, a variant of it—in the Beethoven, V$\frac{8\text{-}7}{6\text{-}5\text{-}}{4\text{-}3\text{-}}$. This type of $\frac{6}{4}$ is very frequently and very appropriately termed *cadential* $\frac{6}{4}$ for it most characteristically decorates the V chord at an authentic or half cadence. Although the cadential use is the most typical, a $\frac{6}{4}$ on the dominant is not restricted to cadences.

2. Origin of the cadential $\frac{6}{4}$. It is easiest to understand the cadential $\frac{6}{4}$ if you realize that it developed out of a very old voice-leading technique: delaying the leading tone at a cadence by means of a suspension. If $\hat{5}$ occurs in the bass, the suspension and its resolution into the leading tone will form the intervals of a 4th and a 3rd (Example 10-2a). Adding another voice in parallel 3rds above gives us the complete $\frac{6}{4}$ chord moving to V in $\frac{5}{3}$ position (10-2b).

10-2 (a)   LT   (b)

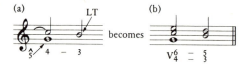

3. Voice leading. The stepwise descending resolution of a 4th to a 3rd forms the basis for the correct treatment of the cadential $\frac{6}{4}$. Stepwise descent is the normal way to resolve suspensions and other accented dissonances, and the 4th is dissonant when it sounds between the bass and one of the upper parts. Because it contains the 4th in this position, the $\frac{6}{4}$ functions as a dissonant chord; thus its resolution requires as much care as that of V^7.

As we noted, the 4th will most often enter as a suspension—held over or repeated from the preceding chord. When this is not possible (for example, coming from II or II^6) the 4th can enter by stepwise descent as an accented passing tone (APT). In either case it will resolve by step to the 3rd of dominant harmony (Example 10-3).

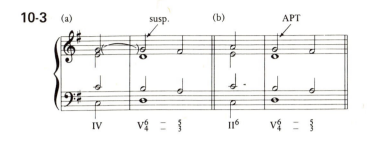

4. **Doubling.** The bass is the best tone to double, for it is the root of the prevailing harmony—V—to which the $^6_4$ resolves. If this doubling is impracticable, the 6th may be doubled. The 4th is not doubled except in very free or complex textures. The cadential $^6_4$ moves easily to V^7. Usually all the upper voices descend by step, thus: $^{8-7}_{6-5}_{4-3}$ (Example 10-4d). Less frequently the 6th above the bass (especially when in an inner voice) can move up to the 7th (10-4e). With the less usual doubled 6th, still another possibility arises: $^{6-7}_{6-5}_{4-3}$ (10-4f).

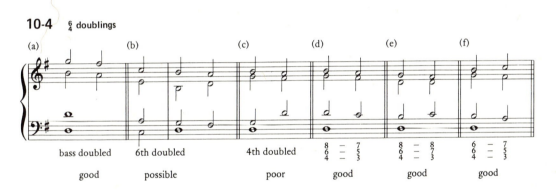

5. **Rhythm.** Because it grows out of a suspension (which, by definition, is metrically accented) and because it resolves over a stationary bass, the cadential $^6_4$ *must* appear in a metrically strong position; no weak-to-strong bass repetitions are permitted. If the chords change every beat or so, the $^6_4$ will appear on a strong beat and will resolve on the following weak beat (duple meter) or on one of the two following weak ones (triple meter). In triple time the second beat is sometimes stronger than the third; therefore a resolution from second to third beat can be a possibility. If the $^6_4$ resolves within a divided beat, the $^6_4$ will appear on the strong part of the beat and its resolution on a weaker part. Sometimes chord changes occur more slowly than one per beat. In such cases the $^6_4$ will appear on a strong beat and its resolution either on a weak or another strong one (for example, from the first to the third quarter of $^4_4$ time). Example 10-5 illustrates the metrical relation between the cadential $^6_4$ and its resolution. Note that the strong-to-weak rhythm can be underscored by the leap of a descending octave in the bass.

10-5   rhythmic position of cadential $\frac{6}{4}$

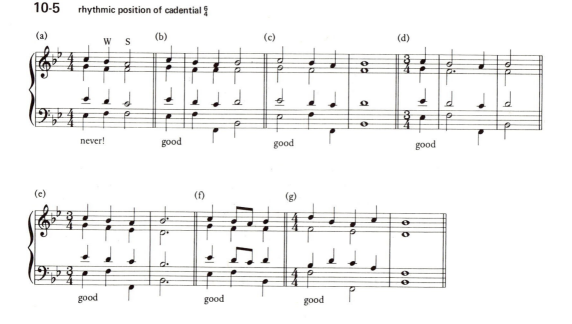

In many musical phrases (for example, the Beethoven excerpt that begins this unit), strong and weak *measures* alternate, creating a metrical pattern similar to strong and weak beats within the measure. In the Beethoven observe that the $\frac{6}{4}$ falls on a strong measure and its resolution on a weak one; also note how the descending bass octave emphasizes the rhythm. Cadential $\frac{6}{4}$ chords that last a whole bar fall, in principle, on a strong or accented bar.

On occasion, cadential $\frac{6}{4}$ chords will last a very long time. Long duration does not alter the meaning or function of the chord; it is still dependent on the dominant to which it resolves. Extending the $\frac{6}{4}$ can generate a great deal of tension, as in Example 10-6, where the musical tension relates directly to Shakespeare's text.

6. Stepwise melodic lines. An important use of the cadential $\frac{6}{4}$ is the stepwise melodic line it permits when IV or II moves to V with $\hat{4}$-$\hat{2}$ or $\hat{2}$-$\hat{7}$ in the soprano. The two excerpts of Example 10-7—one of them from the same Haydn song as our last example—illustrate this.

10-6 Haydn, She Never Told Her Love

10-7 (a) (Haydn)

(b) Bach, Well-Tempered Clavier II, Fugue 9

Using the cadential $^6_4$ effects a significant (though temporary) reversal in the melodic functions of $\hat{1}$ and $\hat{7}$. $\hat{1}$ is, of course, the most stable melodic tone and normally serves as a goal of motion; $\hat{7}$ is an unstable tone with a marked tendency to move to $\hat{1}$. In the cadential $^6_4$, however, $\hat{1}$ functions as a dissonance (4th). It cannot serve as a goal of motion; instead, it must resolve to $\hat{7}$ by stepwise descent. In this situation, therefore, $\hat{7}$ becomes a temporary goal; $\hat{1}$ loses its stability and becomes an active tone dependent on $\hat{7}$. To the perceptive listener, $\hat{1}$ in a cadential $^6_4$ and $\hat{1}$ in a tonic $^5_3$ chord have such contrasting functions that their identical pitch becomes of secondary importance (much as the words "son" and "sun" mean very different things heard in context, though they sound the same). In the cadential $^6_4$, $\hat{3}$ (6th above the bass) also becomes more unstable than $\hat{2}$ (5th of V) to which it normally descends; the relationship between these tones resembles that between $\hat{1}$ and $\hat{7}$. After the resolution of the cadential $^6_4$ to V, $\hat{7}$ and $\hat{2}$ retain their tendency to move on to $\hat{1}$; they function as temporary, not final, goals.

7. Noncadential uses. In Example 10-8, $^6_4$ chords embellish noncadential dominants (bars 95 and 97). With regard to rhythm and voice leading these chords function in the same way as cadential $^6_4$'s.

10-8 Mozart, Piano Sonata, K. 332, I

If a cadential effect is not wanted, the $^6_4$ can move to a $^4_2$ (Example 10-9). A $^6_4$ moving to a $^4_2$ occurs in the last movement of Mozart's String Quartet, K. 499 (Example 10-10). Here Mozart avoids a formal cadence at the end of the phrase and continues the motion into the next group of measures.

10-9

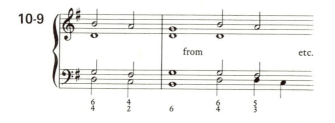

10-10   Mozart, String Quartet, K. 499, IV

These two excerpts from Mozart include techniques that you can profitably apply to your own work. In Example 10-8, the repeated I-V progression of bars 1-4 illustrates a new usage: an incomplete harmonic progression that lacks a *final* tonic (we encountered progressions without an *initial* tonic in Unit 9). The V chords of bars 95 and 97 relate back to preceding tonics; they do not move on to any following ones. (Because of the melodic and rhythmic grouping, we do not hear the V of bar 95 as moving to the I of bar 96; bar 96 starts anew.) The I-V progressions are subordinate to the harmonic framework I (bars 94 and 96)—II⁶ (bars 98-99)—V⁷ (bar 100)—I (bar 101).

Example 10-10 illustrates the technique of forming a larger unit from two phrases by suppressing the first cadence. You can use a similar procedure to extend the duration of a single phrase, as in Example 10-11.

10-11   (a) 4 bars

(b) 6 bars

(phrase extended)

8. Antecedent-consequent construction. Two interdependent phrases that form a larger unit or *period* are in *antecedent-consequent* relation; the first phrase is called the antecedent, and the second is called the consequent. In Example 10-12, two factors working together create the impression of a unified period rather than of two separate phrases. These factors are repetition and the delayed resolution of tonal tension. The second phrase repeats (in sightly varied form) much of the material of the first; the repetition helps to connect the two phrases. An equally important, though less obvious, source of unity is the relationship between the two contrasting cadences. The first phrase closes on V; the tension produced by this semicadence is not dissipated by the tonic of bar 5, which is a new beginning, not a goal. Not until the arrival of I and $\hat{1}$ in bar 8 is tonal equilibrium restored. Cadential $\frac{6}{4}$'s often occur prominently in antecedent-consequent groups; by intensifying the dominant chords, they give emphasis to the cadences.

10-12   Mozart, The Magic Flute, Act I

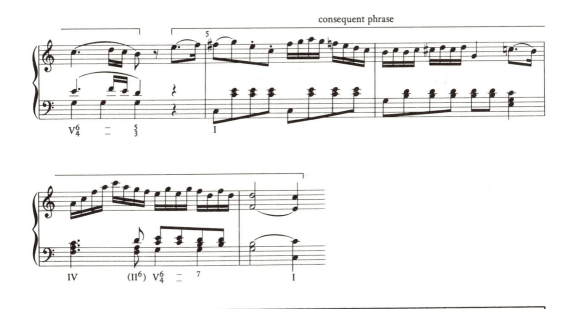

POINTS FOR REVIEW

1. The cadential $^6_4$ is *not* an inversion of I; it is an embellishment and intensification of V.

2. The 4th of the cadential $^6_4$ is dissonant and must resolve downward by step. The 6th usually descends by step as well, thus: $^{6\text{-}5}_{4\text{-}3}$.

3. The cadential $^6_4$ occurs on a strong beat relative to the chord of resolution.

4. The bass is the most frequently doubled tone; *never* double the 4th.

5. The normal resolution to V^7 is $^{8\text{-}7}_{6\text{-}5}_{4\text{-}3}$. Also possible but less frequent is $^{6\text{-}7}_{6\text{-}5}_{4\text{-}3}$.

6. Melodically, the cadential $^6_4$ permits a stepwise descending soprano—$\hat{4}$-$\hat{3}$-$\hat{2}$-$\hat{1}$ or $\hat{2}$-$\hat{1}$-$\hat{7}$-$\hat{1}$—in progressions from $II^{(6)}$ or IV to V.

7. A $^6_4$ on the dominant is not restricted to cadences; the alternative resolution $^{6\text{-}4}_{4\text{-}2}$ avoids a cadential effect.

8. Cadential $^6_4$'s often occur in antecedent-consequent construction, in which two interdependent phrases form a larger group or period. The antecedent ends with a semicadence, the consequent with an authentic cadence.

EXERCISES

NOTE. With the melodic figures $\hat{3}$-$\hat{2}$, $\hat{3}$-$\hat{2}$-$\hat{1}$, $\hat{1}$-$\hat{7}$, and $\hat{1}$-$\hat{7}$-$\hat{1}$, remember that the first melodic tone may require the cadential $^6_4$—*not* tonic harmony, particularly at cadential points. And don't forget that the cadential $^6_4$ must be metrically strong relative to its resolution.

1. Preliminaries.
    a. Write three cadential $\frac{6}{4}$ progressions, each in a different key, containing:
       1. II
       2. IV-V$^{6-5}_{4-3}$ or $^{8-7}_{6-5}$-I.
               $_{4-3}$
       3. II^6
       Be sure the $\frac{6}{4}$ falls on a strong beat!
    b. Write two phrases of at least four measures in length—one in major, one in minor, one in $\frac{2}{4}$, one in $\frac{3}{4}$—each using II, IV, or II^6 moving to a cadential $\frac{6}{4}$.
2. Figured bass.

3. Melody.

*don't harmonize passing tones

4. Melody.

ELEVEN | VI AND IV⁶

11-1 Schubert, Impromptu, D. 899

USES OF VI

1. VI-IV or VI-II⁶ (bass arpeggio). To study harmony and voice leading is to study the expansion of simple patterns into more complex and differentiated ones, creating the possibility for new kinds of tonal motion and new tonal goals. For example, IV and II⁶—chords whose primary purpose is to move on to V—can themselves function as temporary goals of motion. At the beginning of Example 11-1, a bass motion in 3rds—a kind of broken chord or arpeggio—leads down from the tonic to the bass of II⁶ in bar 3: G♭-E♭-C♭. The chord on E♭ is VI, a particularly versatile triad with many possible functions. The function illustrated in the Schubert is one of the most important and characteristic: to connect I with IV or II⁶ by means of an arpeggiated descending motion in 3rds. Usually IV or II⁶ will move on to V and I (as in the Schubert);* sometimes, however, they lead to an inversion of V⁽⁷⁾ or to VII⁶ for a more contrapuntal bass line. Example 11-2 shows some of the most typical possibilities.

11-2   VI leading to IV or II⁶

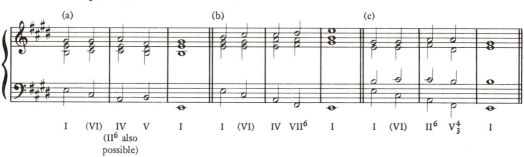

2. VI-II (descending-5th progression). Another very important function of VI is exemplified in the opening idea of Beethoven's "Spring" Sonata for piano and violin (Example 11-3). Two statements of VI occur in this ten-bar phrase (bars 3 and 8); both move to II, the first in root position and the second in ⁶₃ position. The close connection that one feels here between VI and II—especially in bars 3-4—is largely due to the strong harmonic relationship between these chords. VI is built on the scale degree a 5th above II and thus gravitates to it, as II does to V and V to I. This harmonic connection is most strongly evident when both chords are in root position; the "harmonic" motion of a 5th (or its inversion, a 4th) will then occur in the crucial bass part. But a weaker harmonic connection can also be implied when II is in first inversion, as in bar 9 of the Beethoven.

---

*In the Schubert, the I-II⁶-V⁷-I is itself a harmonic expansion of the initial tonic; the phrase as a whole goes from the expanded I to the V of bar 4. The C♮ on the second beat of bar 4 functions as a leading tone to V.

11-3   Beethoven, Violin Sonata, Op. 24 ("Spring"), I

As you add to your vocabulary of chords you will see that progression by falling 5th constitutes a norm—indeed *the* norm of harmonic motion. Thus using VI is the most natural way to lead to II.

Because II$\frac{5}{3}$ in minor is a problematic diminished triad, and because the roots of VI and II in minor form a diminished, rather than a perfect, 5th, the progression VI-II$\frac{5}{3}$ does not have the significance in minor that it does in major. However VI-II^6—where the vertical diminished 5th is softened and the horizontal one eliminated—can and does occur as freely as in major.

In addition to its harmonic role, as discussed above, VI can also fulfill a voice-leading function. It often breaks up the parallel 5ths or octaves that would otherwise occur between I and II, a possibility we will explore closely in Unit 16.

3. VI approaching V from above. I can move to V with either a rising or a falling bass. Both possibilities are good, and both occur frequently, but the rising bass is the more "natural"—that is, it relates more directly to fundamental properties of the tonal system. $\hat{5}$ lies above $\hat{1}$ in the tonic triad and in the overtone series; the normal position of $\hat{5}$, therefore, is *above* $\hat{1}$, and the bass line of a I-V progression will most naturally ascend. The most frequently used intermediate harmonies—

II, IV, and II⁶—have bass tones that lie between 1̂ and the 5̂ above it; these harmonies help to fill in, and thus make partially stepwise, the ascending 5th from 1̂ to 5̂.

However music would not have reached a very high level of development if composers had confined themselves to the simplest and most basic possibilities. Thus, as we know, we can invert the rising 5th and produce a descending 4th. And we will now investigate the possibility of using an intermediate harmony within this descending 4th, thus approaching V from above. The most important of these chords are VI and IV⁶.

VI does not lead directly to V as often as it does to II, IV, or II⁶ but the progression VI-V is nonetheless an extremely useful one. It is particularly well suited to a rising top voice, such as the 1̂-2̂-3̂ in Example 11-4. Example 11-5 is similar, only here we see an incomplete progression VI-V-I instead of one beginning on the tonic.

Another possibility for the top voice is the progression 5̂-6̂-7̂-8̂. This occurs less frequently, perhaps because of the large number of perfect consonances between the outer voices (Example 11-6).

In a progression from VI to V, the top voice can move in parallel 10ths with the bass. This voice leading can be beautiful and is especially suitable for cadential points where a descending soprano is often desirable. It carries with it, however, the threat of parallel 5ths and octaves. To prevent these, *double the 3rd of VI* and move *both* inner voices up, as in Example 11-7.

11-4   Chopin, Scherzo, Op. 39

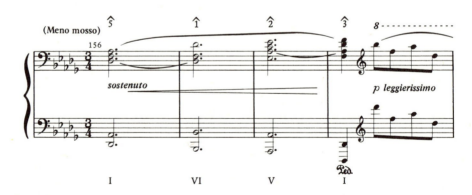

11-5 **Schubert, Wanderers Nachtlied**

War - te nur, war - te nur, - bal - de ru - hest du auch,

translation: Wait, only wait, soon you too will be at rest.

11-6 **Chopin, Impromptu, Op. 36**

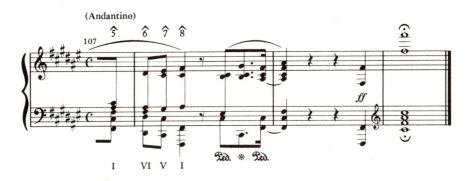

11-7

(a)

(b) Bach, Chorale 47

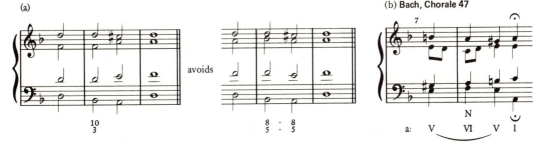

avoids

USES OF IV⁶

4. IV⁶-V. The second important chord whose bass descends by step to V is IV⁶. VI and IV⁶ often appear in similar situations; they relate to each other exactly as do IV and II⁶, sharing two common tones (one of them the bass). To change VI to IV⁶ we use the 5-6 technique, moving the 5th of VI up one step, exactly like changing IV to II⁶.

The two excerpts shown in Example 11-8 demonstrate a most important function of IV⁶: preceding V in a semicadence in minor. This makes a stronger effect than in major because of the bass motion by half step, which intensifies V. The term *Phrygian cadence* is often applied to the semicadence IV⁶-V in minor, not because the piece in question is even partly in the Phrygian mode, but merely because a similar chord progression often appears at cadences in genuine Phrygian compositions (Example 11-9).

11-8 (a) Bach, Chorale 281

(b) Handel, Adagio   (from *Harpsichord Suite No. 2*)

11-9   **Bartolomeo Tromboncino (fl. 1500), Non val aqua**

Phrygian
cadence

When used as a semicadence in minor, the Phrygian cadence occurs most typically in compositions from the Baroque period. Like any semicadence it will most naturally appear within a piece (as in the Bach chorale excerpt of Example 11-8). Quite frequently, however, composers of the Baroque era ended slow movements with such a cadence (thus ending on V rather than I), if the slow movement was not an independent composition but part of a larger work. This is the case in the Handel excerpt of Example 11-8, which ends with a Phrygian cadence on an A major chord. It is followed in the suite by an Allegro in F major, a connection by descending major 3rd that was quite frequent during this period.

When IV⁶ is used in a Phrygian cadence, the usual tone to double is the 3rd above the bass, as in 11-8b and 11-9; this permits a completely stepwise progression into V and reduces the danger both of parallel octaves and of a melodic augmented 2nd (Example 11-10).

11-10

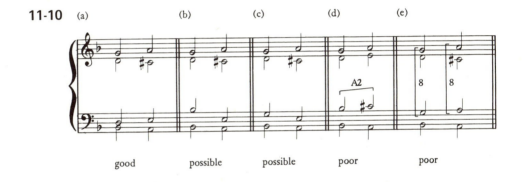

Perhaps you have noticed that all our examples of IV⁶-V include the top-voice progression $\hat{4}$-$\hat{5}$. This is not invariable, but it is typical both for Phrygian cadences and for many other situations where IV⁶ moves to V. IV$^5_3$ could never move to V under a soprano line $\hat{4}$-$\hat{5}$ because of the inevitable parallel octaves. The two excerpts of Example 11-11 illustrate this most useful feature of IV⁶; neither, of course, is a Phrygian cadence.

11-11   (a) Bach, Chorale 256

(b) Brahms, German folksong

Ver - stoh - len geht der Mond auf, blau, blau Blü - me - lein!

IV⁶   V   I

translation: The moon rises stealthily, little blue, blue flower!

Leading to V with the top-voice progression $\hat{4}$-$\hat{5}$ is a specialized function of IV⁶, one that it fulfills more readily than any other chord. In addition to this special function, IV⁶ can serve to *extend* IV (just as I⁶, II⁶, and V⁶ can extend I, II, and V); see the Mozart excerpt in Example 11-12a. IV⁶ can also *substitute* for IV where a lighter sonority, a descending bass, or both are desired (as in the Handel excerpt of 11-12b). In addition, IV⁶ can appear instead of VI in a bass arpeggio leading to IV (11-12a) or II⁶ (11-12c, from the same Handel Air).

11-12   (a) Mozart, Overture to Così fan tutte, K. 588

(Andante)   Presto

IV

(b) Handel, Air   (from *Leçon No. 1*)

IV⁶
instead of IV⁵₃

(c) (Handel)

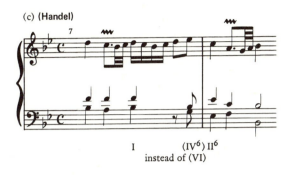

I   (IV⁶) II⁶
instead of (VI)

5. VI and IV⁶ ascending to V⁶ ($\frac{6}{5}$). VI and IV⁶ will normally move to a root-position V, but their use is by no means restricted to such a progression. If a melodic, noncadential bass is appropriate, both chords can move to V⁶ ($\frac{6}{5}$) and then on to I (Example 11-13). In 11-13d, note the beautiful counterpoint between the descending arpeggio of the top voice and the ascending stepwise bass line.

11-13   (a)   (b)   (c)

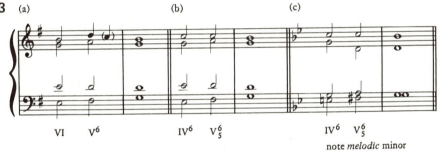

VI   V⁶   IV⁶   V⁶₅   IV⁶   V⁶₅

note *melodic* minor

(d) Mozart, String Quartet, K. 458, III

VI   V⁶   I

(e) Bach, Chorale 222

POINTS FOR REVIEW

1. VI makes possible the bass-arpeggio progression I-VI-IV or I-VI-II⁶.
2. VI leads to II in a descending-5th progression.
3. VI approaches V from above. In this progression, the top voice can ascend (in contrary motion to the bass to avoid parallels) or it can form parallel 10ths with the bass (with the 3rd of VI doubled to avoid parallel 5ths).
4. IV⁶-V in minor forms a Phrygian cadence. A noncadential use for this progression is to support $\hat{4}$-$\hat{5}$.
5. The most frequent doubling of IV⁶ is the 3rd above the bass.
6. IV⁶ can extend or substitute for IV.
7. VI or IV⁶ makes possible the rising-bass progression VI or IV⁶-V⁶($^6_5$)-I.

EXERCISES

NOTE. In setting melodies, keep in mind that a repeated or sustained $\hat{1}$ or $\hat{3}$ may indicate the beginning of a bass arpeggio, that the melodic progression $\hat{4}$-$\hat{5}$ often suggests IV⁶-V, and that the progression $\hat{1}$-$\hat{2}$-$\hat{3}$ can be set VI-V-I.

1. Preliminaries. Melodic fragments.

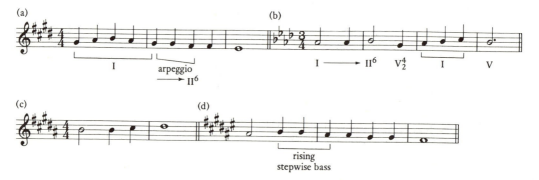

*approach V from above

2. Melody.

3. Figured bass.

4. Melody.

5. Figured bass.

*voice exchange with soprano

TWELVE | SUPERTONIC AND SUBDOMINANT SEVENTH CHORDS

12-1   **Bach, Chorale 99**

$$\text{II}^6_5$$

1. II^7 and IV^7. If we add a 7th to II or IV, we produce II^7 or IV^7; these are among the most frequently used of all nondominant seventh chords. By far the most important positions are II^7, II^6_5, and IV^7. II^6_5, in particular, is an indispensable chord. It occurs in music of many styles and especially often in the works of Bach (Example 12-1). Adding a 7th to II and IV does not change their tendency to move to dominant harmony; on the contrary, the dissonance activates these chords and intensifies their motion toward V. Dissonance treatment greatly resembles that of V^7. As Example 12-1 shows, the process of resolution is exactly the same—*downward and by step.* The way the dissonance is introduced also resembles V^7 but tends to be stricter. Most frequently the 7th enters as a common tone held over or repeated from the preceding chord; it is usually accented and functions as a suspension. Where it is not prepared as a common tone, the 7th generally functions as a passing tone (8-7) within an extended II or IV. Except in rather free or complex textures the 7th will not enter by leap, as sometimes happens in V^7 when the 7th enters unprepared as an incomplete neighbor.

In four-part writing II^6_5, the other inversions of II^7, and the various positions of IV^7 are virtually always complete chords. However, root-position II^7, especially in major, will sometimes appear with 5th omitted and with doubled root or 3rd.

SUPERTONIC SEVENTH CHORDS

2. II$^6_5$. Example 12-1 shows II$^6_5$ in its most characteristic use: as an intermediate harmony connecting I with a cadential V. As the example indicates, the dissonant tone is the 5th above the bass, here the A of the alto. In any position of II^7, the dissonant tone is $\hat{1}$; as a dissonance, $\hat{1}$ cannot serve as goal of motion, but is dependent on $\hat{7}$, to which it resolves by stepwise descent. (We encountered the same reversal in the melodic functions of $\hat{1}$ and $\hat{7}$ with the cadential $^6_4$; see Unit 10, section 6.) Note that the entire chord is accented relative to the V to which it moves. In order to prepare the dissonance as a common tone, Bach has the alto leap up to A on the second beat of the bar. Had he retained E for the second beat, he would have produced an irregular leap into the dissonance.

II$^6_5$ can support $\hat{1}$, $\hat{2}$, or $\hat{6}$ in the soprano; $\hat{4}$ is possible in four parts only if II$^6_5$ is incomplete—a most unusual procedure. At strong cadences, II$^6_5$, like II^6, tends to support $\hat{2}$ in the soprano (as in the Bach chorale). In general II$^6_5$ resembles II^6, of course, but the two chords are not completely interchangeable. II$^6_5$ derives a much richer sonority from the added dissonant tone; its progression to V highlights the leading tone by resolving into it from a dissonance. These features often make it preferable to II^6. On the other hand, II^6 is often to be preferred if a light texture is appropriate. Sometimes the progression of the soprano will determine which of the two chords is better. If the soprano repeats or holds $\hat{2}$ (as in Example 12-1), II$^6_5$ frequently gives a better sonority and (in minor) prevents an augmented 2nd. If the soprano descends from $\hat{2}$ to $\hat{7}$, however (as in Example 12-2a), II$^6_5$ will not readily work—the resolution of the dissonance will be transferred into the wrong voice. For the present, therefore, II^6 remains the only possibility.

Another difference between II$^6_5$ and II^6 is that II$^6_5$ supports $\hat{6}$ in the soprano much more easily; the repetition of $\hat{1}$ (coming from a tonic) removes the danger of parallel 5ths (Example 12-2b).

12-2   II$^6_5$ and soprano

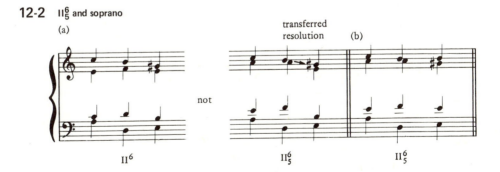

(a)   transferred
                       resolution   (b)

not

II^6 II$^6_5$ II$^6_5$

3. II^7. II^7 (the root position) occurs fairly frequently in composition (Example 12-3), but much less often than II$^6_5$ (just as II is less common than II^6, at least as a cadential chord). In the Mozart, the melody in the second half of bar 3 is an embellished G; the top voice of II^7, therefore, is $\hat{4}$. II^7, like II, very frequently supports $\hat{4}$ in the soprano; the 10th between the outer voices makes for a fluent contrapuntal setting. In the Schumann, the vocal part has the dissonant $\hat{1}$ as top-voice tone for II^7; this is another very frequent possibility and one where the prominence of the dissonance adds to the intensity of the chord. In the Schumann, notice how the addition of the 7th improves the sound of root-position II in minor.

12-3

(a) **Mozart, Piano Sonata, K. 311, I**

(b) **Schumann, Ich will meine Seele tauchen** (from *Dichterliebe*, Op. 48)

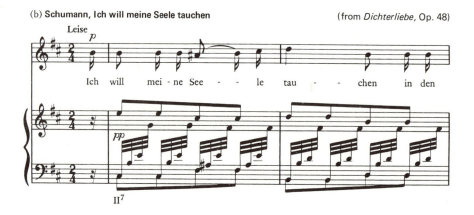

translation: I will dip my soul in the lily's cup.

II^7 presents greater problems in voice leading than II$^6_5$. In moving from I to II^7 in major, the necessity of preparing the 7th and the danger of parallel 5ths make it almost obligatory to omit the *5th* of II^7 and to double the *root* or *3rd* (Example 12-4a and b). In minor, the diminished 5th of II^7 eliminates the danger of parallels and, at the same time, lends a characteristic sonority to the chord (12-4c). For these reasons the complete chord occurs more frequently in minor than in major. Nevertheless, securing a smooth introduction for the 7th of V^7 often makes it advisable to use the incomplete chord in minor as well (12-4d). Coming from I^6, a complete chord is possible in both major and minor (12-4e and f).

12-4   II^7 : voice leading and doubling

4. **Moving to V^7.** In Examples 12-3 and 12-4, II^7 moves to V^7 rather than V$^5_3$. If we move from II^7 to V^7 we interlock two dissonant chords; the immediate succession of two dissonant chords is perfectly correct as long as the dissonant *tones* resolve correctly. Especially when $\hat{4}$ is the soprano tone of II^7, moving to V^7 makes for logical and connected voice leading; $\hat{4}$ holds over to become the 7th of V^7 and then resolves to $\hat{3}$, usually over I (Example 12-5a). And, in fact, if $\hat{4}$ in the soprano is not held as a common tone (if, for instance, it leaps down to $\hat{2}$), then it is usually best to double $\hat{4}$ (3rd of II^7) in an inner voice in order to secure a good preparation for the 7th of V^7 (12-4b and the piano accompaniment to 12-3b).

II$^6_5$ can also move to V^7, but it does so less readily than II^7. In four-part texture, II$^6_5$ does not contain $\hat{4}$ in any of the upper voices ($\hat{4}$, of course, is in the bass). This means that the 7th of V^7 must enter through the leap of a 3rd (12-5b and c). Although not incorrect, these voice leadings are less smooth than the completely stepwise progression of II$^6_5$ to V (as in Example 12-1), a voice leading that provides a particularly good accompaniment to the resolution of the suspension. Of the two possibilities shown in Example 12-5, c is the more natural, for $\hat{6}$ (as in 12-5b) has so strong a tendency to move by step to $\hat{5}$ that the leap can sound forced. And in any case we can always introduce a 7th over V as a passing tone (8-7) as in Example 12-1.

12-5   moving to V^7

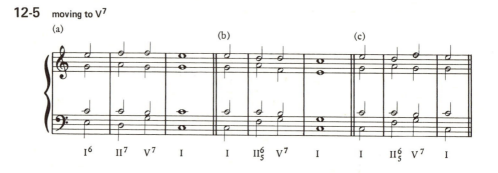

5. Metric position. In all the examples from the literature that we have presented so far, II$^6_5$ and II^7 have appeared on strong beats, the dissonant tone functioning as a suspension. And the dominant chord that follows has been metrically weaker than the II^7. This is the usual situation, but by no means an invariable one. Sometimes II^7 ($^6_5$) appears on a weak beat and leads to an accented dominant. Such is the case in Example 12-6, an excerpt from a Schubert Impromptu. In this instance and in similar ones, although the dissonance is repeated as a common tone it is not really a suspension, for it is metrically weak. As the explanatory sketches indicate, the dissonance is derived from a passing tone within II^6; the passing motion is contracted from three tones to two, through the omission of the first tone.

12-6   Schubert, Impromptu, D. 935

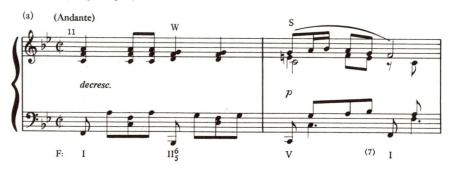

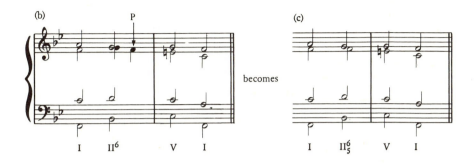

6. **Moving to a cadential $^6_4$.** II^7 or II^6_5 can move to a dominant embellished by a cadential $^6_4$ (Example 12-7). The 7th of II^7 ($^6_5$) is repeated to become the 4th of the $^6_4$ chord before resolving down to the 3rd of V; thus the $^6_4$ effects a delay in the resolution of the dissonance.

12-7   Schubert, String Quartet, D. 804, III

some possibilities in 4 voices

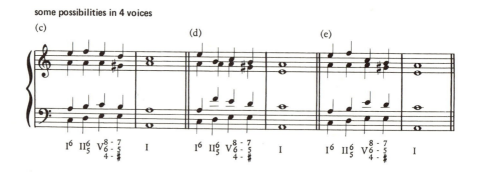

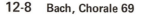

7. VI-II$^6_5$. Any chord that can lead logically to II can also lead to II^7 or its inversions as long as it allows the dissonance to enter correctly. A particularly frequent and idiomatic progression is I-VI-II$^6_5$ with a bass descending in 3rds. We see an example of this progression in the closing cadence from Bach's Chorale 69 (Example 12-8); note that the bass of II$^6_5$ skips down to the root before moving on to V.

12-8   Bach, Chorale 69

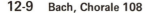

8. II^7 expanding supertonic harmony. Composers often elaborate and extend supertonic harmony before moving on to V. In Example 12-9, also from a Bach chorale, II first appears in $^6_3$ position. On the second beat of the bar, the bass moves down to the root; at the same time, the soprano brings in the 7th as a passing tone.

12-9   Bach, Chorale 108

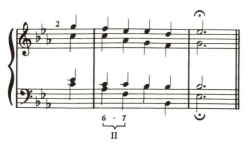

A phrase from an etude of Mendelssohn (Example 12-10) shows II⁶₅ moving to II⁷ with voice interchange between the bass and melody (here the melody is in the middle, not at the top). Such motions between II⁶₅ and II⁷ (in either direction) occur frequently. In this excerpt the 4th of the cadential ⁶₄ moves up to the 5th of V; we will discuss such "irregular" resolutions of the ⁶₄ in Unit 19.

12-10   Mendelssohn, Etude, Op. 104/1

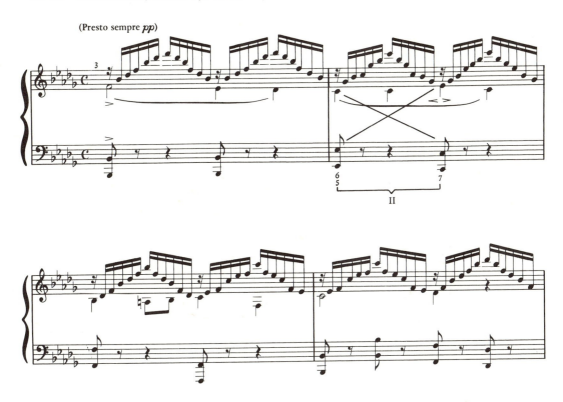

In general, dissonant chords have far fewer possibilities for extended duration than consonant ones. II⁷, however, is so strongly directed toward dominant harmony that it can be extended over fairly broad stretches of time without any loss to the music's coherence. In the latter part of Example 12-11, for example, the II⁶₅ spans 2¼ bars compared with just half a bar for the V⁶⁻⁷₄ to which it leads; also interesting is the voice exchange between the two lowest parts.

12-11   Mozart, String Quartet, K. 428, I

A passing "I⁶" can move between II⁷ and II⁶₅ or, as in Example 12-12, between II and II⁶₅; compare the very similar progression discussed in Unit 9, section 8. The reverse of this progression can also occur: from first inversion to root position (12-12c).

12-12   Chopin, Etude, Op. 10/II

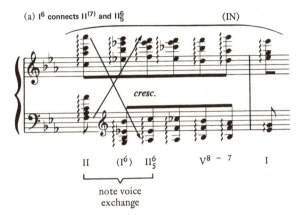

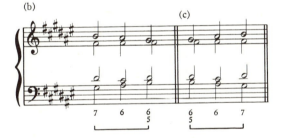

9. **Noncadential uses of II⁷ and II⁶₅.** II⁷ and II⁶₅ can lead to noncadential as well as cadential dominants. The noncadential ones need not be in root position. A particularly characteristic progression contains II⁶₅ moving to V⁴₂ over a common bass tone, as in Example 12-13. This progression is, in principle, the same as IV or II⁶ moving to V⁴₂; if the bass tone of the ⁴₂ receives an accent, it functions as a suspension.

12-13   Bach, Menuet   (from *Partita No. 4*)

10. Other inversions of II^7. Of the two remaining inversions of II^7, $\frac{4}{2}$ is the more important. It occurs very frequently in noncadential situations, especially at the beginning of a composition, where staying close to the tonic in the bass is often more appropriate than moving abruptly away from it. II$\frac{4}{2}$ leads from I to V^6 or, more often, V$\frac{6}{5}$. The opening of the first Prelude from *The Well-Tempered Clavier I* is a familiar example (Example 12-14).

12-14   Bach, Well-Tempered Clavier I, Prelude 1

II$\frac{4}{2}$ leads from I to V^6 or,

V$\frac{6}{5}$

II$\frac{4}{3}$, like VI or IV^6, can be used to lead to V$^{(7)}$ from above. In Example 12-15a, II$\frac{4}{3}$ moves into a cadential $\frac{6}{4}$; the eventual resolution of the $\frac{6}{4}$ is not shown in the example.

12-15   (a) Mendelssohn, String Quartet, Op. 13/1, I

II$\frac{4}{3}$

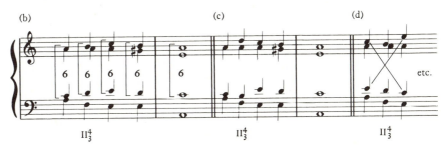

some possibilities in 4 voices

SUBDOMINANT SEVENTH CHORDS

11. IV^7. As we know, IV and II are closely associated; they share two common tones and a common goal—V. It follows as a logical consequence that the seventh chords based on these triads—II^7 and IV^7—will also have many features in common. The most important position of IV^7—the root position—differs by only a single tone from II$^6_5$ and moves to V in a very similar manner. Thus in Example 12-16, merely substituting an F♯ for the G in the IV^7 would transform it into a II$^6_5$. The harmonic direction of the phrase would remain much the same but the *sound* of the chord in question would change in a way easier to hear than to describe in words. And, in bars 2-3, Schumann's imitative counterpoint (the repetition of a melodic idea in different voices) would suffer distortion.

12-16   Schumann, Auf einer Burg, Op. 39

translation: The old knight has fallen asleep during his watch.

IV^7 shows less resemblance to II$^6_5$ when the 7th of the chord is in the soprano, for this tone ($\hat{3}$) is the only member of the chord that does not also belong to II^7. As it happens, $\hat{3}$ occurs very frequently in the soprano, more frequently than any of the other tones. This disposition gives us an alternative to the cadential $^6_4$ when $\hat{3}$ moves to $\hat{2}$ at a cadence, as in Example 12-17. In this excerpt IV^7 comes from a IV^6 in the previous beat; the 7th functions as a passing tone within an expanded subdominant.

12-17   Bach, Chorale 117 (end)

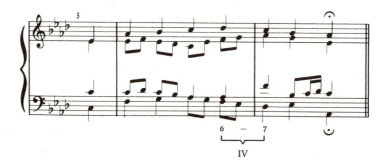

As Example 12-16 has shown, IV^7 can appear on a weaker beat than the V to which it moves; however it appears much more characteristically in strong metrical position, as in Example 12-17. The chord presents the problem of parallel 5ths in moving to V, especially when $\hat{3}$ occurs in the soprano. Example 12-18 indicates various ways of preventing 5ths. In 12-18d, IV^7 moves to II$^6_5$ (by anticipating $\hat{2}$ in the soprano) before going to V. Note that in all progressions the 5th of IV^7 descends by step into the leading tone. This detail of voice leading is characteristic of IV^7, whose 5th and 7th tend to move to V in parallel 3rds, 6ths, or 10ths.

12-18

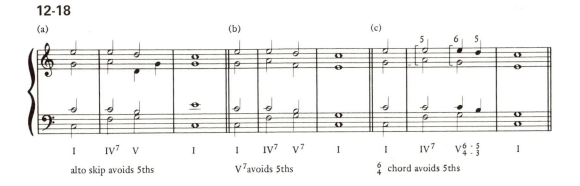

(a)   (b)   (c)

I   IV^7 V   I   I   IV^7 V^7 I   I   IV^7 V$^{6\ -\ 5}_{4\ -\ 3}$ I

alto skip avoids 5ths   V^{7}avoids 5ths $^6_4$ chord avoids 5ths

(d) Bach, early version of Prelude 1, WTC I

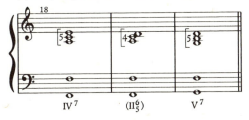

IV^7 (II$^6_5$)   V^7

12. Inversions of IV^7. Of the three inversions, the $^6_5$ is by far the most important. Its most useful function is to lead to V$^6_5$ (less often V^6) and I with a stepwise ascending bass—a beautiful alternative to IV-V-I where a strong harmonic cadence is not needed (Example 12-19). This use of IV$^6_5$ is closely related to that of IV^6 described in Unit 11, section 5.

12-19   Bach, Chorale 117

IV$^6_5$ V$^6_5$ I

POINTS FOR REVIEW

1. II^7, IV^7, and their inversions move to dominant harmony. All positions are usually complete except for root-position II^7 in major. The most important position is II^6_5; II^7 and IV^7 also occur frequently.

2. The motion to V is intensified by the dissonant 7th, which resolves downward by step. The 7th is most often introduced as a common tone, but sometimes as a passing tone.

3. II^6_5 is better than II^6 if the soprano repeats $\hat{2}$; II^6 is better if the soprano moves $\hat{2}$-$\hat{7}$. II^6_5 provides better support for $\hat{6}$ than II^6.

4. In minor, the 7th of II^7 improves the root-position sonority of II.

5. Frequent progressions leading to a cadential dominant are I-VI-II^6_5 (or II^7) and I-VI-IV^7. II^6_5-V^4_2 is an important noncadential progression.

6. II^4_3 can approach V from above. A more important progression is II^4_2 (often from root-position I) leading to V^6 or V^6_5. (This progression is particularly frequent at the beginning of a piece.)

7. IV^7 is sometimes an alternative chord to II^6_5 ($\hat{1}$ or $\hat{6}$ in soprano), but the most important use of IV^7 is to support $\hat{3}$ in the soprano. *Warning:* Be careful of parallel 5ths in the progression IV^7-V^5_3 (see Example 12-18).

8. The most important inversion of IV^7 is IV^6_5 in the progression IV^6_5-V^6_5-I with ascending bass; compare IV^6-$V^6(^6_5)$-I.

EXERCISES

1. Preliminaries. Write the following progressions, each in a different major or minor key.

   a. I-II^6_5-$V^{6\text{-}5}_{4\text{-}3}$-$I$. II^6_5 should have $\hat{2}$ in the soprano.

   b. I-II^6_5-$V^{8\text{-}7}$-I. II^6_5 should have $\hat{6}$ in the soprano.

   c. I-VI-II^6_5-V-I. II^6_5 should have $\hat{1}$ in the soprano.

   d. II^6_5-noncadential V^7-resolution.

   e. I^6-II^7-V^7-I.

   f. I^5_3-II^7-V^7-I.

   g. I-$\underbrace{II^6_5\text{-}II^7}_{\text{voice}}$-$V^{6\text{-}5}_{4\text{-}3}$-$I$.
      voice
      exchange

   h. I-II^4_2-resolution-I.

   i. I-IV^7-V-I. IV^7 should have $\hat{3}$ in the soprano.

   j. I-IV^6_5-V^6_5-I.

2. Melody.

bass:

II⁶ or II⁶₅ ?

*voice exchange, bass and soprano

3. Figured bass.

4. Melody.

THIRTEEN | OTHER USES OF IV, IV⁶, AND VI

13-1 Bach, Chorale 32

IV AND IV⁶

1. I-IV-I expanding tonic harmony. In the first two bars of Example 13-1, we encounter a new and characteristic function of IV. Instead of leading to V, this IV moves from tonic to tonic. Comparing the basses of I-IV-I and I-V-I (in A major, A-D-A and A-E-A), we discover that the latter unfolds the 5th of tonic harmony (A-E) whereas the former does not. For this reason, I-IV-I does not express the key nearly as strongly as I-V-I, and is thus a distinctly subordinate progression. I-IV-I generally occurs either before or after a progression in which the tonic is securely established by a strong dominant.

It would be quite possible to harmonize the tune in 13-1 with I-IV-V in the first two bars (Example 13-2). The effect, however, would differ greatly from that of Bach's setting; the temporary stop on V would introduce a much higher degree of tension. By extending tonic harmony without using V (or any chord containing the leading tone), I-IV-I constitutes an important source of variety; through contrast, it enhances the directional pull of dominant harmony once the latter arrives.

13-2

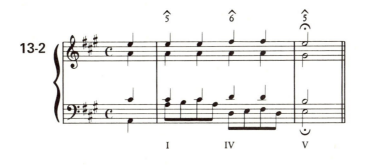

Our Bach chorale illustrates a most important aspect of I-IV-I: its frequent association with a neighboring progression in the melody, here the upper-neighbor figure $\hat{5}$-$\hat{6}$-$\hat{5}$. IV, which contains the upper neighbors to $\hat{3}$ and $\hat{5}$ plus $\hat{1}$ as a common tone, works particularly well as a neighboring chord to I. (II also contains 4 and $\hat{6}$ as upper neighbors to $\hat{3}$ and $\hat{5}$, but the absence of a common tone makes it almost impossible to secure good voice leading for the progression I-II-I.) Another important neighboring motion, $\hat{3}$-$\hat{4}$-$\hat{3}$, can also be supported by I-IV-I, as in the Schumann excerpt of Example 13-3.

13-3   Schumann, Sheherazade   (from *Album for the Young*, Op. 68)

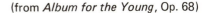

Although I-IV-I most often supports a neighboring motion in the soprano, other possibilities exist. In bar 5 of Schubert's "Des Fischers Liebesglück" (Example 13-4), the neighbors are in the middle voices while the melody stays around Î. Here the effect is that of an incomplete progression IV-I rather than the usual I-IV-I. Although the preceding bar ends with I, the entrance of the singer, together with the fermata and rest, makes the IV sound like a new beginning. In bar 6, beat 2, the passing tone B transforms the IV into an apparent II^6. This "II^6" should be regarded as a contrapuntal derivative of IV (through the 5-6 technique) rather than representing supertonic harmony, for a root-position II would never occur in this context (review the relation of II^6 to IV in Unit 9).

13-4   Schubert, Des Fischers Liebesglück

translation: Through the willows a glimmer winks and beckons.

In the progression I-IV-I, I^6 can represent either or both of the tonic chords, frequently with 10ths between bass and soprano (Example 13-5).

13-5   Handel, Air   (from *Harpsichord Suite No. 5*)

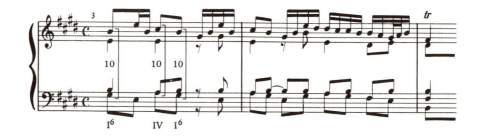

2. Plagal cadences. The progression IV-I, used as a cadential formula, is called a *plagal cadence.* Because motion between IV and I lacks the key-defining power of the V-I progression, plagal cadences have a much more limited function than authentic (V-I) cadences. They typically occur at the very end of a composition, as in the Amen at the close of a hymn. Emphasis on the subdominant can be very beautiful at the end of a piece, for this chord (a 5th below the tonic) often generates a feeling of repose (Example 13-6). In such cases the "finality" of the closing tonic has already been established by stronger tonal forces earlier in the piece.

13-6   Chopin, Nocturne, Op. 27/1

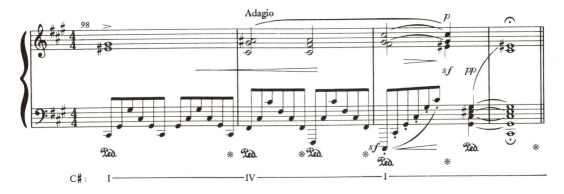

Often, as in Example 13-7, a plagal cadence follows immediately on an authentic one and gives added emphasis to the tonic.

13-7   Handel, And the Glory of the Lord   (from *Messiah*)

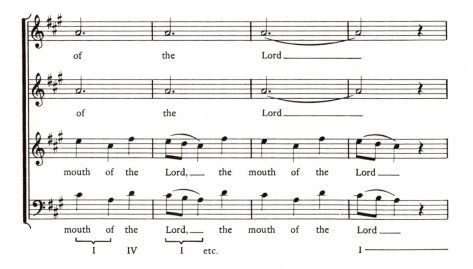

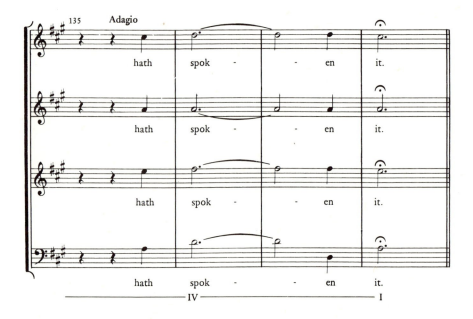

3. I-IV⁶-I⁶. IV⁶, like IV, can move within an expanded I, leading directly from one tonic to another. It does so in the context of a progression shown in Example 13-8, the beginning of the last movement of Haydn's "Clock" Symphony. In this very important progression, IV⁶ supports a passing tone ascending from $\hat{3}$ to $\hat{5}$; the bass moves from I to I⁶, not up a 3rd as is usual, but down a 6th.

13-8 **Haydn, Symphony No. 101 (Clock), IV**

This characteristic function of IV^6 can be most valuable, especially if a leading-tone chord (VII^6 or V$^4_3$) is not wanted as the support for $\hat{4}$ (Example 13-9). Incidentally, IV$^5_3$ does not work very well in this situation; the root-position chord following a large leap in the bass creates too heavy an effect for the passing function of the chord.

13-9

(a)

(b)

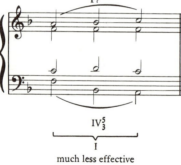

Motion between I and I^6 with a stepwise bass works well in both directions (I-VII^6-I^6 or I^6-VII^6-I). But the progression I-IV^6-I^6 is not reversible; I^6-IV^6-I does not occur. Nor will I-IV^6-I^6 appear with the bass rising a 5th from IV^6 to I^6. The reason is that $\hat{6}$ between two tonic chords is heard as upper neighbor to $\hat{5}$. Now if $\hat{6}$, as bass tone of IV^6, leaps *down* to I^6, we hear it resolving to an inner-voice $\hat{5}$, either actually present or implied. But if $\hat{6}$ leaps *up* (either to I or I^6), it is left exposed and unresolved. And a leap of a 6th from IV^6 down to I creates a needlessly discontinuous bass (Example 13-10).

13-10 IV⁶ supports P within tonic harmony

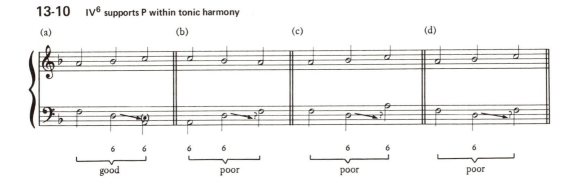

4. IV⁶ as a passing chord within V. Another contrapuntal function of IV⁶ is to move between the root position and the first inversion ($\frac{6}{3}$ or, more frequently, $\frac{6}{5}$) of dominant harmony. IV⁶ often introduces the 7th in an elaboration of V⁸⁻⁷, as in Example 13-11.

13-11 IV⁶ passing between V and V⁶₅

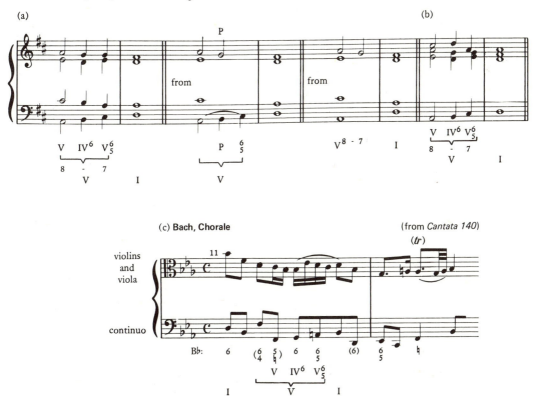

VI

5. VI as substitute for I. VI and I share two common tones, $\hat{1}$ and $\hat{3}$. Therefore VI can substitute for I where the latter might be expected—after V or V^7. This substitution can forestall excessive repetitions of I, as in an excerpt from Beethoven's "Waldstein" Sonata (Example 13-12a), in which the soprano descends from $\hat{4}$ (over V^7) to $\hat{3}$ (over VI), a frequent melodic pattern when VI substitutes for I.

Another quotation from the same sonata (13-12b) shows a different possibility for the top voice. Here the soprano for V^7-VI is the same as for V^7-I two bars later—both end on $\hat{1}$. The two contrasting harmonizations of $\hat{1}$ create variety in a most beautiful way; in addition, using VI the first time prevents a cadential effect too early in the passage.

13-12

(a) Beethoven, "Waldstein" Sonata, Op. 53, II

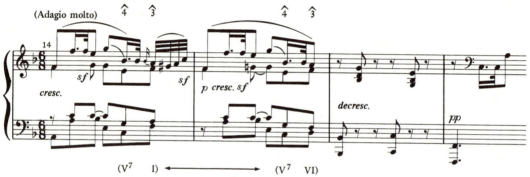

(b) Beethoven, "Waldstein," I

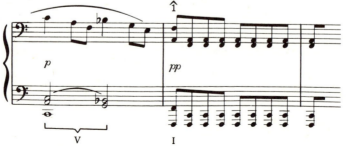

In both "Waldstein" excerpts, the 3rd of VI is doubled. In moving from $V^{(7)}$ to VI in four parts, one normally doubles the 3rd of VI in order to prevent parallel 5ths or, in minor, an augmented 2nd (Example 13-13).

13-13

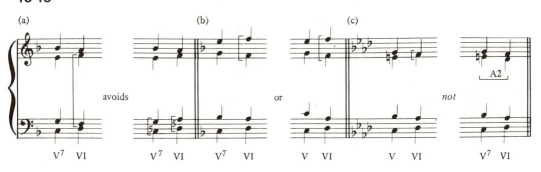

6. **Deceptive cadences.** If a substitution of VI for I occurs where a cadence is expected, we call the progression a *deceptive cadence* (V-VI or V^7-VI). Deceptive cadences are inconclusive. They create no sense of repose; on the contrary, they produce a suspense that dissipates only when tonal stability is regained, usually through an authentic cadence. The deceptive effect is strongest if the soprano is the same as in a perfect authentic cadence—$\hat{2}$-$\hat{1}$ or $\hat{7}$-$\hat{8}$. In the music of the great composers, deceptive cadences fulfill a variety of functions. Examples 13-14 and 13-15 show two of the most important possibilities.

In Example 13-14, the deceptive cadence provides the impulse for a varied repetition of the whole four-bar phrase in a kind of antecedent-consequent grouping.

13-14   Mozart, Trio, K. 498, I

In Example 13-15, the VI of the deceptive cadence forms part of a rising-bass progression that leads chromatically from V to I. (The chords over D♮ and E♭ result from this chromatic progression; they will be discussed in later units.)

13-15   Handel, Courante   (from *Harpsichord Suite No. 8*)

7. Relationship between IV⁶ and VI. As we noted in Unit 11, VI and IV⁶ are closely related chords that frequently appear in similar situations. Thus IV⁶ will sometimes appear instead of VI at a deceptive cadence, as in Example 13-16. Similarly, VI will sometimes replace IV⁶ in leading down a 6th from I to I⁶ (Example 13-17; compare 13-8).

13-16   Handel, Sonata No. 5 for Flute and Thoroughbass

13-17   Mozart, Piano Sonata, K. 545, II

As we saw in 13-15, VI, like IV⁶, can function as a passing chord between the root position and first inversion of V (also compare 13-11).

8. Harmonizing ascending scales. If you memorize the standard patterns for harmonizing scales shown in Examples 13-18 and 13-19—and, in particular, if you learn to play them in all keys—you will find it much easier to harmonize melodies, to realize figured and unfigured basses, and, eventually, to improvise at the keyboard. In these two examples, pay special attention to the treatment of $\hat{6}$ and $\hat{7}$ in minor.

As is true with most formulas, the standard scale harmonizations offer only limited insight into the music of great composers. To be sure, the textbook patterns will sometimes appear in a composition. But the meaning—the inner group-

13-18 harmonizing the ascending scale in the soprano

(a) major

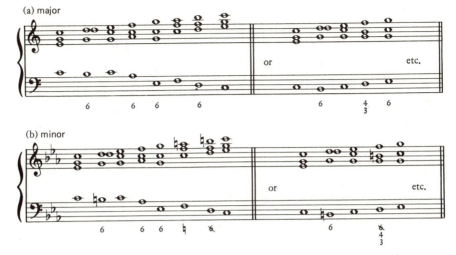

(b) minor

13-19 harmonizing the ascending scale in the bass

(a) major

(b) minor

ings and the relation to larger context—will depend largely on the individual character of the passage. Thus in the last movement of Haydn's Symphony No. 98 (Example 13-20), we find a passage very similar to 13-18a except for the fact that I appears only in $\frac{6}{3}$ position. As it happens, this "exception" is one of the most significant aspects of the passage, which follows an extended V^7 with the 7th very prominent in the soprano (bars 64-71); the 7th then moves to the bass (bars 74-75), necessitating a resolution to I^6. That is why the scale in the soprano is harmonized in such a way that I^6 rather than I represents tonic harmony.

13-20   Haydn, Symphony No. 98, IV

POINTS FOR REVIEW

1. I-IV-I expands tonic harmony, usually with a neighboring figure ($\hat{5}$-$\hat{6}$-$\hat{5}$ or $\hat{3}$-$\hat{4}$-$\hat{3}$) in the soprano. I⁶ can replace either or both of the root-position tonic chords.

2. IV-I is the plagal (or Amen) cadence. It usually occurs at the end of a composition or section, often following an authentic cadence.

3. IV⁶ leads from I *down* to I⁶ with the melodic line $\hat{3}$-$\hat{4}$-$\hat{5}$. IV⁶ also connects V⁽⁷⁾ and V⁶ ($^6_5$).

4. VI substitutes for I following V or V⁷, preventing excessive repetition of I. In the

progression V⁽⁷⁾-VI, the 3rd of VI should be doubled.

5. V⁽⁷⁾-VI forms a deceptive cadence if it occurs where an authentic cadence is expected. This cadence is strongest with $\hat{2}$-$\hat{1}$ or $\hat{7}$-$\hat{8}$ in the soprano.

6. IV⁶ and VI are sometimes interchangeable:

   a. IV⁶ can replace VI in a deceptive cadence: V⁽⁷⁾-IV⁶.

   b. VI can replace IV⁶ in moving down from I to I⁶: I-VI-I⁶.

   c. VI can replace IV⁶ as a passing chord between V⁽⁷⁾ and V⁶($^6_5$).

EXERCISES

NOTE. In setting both melodies and basses, keep in mind the relation between characteristic soprano figures and the chord progressions presented in this unit. For example, $\hat{7}$-$\hat{1}$, $\hat{2}$-$\hat{1}$, or $\hat{4}$-$\hat{3}$ may suggest V⁽⁷⁾-VI as well as V⁽⁷⁾-I.

1. Preliminaries.
   a. Write a phrase with a final tonic that is extended through a plagal cadence.
   b. Write a phrase with a deceptive cadence leading to an authentic cadence.
2. Melody.

*don't use tonic

3. Unfigured bass.

soprano: $\hat{5}$

4. Figured bass.

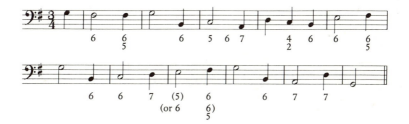

5. Melody. Set in keyboard style.

6. Unfigured bass.

scalar soprano

7. Melody.

bass: etc.   expand
                                      $V^{8\text{-}7}$

FOURTEEN | V AS A KEY AREA

14-1 Schubert, Heidenröslein

sah's mit vie - len Freu - den. Rös - lein, Rös - lein, Rös - lein rot,
Rös - lein auf der Hei - den.

translation: A boy saw a wild rose, as fresh and lovely
as the morning. He ran to it quickly to gaze
on it closely with great joy. Little rose, little
red rose, little wild rose.

TONICIZATION AND MODULATION

1. Nontonic key areas. So far, all the chords we have studied result from harmonic progressions or voice-leading connections that are under the immediate control of the tonic triad. Most compositions, however, contain at least one passage that centers temporarily on a tone other than the tonic. In that new *key area* we hear another scale degree as $\hat{1}$ and another chord as the tonic triad. In Schubert's familiar song "Heidenröslein" (Example 14-1), the first phrase (bars 1-4) gravitates to the tonic G. The second phrase starts out as though it will simply repeat the first one. In its second bar, however (bar 6), a single change—C♯ instead of C♮—shifts the music temporarily into the orbit of D major. Until the end of the phrase, the progression of chords and the motion of the melodic line direct themselves to D. In making a chordal analysis of the phrase, we would count the D triad, not the G, as I; D has for the moment taken over the function of tonic.

The Schubert song illustrates a new and most important way to emphasize non-tonic chords: they can simulate the effect of a tonic and expand into temporary key areas; in the Schubert, the key area of the second phrase is the dominant.

2. Temporary tonics. We have two terms for the process of making scale degrees other than $\hat{1}$ sound temporarily like tonics: *tonicization* and *modulation.* The first implies a temporary "tonic" of brief duration; the second implies a longer-lasting and more significant change. The two terms overlap to a considerable extent; we cannot precisely determine where one stops and the other begins. From a broad perspective—one that takes in the composition as a whole—even the most firmly established key areas function as offshoots of the main key, if the composer has conceived the piece as a unified whole. In the Schubert song, which is only 16 bars long, it scarcely matters whether we think of the area in D as a large-scale tonicization of the dominant, or a brief modulation to it. This is often the case in very short pieces where there is hardly room for an extensive modulation.

3. Tonicizing V in major. Tonicizations and modulations can be organized around any scale degree and around any major or minor triad. Since V is the chord most closely related to I, tonicizing V helps to express the main key; consequently pieces in major move to V as a key area more readily than to any other scale degree—one more instance of the controlling influence that the relationship between tonic and dominant exerts on tonal structure. (Pieces in minor tend to tonicize III, as we will see in the following unit.) In this unit we will study only tonicizations of, and modulations to, V in major; however most of the techniques that we will discuss are easily applicable to other tonicizations and modulations.

4. The pivot chord. Occasionally composers will introduce their new key area abruptly and without preparation. Much more often, however, they will try to effect a smooth transition from the old key to the new. An important way of achieving this transition is by using a *pivot chord,* a chord that occurs in both keys. In the Schubert song, for example, we first hear the G chord of bar 5 as I. But the chord in bar 6—V_2^4 of D, leading to I^6—makes us reinterpret in retrospect the harmonic meaning of bar 5. In relation to what follows it, the G chord functions as IV in D; in relation to what has preceded it, the chord is a I in G major. Because it effects the transition from one tonal area to the other, the G chord is indeed the "pivotal" event of the modulation.

The pivot chord need not be the tonic of the main key; any major or minor triad that belongs to both keys will serve. In tonicizing V, VI in the main key (II in the new key) makes a particularly effective pivot (Example 14-2).

Sometimes the transition consists not of a single pivot chord, but of a group of two or more chords. The opening theme of Haydn's "Emperor" Quartet tonicizes V in its second measure. In that measure, both the C major and A minor chords function as elements common to both keys (Example 14-3).

14-2   Freylinghausen, Figured-Bass Chorale, *Morgenglanz der Ewigkeit*

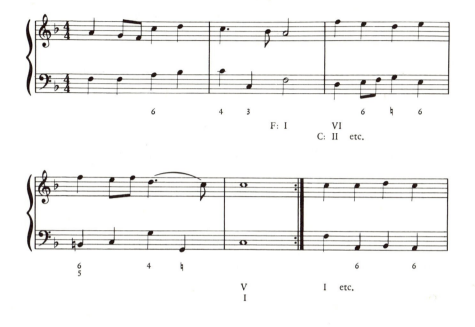

14-3   Haydn, "Emperor" String Quartet, Op. 76/3

In Example 14-4, the C chord appears first as the goal V in a semicadence in F (bar 26). In the next bar it is repeated, this time as I of C; contrasts in dynamics, register, and texture direct the listener's ear to this change in harmonic function. Here the modulation is effected by *repeating* the transitional chord rather than by changing its meaning in retrospect as in Examples 14-1 and 14-2. For this reason, the C chord is not a pivot—at least not in the same sense as in the earlier examples. In the Mozart the change of key occurs suddenly, rather than after a smooth transition.

14-4 Mozart, Piano Sonata, K. 280, I

5. Cadencing in the new key. Most modulations and many of the more extensive tonicizations confirm the new tonic by means of an authentic cadence. In Example 14-3, the transitional chords—IV and II of G—lead directly to a V and form part of the cadence. Thus the pivot chord(s) can move immediately to the cadential dominant. At other times, however, the pivot chord will form part of a noncadential progression, and the cadence will occur later. In Example 14-1, the pivot chord leads to V_2^4 and I^6; the I^6 moves first to a deceptive, then to an authentic cadence. In Example 14-2, the pivot chord leads to a noncadential V, with the cadential dominant coming later, in bar 4. The Mozart excerpt (14-4) differs from all the others in that the new key is confirmed by the new theme and by contrasts in sonority rather than by a cadence.

6. Returning to the tonic. After a brief sojourn in the area of the dominant, a return to the tonic requires no special preparation. If V has not been tonicized for long, the listener still feels the strong pull of the main tonic. The composer, therefore, can simply introduce the I chord in a place of some prominence and continue in the tonic. The last chord in the dominant area will have a double meaning: I of V and V of I. In Example 14-2 the tonic returns with the first chord of the new phrase that begins in bar 6.

If the dominant has been maintained as a key area for a longer time, it may be necessary to make it clear to the listener that the tonicized V is reverting to its permanent and basic function—that of dominant in the main key. This is best accomplished by turning the chord into a dominant seventh by adding a minor 7th ($\hat{4}$ in the main key). As a seventh chord, V no longer sounds like a tonic; besides, V^7 has so strong a drive toward I that the listener is prepared for the return of the tonic. And finally, $\hat{4}$ is the one scale degree in the tonic key that does not appear in the key of the dominant. Therefore the appearance of this tone helps to neutralize the temporary key at the same time as it prepares the return of the main one. In the Schubert song, the 7th appears as the bass of a V_2^4 chord (bar 11).

7. V as a key area and musical form. The *form* of a piece results from its articulation into parts of various dimensions—rhythmic groups, phrases, groups of phrases, sections—and from the relationship of part to part and of part to whole. A new key area makes for contrast with what has already happened; this contrast, in turn, can help to differentiate one section from another. Modulation, therefore, can be an important means of articulating the large divisions of form; tonicization can help to articulate some of the smaller segments. Because of the special importance of the tonic-dominant relationship, the use of V as a key area is of particular importance in creating musical form.

The form of Example 14-1, for example, grows out of its division into three phrases. The first of these moves within the tonic; the second tonicizes V and confirms it with a strong cadence; the third returns to the tonic and refers back to some of the opening material—note the resemblance between bars 11-12 and 3-4. The tiny *coda* or postlude rounds off the ending with a varied repetition of the final cadence. Without the contrast of the tonicized V, there would be no impression of departure and return; the form would lose much of its plasticity.

Tonicizations of V often occur within a group of two phrases in antecedent-consequent relation. Sometimes, as in Example 14-5, the antecedent phrase closes with an authentic cadence in the dominant area, as an intensified replacement of the usual semicadence. (In the Chopin excerpt, a cadential $^6_4$ occurs on a weaker beat than the V^7 to which it moves; this rhythmic irregularity will be discussed in Unit 19, section 12.)

14-5 **Chopin, Prelude, Op. 28/13**

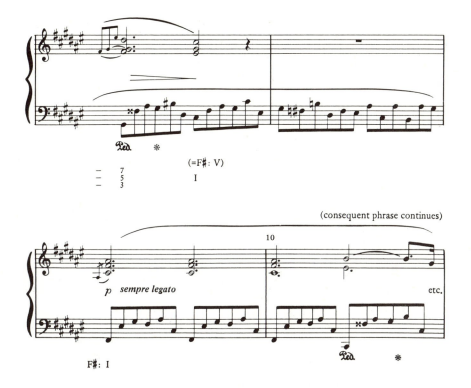

Another possibility is for the *consequent* phrase to end with an authentic cadence in the dominant instead of the expected final tonic (Example 14-6). This procedure gives the consequent phrase a very different function from its usual one. It does not resolve the tension generated by the nontonic ending of the antecedent phrase; on the contrary, the level of tension is increased by the shift to a new key area. After such a modulating consequent phrase, the tonic may return immediately. But the dominant may also remain as a key area, or the ending of the consequent phrase may serve as a springboard for a modulation to yet another key area.

14-6 **Mozart, In diesen heil'gen Hallen**   (from *Die Zauberflöte,* K. 620)

translation: In these sacred halls revenge is unknown, and if a person
should be tempted, love will lead him to his duty.

A German dance by Mozart (Example 14-7) shows another important possibility: a tonicized V as the harmonic basis for the B section in an ABA or A :‖:BA :‖ form. In this piece, the middle (B) section starts off immediately in G, the dominant area (bar 9). This creates a more sharply sectionalized form than in the Schubert song, where the second phrase makes a gradual transition into the new key area. In analyzing a piece like the Mozart, the notion of a pivot chord is not very helpful. To be sure, the G chord of bar 9 might possibly be understood as a pivot, but the strong contrasts in rhythm and texture (and also the F♯ in the upbeat to bar 9) make it sound as though the section in G begins anew, without any transition from the preceding.

14-7   Mozart, German Dance, K. 509/6

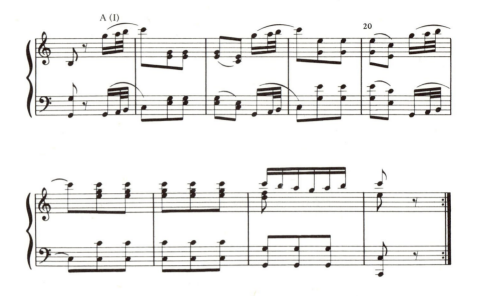

Longer and more elaborate pieces than Examples 14-1 or 14-7 articulate their form by means of modulation to V. Among the most important are movements in sonata-allegro form in a major key. These usually modulate to the dominant in the bridge section that follows the first theme or thematic group. The latter part of the exposition remains in the dominant key; the return to the tonic is effected by the events of the development section.

APPLICATIONS TO WRITTEN WORK

8. Harmonizing modulating melodies; realizing modulating basses. Melodies sometimes signal a modulation with accidentals. In the Schubert song, for example, the C♯'s in the vocal line clearly indicate D as temporary tonic. Such melodies are not always easy to harmonize well, but at least recognizing that a modulation is taking place should not be a problem. Other melodies are less obliging. In the chorale of Example 14-2, for instance, the soprano line of bars 3-5 contains not a single accidental; the B♮ in the bass line is the only one. Harmonizing a melody of this kind can be difficult; you must use your ear and brain to recognize modulations where the melodic line does not hold up a sign, so to speak, to announce them. Always listen for the long-range goals of the line; in particular observe the cadential points. In the chorale melody, the motion from D to C (bars 4 and 5) implies $\hat{2}$-$\hat{1}$ in C rather than $\hat{6}$-$\hat{5}$ in F; strong cadences do not normally support the melodic progression $\hat{6}$-$\hat{5}$, but they *do* support $\hat{2}$-$\hat{1}$.

The realization of modulating figured and unfigured basses is usually easier than harmonizing melodies. The figured basses normally indicate all the necessary chromatic adjustments, and even in unfigured basses, modulations are easy to recognize because of the unmistakable V-I progressions, especially at cadences.

9. **Writing phrase groups that tonicize V.** Writing short phrase groups that begin on I, tonicize V, and return to and conclude on I can be one of the most valuable exercises for learning to hear and understand modulations. Example 14-8 includes three such groups that can serve as models. All three are eight bars long and have the following in common:

1. They establish the initial tonic (bars 1-2).
2. A pivot chord introduces the key change (bar 3 or bars 2-3).
3. An authentic cadence confirms the new key (bars 3-4).
4. The new "tonic" is transformed into a V (bar 5 in a; bar 6 in b; bar 4 in c).
5. The initial tonic returns and leads to a closing cadence.

14-8 (a)

Follow these procedures closely when you begin to write such phrase groups. You can vary the pacing of the tonal motions from one exercise to another, but you should achieve the cadence in the dominant key midway through the exercise. Strive for a clear texture in which the larger harmonic direction is not obscured by unnecessary complexities of voice leading or chord succession. You are writing exercises, not compositions, but they can sound very good if you direct your attention to the contour of the melodic line and to the balance among rhythmic groups.

POINTS FOR REVIEW

1. The terms *tonicization* and *modulation* refer to the process of making scale degrees other than $\hat{1}$ sound like temporary tonics.

2. In major, V is the most frequently tonicized area.

3. A pivot chord is a chord belonging to both the original and the new keys. Sometimes the pivot consists of more than one chord.

4. In tonicizing V, frequent pivot chords in the new key are II, IV, and I.

5. The new key area is generally confirmed by an authentic cadence.

6. The return to the main tonic is often effected by adding a 7th to the tonicized V, so that it becomes V^7 of the main key.

7. There are several ways in which tonicizing V has an important influence on musical form. These include:

   a. using a tonicized V at the end of an antecedent or consequent phrase.

   b. using a tonicized V for the middle section of ABA form.

   c. modulating to V in the exposition of a sonata-allegro movement in major.

EXERCISES

1. Preliminaries. Write short progressions in different major keys that begin on I and modulate to V. Show at least two different ways of using the following pivot chords.

       main key   *new key*
   a. I   =   IV
   b. VI$^{(6)}$ =   II$^{(6)}$
   c. V   =   I

2. Expand the progressions you wrote in Exercise 1 into phrase groups that incorporate the five features listed on page 189. See Example 14-8 for models.

3. Chorale melody.

4. Chorale melody.

5. Chorale melody.

6. Figured bass.

FIFTEEN III AND VII

Schumann, Armes Waisenkind (from *Album for the Young,* Op. 68)

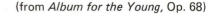

USES OF III

1. I-III-V in minor. Example 15-1 illustrates some of the most important characteristics of III and, in addition, shows a typical function of VII in minor. The section consists of two phrases in antecedent-consequent relation. In the first phrase the harmonic focal points are I (bars 1-2), III (bars 2-3), and V (bar 4). The second phrase retraces the same steps but adds a final tonic, thus answering the semicadence with an authentic one. Example 15-2 extracts the harmonic structure. Note that III forms a resting place almost midway between I and V (hence the term *mediant*) and that the bass lines of I-III-V and I-III-V-I arpeggiate the tonic triad.

15-2

        (♮VII)   (II⁶)   (♮VII)   (II⁶)

   I   III   V   ‖ I   III   V   I

As in the Schumann piece, III often forms an important part of a large-scale harmonic plan. Like II, IV, and sometimes VI, it leads from an opening tonic to a dominant. However, III differs from these other triads in an important way: the direct progression I-III-V *without intervening chords* occurs infrequently. This is because a root progression by rising 3rd connects two chords with two common tones, one of them the root of the second chord. There is little contrast, and the second chord receives too little emphasis to sound like a goal. In the direct progression I-III-V, therefore, both III and V will come in rather weakly.

Composers frequently move from I to III through VII. In the Schumann, the G triad has two meanings. On the one hand it is an element of the A minor tonality (natural VII); on the other, it sounds like a dominant of the C chord (III) and makes C sound like a goal. In moving from III to V composers most often make use of a passing tone in the bass supporting IV or (as in the Schumann) II⁶. The directional quality of the bass line and the elimination of $\hat{5}$ as a common tone intensify V and make the progression a very satisfactory one. As Example 15-3 shows, such a progression usually supports a top voice that descends by step. Other options exist, however. In the Schumann, for example, the leap of the diminished 5th in an otherwise conjunct melody enhances the poignant expression of the cadences.

15-3

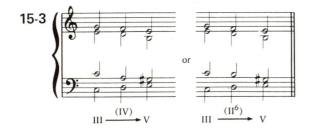

                     or

        (IV)   (II⁶)

III ⟶ V   III ⟶ V

2. Modulation to III in minor. Because of the position of the tritone in the natural form of minor, the minor mode has an inherent tendency to gravitate to III. Thus, III in minor is very frequently expanded into a key area. In addition, the major quality of III makes a welcome contrast to the minor tonic—a contrast beautifully evident in the Schumann excerpt of Example 15-1. Furthermore, the minor mode can tonicize III without any chromatic alteration; thus the chords in bar 2 of the Schumann suggest a cadential progression (VI-V-I) in C major without the use of any accidental signs.

Pieces in minor therefore tend to modulate to III more often than to V, but without any weakening of the tonic-dominant relationship, for the expanded III functions as a stopover on the way to V. In an excerpt from a figured-bass chorale of Bach (Example 15-4), III arrives in bar 3 and is confirmed by a strong cadence. Just as in the Schumann—only over a longer span—the III moves up by step to a strong V-I cadence.

15-4   Bach, Figured-Bass Chorale, No. 29

(Inner voices supplied by the authors.)

3. I-III-V in major. An excerpt from a Chopin etude (Example 15-5) shows III functioning as part of a broad harmonic progression in the major mode. This usage of III is much less common in major than in minor, especially in music before the nineteenth century. Unlike minor, the major mode contains no inherent tendency to gravitate to III; the tritone in major leads unequivocally to I. And

III in major cannot be tonicized without the use of accidentals in the altered VII or V of III (note the F♯ in bar 7 of the Chopin; a complete chord would require a D♯ as well). A progression leading from III to V in major usually proceeds exactly as in minor—through a passing IV or II.

Sometimes, as in the Chopin, V in the progression III-V-I will appear in a weak metric position compared with III and I; this can occur both in major and in minor. The force of dominant harmony is so great that it does not always require special emphasis through duration or accent.

15-5   Chopin, Etude, Op. 10/7

As we have seen, I-III-V does not typically occur in direct progression, especially in music written before the nineteenth century. During that century, composers increasingly began to exploit chord progression by ascending 3rds, sometimes moving directly from III to V without a passing IV or II⁶. But they would seldom write the entire progression I-III-V without intervening chords. Brahms did, however, in his Intermezzo, Op. 119, No. 3 (Example 15-6), in a most unusual passage. With both poetry and wit Brahms leads us from I to V^7 by almost imperceptible degrees, so that we are hardly aware that we have arrived at the dominant in the bass (beginning of bar 44) until the *sforzando* and the rush of quick notes bring the V^7 forcefully to our attention.

15-6   Brahms, Intermezzo, Op. 119/5

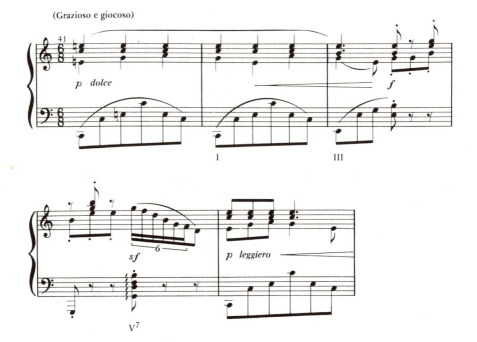

4. III moving to I through an inversion of V(7). The first main part of Mozart's Rondo in A minor, K. 511, divides into three subsections, the first and last in the tonic, the second in the mediant (C major) expanded into a key area. Example 15-7 shows the end of the C major section and the transition back to the tonic. Note that Mozart does not lead to I through a root-position V; the dominant chord is an inverted one, a $\frac{4}{3}$. As in the Mozart, III frequently moves to I through an inverted dominant (most often $\frac{4}{3}$, $\frac{6}{5}$, or $\frac{6}{3}$). The stepwise connection to I gives these progressions a decidedly melodic, contrapuntal character.

15-7   Mozart, Rondo in A Minor, K. 511

Inverted dominants do not normally constitute goals of motion and need not receive as much emphasis as those in root position, so intervening chords are not required here (Example 15-8). In major, there are two common tones between III and V; in minor, one common tone and one chromatic half step. The greater tonal contrast makes the progression stronger in minor than in major.

The use of V$^6_3$ or V$^6_5$ in minor creates a *cross-relation* between the bass and an upper part; that is, the chromatic succession takes place between *two* voices rather than in a single one. The cross-relation is unduly harsh if natural $\hat{7}$ occurs in the soprano voice (15-8c), but creates no problem if natural $\hat{7}$ is in one of the inner voices (15-8d).

15-8

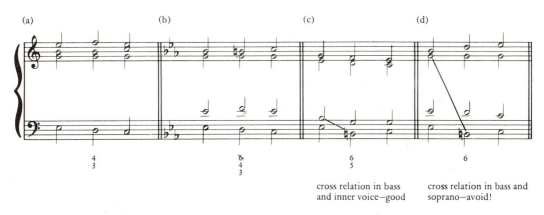

cross relation in bass and inner voice—good

cross relation in bass and soprano—avoid!

5. III as upper 5th of VI; III-VI-II-V-I. The addition of III to our vocabulary of chords allows us to add another link to the chain of progressions by descending 5th. III can move to VI in the same way that VI moves to II or II to V. As we know, VI does not usually function as a goal but instead moves on to some other chord—IV, perhaps, or II, or V. For this reason the descending 5th III-VI does not normally occur by itself but leads on through II to V and, often, I. We can observe such a progression in Example 15-9. Note that II appears in $^6_3$ position—partly, perhaps, to avoid a diminished $^5_3$, but mainly to allow a large-scale stepwise bass line F-G-A (III-II^6-V). In this excerpt the VI sounds subordinate to the other chords, which are emphasized by fuller texture and greater rhythmic activity. Incidentally, the root-position II (diminished $^5_3$) and the dissonant bass progression VI-II (diminished 5th or augmented fourth) sound better in the middle of a progression (as in III-VI-II-V-I) than when the progression begins on VI. Handel avoids the root position here, but, as it happens, uses it in the next variation.

15-9   **Handel, Air and Variations, Variation 3**   (from *Suite No. 3*)

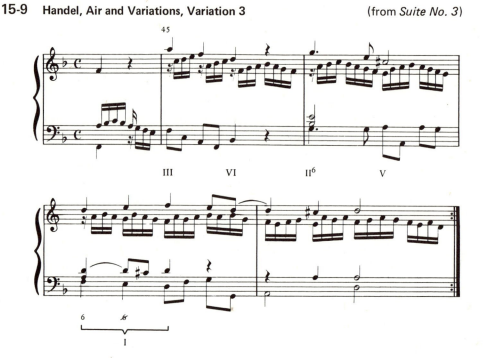

6. III in smaller contexts. Important though it is in large-scale progressions, III does not frequently appear in smaller contexts—much less frequently, indeed, than II, IV, or VI. When it does so it usually follows I, and because of the common tones of the two chords, III sounds less like an independent chord than like an offshoot or extension of tonic harmony. As such it has one highly important and characteristic function: to support a passing $\hat{7}$ in a descending line, usually in the soprano. This usage occurs in Schubert's song "Im Frühling" (Example 15-10a). Schubert's succession of chords—I-(III)-IV, and so on—is the typical one; another important possibility is moving to II[6] with the melodic progression $\hat{8}$-$\hat{7}$-$\hat{6}$ in an inner voice (15-10b). Less frequently VI supports $\hat{6}$ (15-10c).

15-10   **Schubert, Im Frühling**

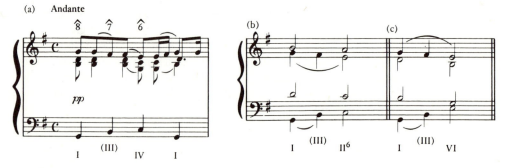

III's support of $\hat{7}$ makes it possible to harmonize a descending scale in the soprano (Example 15-11). Note that in minor the natural form must be used.

15-11   harmonizing the descending scale in the soprano

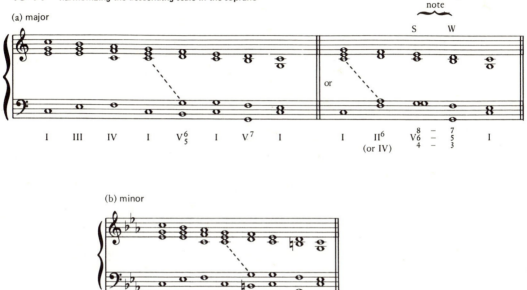

(a) major

I	III	IV	I	V$^6_5$	I	V^7	I	I	II^6 (or IV)	V$^{8-7}_{6-5}_{4-3}$	I

(b) minor

7. **III as equivalent to I^6.** III is related to I^6 through the contrapuntal motion 5-6 above a stationary bass (like IV and II^6 or VI and IV^6). Sometimes, therefore, III can occur in contexts where the bass would usually suggest I^6. Such is the case in the opening of Bach's Chorale 365 (Example 15-12a) as well as in the other progressions of 15-12. In most situations where a choice between I^6 and III exists, I^6 is preferable; by unequivocally prolonging tonic harmony I^6 can help to define the tonality. But III can be preferable when the stepwise descent $\hat{8}$-$\hat{7}$-$\hat{6}$ in the soprano or in an inner voice is wanted, or when excessive repetitions of $\hat{1}$ in any of the upper voices would otherwise result.

15-12   (a) Bach, Chorale 365

(III)

(b)

(III)

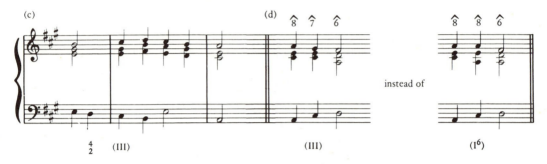

(c)

(d)

instead of

$\frac{4}{2}$ (III)

(III)

(I⁶)

As a general rule, avoid moving from I to III in weak-to-strong rhythm. Because of the lack of tonal contrast, chord succession by ascending 3rd sounds almost like motion within the same chord; using it to move from a weak to a strong beat tends to contradict the meter.

8. III in minor as an augmented triad. III does not tend to move directly to I. In minor, therefore, there is usually no reason to raise $\hat{7}$ when it is part of III. This means that the augmented form of III—derived from the harmonic form of the minor scale—does not play an important role in pieces written in minor. Most of the apparent instances of III as an augmented triad are in $\frac{6}{3}$ position and express dominant rather than mediant harmony (see Unit 18).

USES OF VII

9. Natural VII in minor. Example 15-1 shows root-position VII in minor (natural form) as V of III. This is an important usage. In first inversion, as in Example 15-13, the chord leads from I to III by stepwise ascent (passing function) and provides a new way to move from I up to V.

15-13 (a)

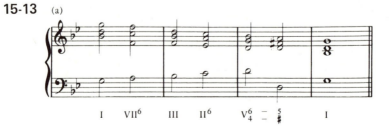

I   VII⁶   III   II⁶   V⁶₄ — ⁵₃♯   I

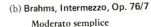

(b) Brahms, Intermezzo, Op. 76/7

Moderato semplice

I   (VII⁶)   III   III

I   (VII⁶)   III   II⁶   V   I

Sometimes—especially in Baroque music—natural VII appears as a chord leading to V^7. Because its two upper tones also belong to V^7 and because its lowest tone needs only a chromatic inflection to become the 3rd of V^7, natural VII becomes absorbed into the V^7 chord. Because of the contrast between natural $\hat{7}$ and raised $\hat{7}$, on the one hand, and the common tones, on the other, the progression natural VII-V^7 can sound both unexpected and, in retrospect, logical. And the chromatic inflection of $\hat{7}$ can produce a particularly expressive effect. Example 15-14 shows natural VII as part of a bass line descending from I to V^7; the 5th of natural VII ($\hat{4}$ in the soprano) forms a good preparation for the 7th of V^7.

15-14

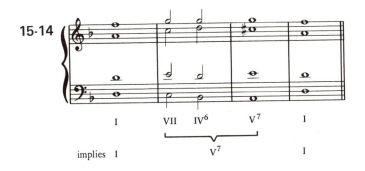

I   VII IV⁶   V⁷   I

implies I   V⁷   I

In Example 15-15, natural VII follows a tonicized III and functions, at first, as its dominant. Note the passing IV⁶ to connect natural VII and V⁷. This usage is very frequent; so is the use of parallel 10ths between the outer voices.

15-15 Handel, Concerto Grosso, Op. 3/1, II

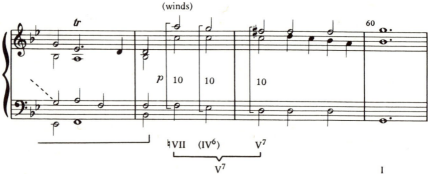

Natural VII often moves chromatically to I through V^6 or V^6_5, as in Example 15-16.

15-16

10. VII⁵₃ in major; raised VII⁵₃ in minor. Diminished triads on the leading tone are seldom satisfactory in ⁵₃ position. As we will see in Unit 17, the diminished triad occurs freely in some sequential passages. In most other situations, V^6_5 (which contains all three tones of the diminished VII) creates a far more pleasing sonority and is to be preferred. Occasionally, however, V_5^6 proves impracticable, and VII_3^5 forms the only possible alternative. Such cases arise most frequently in three-part texture. In a posthumously published composition of Brahms (Example 15-17) the diminished triads would doubtless have been $_5^6$ chords if the pianistic setting permitted a fourth voice to sustain an E. Here the diminished chords form part of passing motions within I-V-I; they are of very brief duration and receive no emphasis.

15-17   Brahms, Gigue (1855)

(VII_3^5) (VII_3^5) (VII_3^5) (VII_3^5)

In the trio sonatas of the Baroque period, diminished VII chords sometimes appear in the three-part setting formed by the two melody instruments and the bass. This occurs in a passage from Corelli (Example 15-18) where VII clearly represents an incomplete V_5^6; the 6th above the bass tone must be sacrificed to allow the resolution of the dissonant 5th of the preceding IV_5^6 chord. A good continuo player, however, would supply the missing 6th in the accompaniment, knowing that composers of the period frequently wrote the figure $5\flat$ as an abbreviation for $_5^6\flat$.*

15-18   Corelli, Sonata V, Op. 1, Allegro

*See C. P. E. Bach, *Essay on the True Art of Playing Keyboard Instruments,* translated and edited by William J. Mitchell (New York: W. W. Norton, 1949), pp. 222, 243-252.

In four-part writing IV$_3^6$ is generally best followed by V$_5^6$; occasionally VII$_3^5$ will occur for the sake of a smoother line in the inner voices. In Example 15-19 the vocal parts form a diminished $_3^5$; Bach's figures expressly indicate that the missing 6th should be played in the continuo accompaniment. Note that Bach doubles the 3rd of the diminished chord; this is the preferred doubling, the 3rd being the one tone not involved in any dissonant relationship.

15-19   Bach, Chorale 83

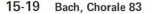

note   (The figures are Bach's.)

In Example 15-20, also from a Bach chorale, the first bar consists of an extended dominant chord; the bass moves down a 6th from the root to the 3rd while the top voice ascends from $\hat{2}$ to $\hat{4}$. Normally the last beat of this bar would contain a $_5^6$ chord. Here, however, Bach allows the tenor to accompany the bass at the upper 3rd, creating a "polarized" texture (SA up, TB down). This prevents the tenor from sounding the 6th, B♭, of the V$_5^6$ and produces a diminished $_3^5$ as a substitute. Because it grows out of the strong V at the beginning of the bar, the diminished chord would be heard as representing a V$_5^6$ even if the continuo player failed to provide the missing 6th (the bass is unfigured).

15-20   Bach, Chorale 22

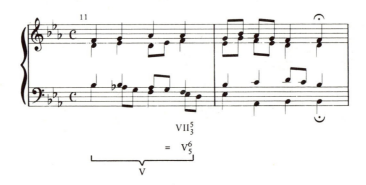

POINTS FOR REVIEW

1. In minor, III frequently leads from I to V in a large-scale harmonic progression. Typically introduced by natural VII, III is often expanded into a key area and generally moves to V through a passing IV or II^6 (descending stepwise soprano).

2. In major, a large-scale I-III-V is less common, as chromatic alteration is necessary to tonicize III. As in minor, III in major typically progresses to V through a passing IV or II^6.

3. III, in either a large- or small-scale progression, can move through an inverted V ($^4_3$, $^6_3$, or $^6_5$) to I. In this progression, which is most frequent in minor, no intervening chord is necessary between III and V, and a cross-relation is acceptable if not between soprano and bass.

4. III functions most characteristically in large contexts. Its most important small-scale use is to support $\hat{7}$ in a descending soprano line while leading the bass from I to IV. The progression III-VI-II-V-I is also possible.

5. In minor, natural VII often leads to III and functions as its dominant. In $^6_3$ position, natural VII forms a logical passing chord between I and III; the bass line will often continue by step to V. Natural VII can also lead to V^7 through a descending bass (with passing IV^6) and up to I through a chromatically inflected bass supporting V^6 or V$^6_5$.

6. Because of their poor sonority, VII$^5_3$ in major and raised VII$^5_3$ in minor are to be avoided; a leading tone in the bass will generally support V$^6_5$. Sometimes, especially in three-part texture, VII$^5_3$ substitutes for V$^6_5$.

EXERCISES

1. Preliminaries. Write the following progressions:
   a. III moves to root-position V through a passing IV or II^6 (minor only—two versions)
   b. III moves contrapuntally through an inversion of V^7 to I (minor only—two versions)
   c. $\hat{8}$ - $\hat{7}$ - $\hat{6}$
      I-(III)-IV (major and minor)
   d. III-VI-cadence (minor only)
   e. I moves to III through a passing natural VII^6 (minor)
   f. I moves to III through a natural VII$^5_3$ (minor)
   g. natural VII moves to V^7 through a passing IV^6 (minor)

2. Melody.

3. Figured bass.

4. Melody.

5. Figured bass. Find a soprano line that will work for both bars 1-4 and 5-8.

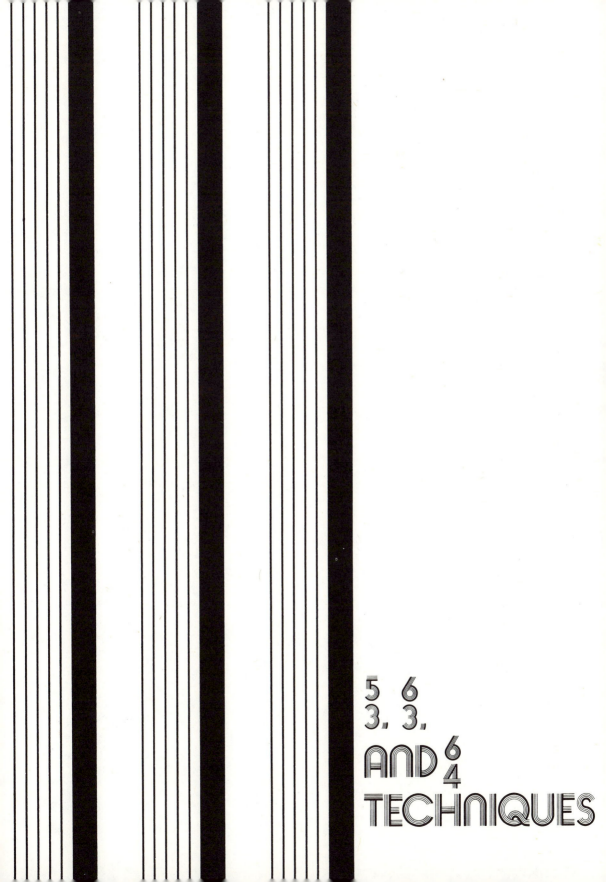

SIXTEEN | $\frac{5}{3}$=CHORD TECHNIQUES

Now that all seven diatonic triads have been introduced, we can begin to deal with some new procedures of harmony and voice leading and to broaden the application of those we have already discussed. For the moment we will discuss $\frac{5}{3}$ chords only; later units will show how the principles investigated here apply to work with other chords.

PROGRESSIONS BY 5THS AND 3RDS

1. **The principle of descending 5ths.** The basic progression of harmony is by 5th, so we can form a logical harmonic succession by arranging a group of triads in the order of descending 5ths. Sometimes, in fact, we encounter all seven triads so arranged: I-IV-VII-III-VI-II-V-I. When the complete progression occurs in a composition, some of the descending 5ths will appear in inversion as ascending 4ths in order to keep the bass in a reasonable register. We can see this quite clearly in Example 16-1. In the complete series of descending 5ths, one diminished 5th (or its inversion, the augmented 4th) must appear. In major it occurs between IV and VII; in minor, between VI and II. Without this diminished 5th, tones foreign to the key would appear, and the progression would not arrive at the tonic at the desired time. Thus, in the Handel, substituting a perfect 5th for the diminished 5th would produce the bass line E♭-A♭-D♭-G♭ instead of E♭-A-D-G. In a chain of descending 5ths, some chords may be more significant than others. In the Handel the emphasized chords are I (beginning of motion, full voicing), III (low bass register, return to initial melody tone), and the cadential II-V-I (end of motion, bass register, increased rhythmic activity). The other chords do not function on an equal level of importance; IV and VII form a transition from I to III and VI leads from III to the final cadence.

16-1 Handel, Passacaglia   (from *Harpsichord Suite No. 7*)

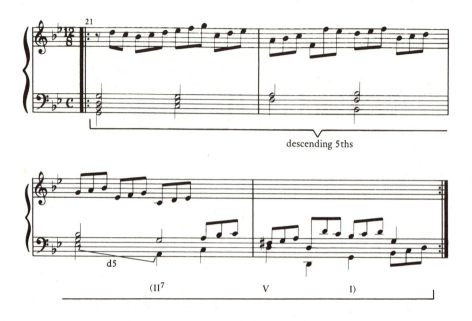

The technique of descending 5ths is a most useful and important one. Variants of it can accommodate triads in $\frac{6}{3}$ position and seventh chords as well (in the Handel, II occurs as a seventh chord). It lends itself to contrapuntal elaboration of various kinds, ranging from suspensions to canonic imitation. And with chromatic alterations, the technique can produce applied dominants and can help to effect modulations. In later units we will often use this technique.

2. The principle of ascending 5ths. Progressions of ascending 5ths occur much less frequently and play a much less important role in tonal composition. The complete progression, I-V-II-VI-III-VII-IV-I, is virtually useless, for the chords before the final I do not establish it as a goal. However segments of the progression can make a convincing transition to chords other than the tonic. The two main possibilities are I-V-II-VI-III in major (which will be illustrated in Unit 17) and III-VII-IV-I-V in minor, as shown in Example 16-2. (Note that both these possibilities avoid the diminished triads VII in major and II in minor.)

The excerpt from the Bach chorale shows the first two phrases. The ascending 5ths lead from III (tonicized in the first phrase) to the cadential V. The main link between III and V is, typically enough, the E minor chord, IV. The stepwise line III-IV-V fits into the larger harmonic scheme; these chords take precedence over VII and I, whose function it is to make a smooth connection from one main chord to the next. In general, as in this phrase, a series of ascending 5ths consists of a rising stepwise line decorated harmonically by the upper 5ths of the main chords. In this example, consequently, the I chord before the cadential V is a I in name only, not in behavior, for it does not form part of the harmonic framework.

16-2   Bach, Chorale 265

(a)

I   III ————————

VII   IV ——————— I   V

ascending 5ths
——————————————————→ V   I

(b) **reduction of bars 2-4**

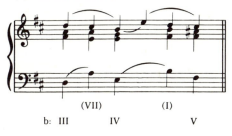

(VII)   (I)

b: III   IV   V

3. Bass motion by 3rds. We already know two important examples of this technique: I descending through VI to IV (or II⁶) and I rising through III to V. Progressions like I-VI-IV and I-III-V connect the beginning and goal chords by means of arpeggiation. In I-VI-IV the bass line arpeggiates the goal chord (in C major, C-A-F or IV); when the goal arrives the ear connects it with the preceding bass motion, which it sums up. In I-III-V the bass line arpeggiates the beginning chord (in C major, C-E-G or I); the V, therefore, does not sound so much like a goal. And, as we saw in Unit 15, the root of each new chord has already appeared in one (or even two) of the preceding chords, so that the chord's impact is weakened. For this reason, I-III-V does not usually occur in immediate succession without intervening chords (such as II⁶ or IV between III and V). In progressions by rising 3rds other than I-III-V, the intervening chords are usually applied dominants, which we will discuss in Volume 2.

An interesting instance of descending 3rds occurs at the end of a Chopin mazurka (Example 16-3), where the bass moves from V through III to I; the motion as a whole arpeggiates I. III as a divider between V and I sometimes appears before reprise sections and sonata recapitulations, but its appearance at the end of a piece is quite unusual; here it emphasizes the major tonic with which this mazurka in B♭ minor ends, by bringing $\hat{3}$ into the bass.

16-3   Chopin, Mazurka, Op. 24/4

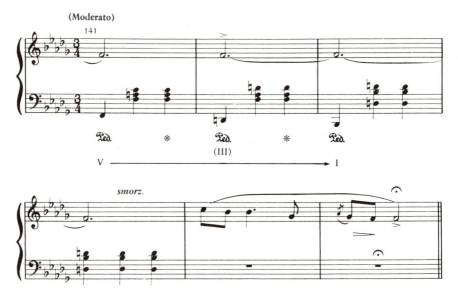

A more extended motion in descending 3rds occurs in a phrase from Chorale 101 of Bach (Example 16-4). Here the bass moves down a 9th from I to V⁶. Passing tones create a completely stepwise bass line, but the organization of this stepwise motion by 3rds can be clearly heard. As the slurs connecting the roman numerals show, the motion of a 9th is subdivided by E♭ (IV) into two stages; the IV is emphasized by meter and by change of melody tone. In the first stage VI connects I and IV; in the second, II connects IV and V⁶.

16-4   Bach, Chorale 101

One sometimes encounters bass motions by descending 3rd leading down a 7th from I to II. Example 17-1, bars 1-2, will show such a progression in slightly elaborated form.

4. Chords built on the upper 5th. Example 16-5 shows a beautiful Chopin cadence. A literal interpretation of the first bar as V-II-V^7 would be correct as far as it goes, but it would tell us little about the meaning of the "II." This chord does not fulfill the usual function of supertonic harmony—to lead to V—for it appears *after* the cadential V has already been introduced. Furthermore this "II" does not *sound* like a harmonic entity but rather like the result of motion within the expanded V. Therefore we can best understand it as the upper 5th of V, arrived at through a bass progression down from root to 5th to root. While the bass moves down through chordal tones, the melody moves up a 3rd to introduce the 7th of dominant harmony.

16-5 Chopin, Mazurka, Op. 17/3

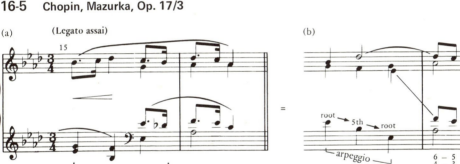

Chopin's cadence provides a good illustration of the principle that not every chord can be taken at face value as a harmonic entity. The possibility of a chord's functioning primarily as part of another, more extended, chord, as in the Chopin, is one you should bear in mind. The principle can be applied to other chords; thus I can function as the upper 5th of IV, VI as the upper 5th of II, and so on.

5. Chords built on the upper 3rd. A phrase from another Chopin mazurka (Example 16-6) shows a progression from a chord in B major to one in D♯ minor and (at the beginning of the next phrase) back to the B chord. Here, too, a literal analysis (I-III-I in B major) would fail to capture the specific meaning of the chord progression. Like the II of the preceding example, the III of this one is best understood as resulting from a motion within the governing B major chord, only this time between root and 3rd rather than between root and 5th. It helps to extend the tonic much as I^6 might, a further instance of the connection between III and I^6 mentioned in the preceding unit. The use of III as upper 3rd of I, of IV as upper 3rd of II, and so on, represents another important chordal function. Nineteenth-century composers sometimes wrote progressions that move back and forth between two ⅗ chords with roots a 3rd apart—such as II-IV-II or IV-VI-IV. This sort of oscillating movement within a 3rd is not characteristic of eighteenth-century music.

16-6   Chopin, Mazurka, Op. 41/2

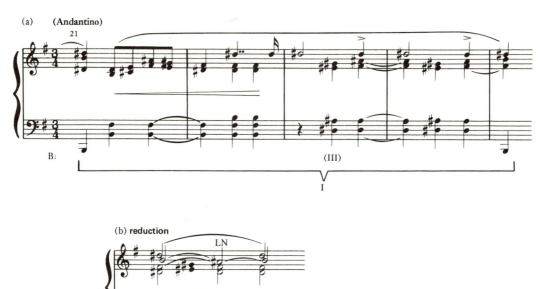

CONTRAPUNTAL CHORD FUNCTIONS

6. Chords as voice-leading correctives. Understanding that chords can act as voice-leading correctives—that is, that they can break up parallel 5ths and octaves—can help you reduce the number of errors in your written work. Much more importantly, it can also deepen your awareness of the interplay between harmony and voice leading in great music—voice leading as the composers conceived it, not narrowly, chord by chord, but comprehensively, over both small and large musical spans.

The first phrase of Bach's Chorale 280 (Example 16-7) illustrates how a chord can prevent voice-leading errors. The melody contains, in slightly decorated form, the progression 5̂-6̂-7̂-8̂; the main harmonies are I, IV, V, and I. We know from Unit 9 that a motion from IV to V entails the risk of parallels unless the upper voices move down, not up as they do here. And indeed if we glance from IV to V we shall soon find the parallels: 5ths between bass and alto, octaves between tenor and soprano. We do not *hear* the parallels because of the II on the fourth beat of the first bar; this chord interpolates a 10th between the 5ths and a 5th between the octaves. In addition to permitting good voice leading, the II here also plays its characteristic harmonic role of intensifying V.

16-7   **Bach, Chorale 280**

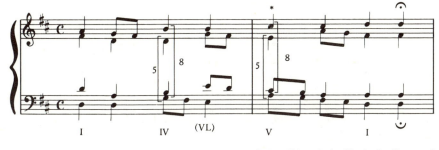

*Why did Bach double the leading tone?

In this connection, look again at the beginning of Beethoven's "Spring" Sonata (Example 11-3). In addition to its harmonic function, the VI chord of bar 3 breaks up parallels between I and II (compare bars 1 and 4). The voice-leading function of VI is frequently a factor in the progression I-VI-II-V-I. Example 16-8 supplements the Bach and Beethoven excerpts by showing some other important possibilities. Voice-leading chords can be particularly useful in progressions involving chords with roots a 2nd apart (such as I-(VI)-II), but their use is not restricted to such situations. We will return to voice-leading chords later to discuss other functions they often fulfill.

16-8   (a)

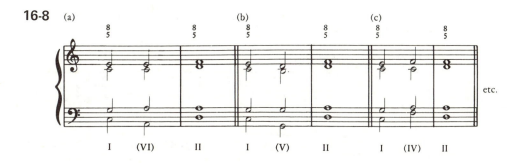

etc.

7. Chords as support for passing tones. Some chords function mainly as support for passing tones in an upper part, usually the soprano. We have already encountered this chord function, most recently in connection with III as support for $\hat{7}$ in $\frac{\hat{8}\text{-}\hat{7}\text{-}\hat{6}\text{-}\hat{5}}{\text{I-III-IV-I}}$ (Unit 15). Example 16-9 from a Brahms lied (song), demonstrates an exactly analogous use of IV. An extension of the preceding II, rather than a self-sufficient harmony, the IV gives support and a measure of emphasis to the passing tone, E, of the melody. If this chord were not there, the E would be a dissonant passing tone (7th) above the II; the IV transforms it into a consonance. Incidentally, the C♮ in the piano part is an element of E minor used in an E major context, an instance of *mixture* (see Unit 1, section 21).

16-9   Brahms, Geliebter wo zaudert, Op. 33/13

Quite often an apparent tonic—that is, a tonic in name but not in function—appears between IV and V in order to support a passing tone in the soprano. The characteristic soprano progression is $\hat{4}$-$\hat{3}$-$\hat{2}$; $\hat{3}$, of course, is the supported passing tone. This progression usually occurs when $\hat{3}$ is metrically weak; when it is strong, the cadential $\frac{6}{4}$ becomes possible. Example 16-10 illustrates.

16-10   Schubert, Piano Sonata, D. 958, I

A V interpolated between I and VI frequently supports a descending passing tone in the soprano and may serve as a voice-leading corrective as well. Any bass progression of a descending 3rd can be similarly elaborated—for example, VI-(III)-IV or IV-(I)-II. We will see a very clear example of this technique in Example 16-17a.

8. Chords above a bass passing tone. In small contexts $\frac{6}{3}$ or $\frac{6}{4}$ chords are often preferable to $\frac{5}{3}$'s as passing chords, especially when moving between the root position and first inversion of a triad. In connecting I and I^6, for instance, VII^6 generally works better than II, whose greater stability and "weight" tend to contradict its transitional function. For one reason or another, however, $\frac{5}{3}$'s do sometimes appear as short-range passing chords. In the last phrase of Bach's Chorale 102 (Example 16-11), the chord labeled (V) passes from IV to IV^6. A $\frac{6}{4}$ chord, with B in the tenor instead of A, would produce 5ths between the inner voices and is not a possibility here. The chord at the beginning of bar 21, incidentally, is not a functional tonic; it supports the passing tone B of the soprano; the hemiola rhythm makes us hear the B as an unaccented passing tone.

16-11   Bach, Chorale 102

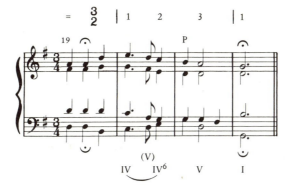

$\frac{5}{3}$ chords will more often appear above passing tones in the bass when the motion is within a seventh chord rather than a triad. A passing $\frac{5}{3}$ fits very naturally in the space between the $\frac{4}{3}$ and the $\frac{6}{5}$ positions, most typically in an expansion of V^7—also, sometimes, within II^7. Another possibility is between V^6 and V^4_3 (Example 16-12).

16-12   Beethoven, Piano Sonata, Op. 111, II

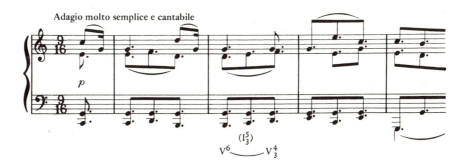

Stepwise bass motions can play an important part in creating continuity over longer spans; such bass progressions can be considered expanding passing motions. $\frac{5}{3}$ chords frequently appear in the course of such passing motions; thus they function as passing chords. Look again at Example 16-2: from a broad perspective the E minor (IV) chord is passing—that is, it connects the beginning of the stepwise motion, III, with the goal, V. Long-range passing motions, by their very nature, seldom proceed consecutively from one main chord to another. Subordinate tones and chords, such as the A major and B minor chords in 16-2, will appear between them.

9. Chords as support for neighboring tones. $\frac{5}{3}$ chords often support neighbors—especially upper neighbors—in the soprano, less often in one of the inner voices. Typically the root of the neighboring chord is a 5th below that of the main chord: IV supporting upper neighbors within an expanded I is the most frequent and important possibility. The same relationship can extend to other chords; in Example 16-13 we see a "I" supporting neighbors within a prolongation of V; this "I", like several others we have observed in this unit, is not a functional tonic but a detail within the expansion of V.

16-13   Mozart, Piano Sonata, K. 310, I

In some nineteenth-century music, starting around the time of Schubert, we now and then find neighboring chords whose root is a 3rd below that of the main chord—I-VI-I, for example. The D minor chord in Example 16-14 arises mainly as support for the D of the first violin part (upper neighbor to the 5th of I).

16-14 Brahms, String Quartet, Op. 51/1, III

10. Chords above a bass neighboring tone. These are usually easy to recognize and do not require much discussion. In immediate chord successions, neighbors in the bass tend to support $^6_3$'s rather than $^5_3$'s (such as I-VII⁶-I rather than I-II-I). This is because a series of consecutive root-position chords, especially where there are no common tones, does not create an effect of flowing motion. Over longer spans (with intervening chords), neighboring $^5_3$'s become very useful. The most important possibility is VI as upper neighbor to V, an idiom that sometimes also occurs in immediate succession, as in Example 16-15. In this excerpt, VI also supports a passing tone in the soprano.

16-15 Bach, Chorale 102

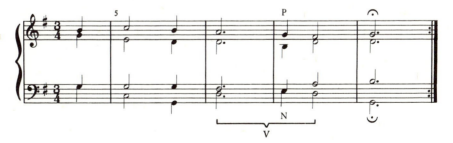

11. V as a minor triad. As we know, the natural form of minor generates a minor triad on the 5th scale step (symbol: -V). Because it lacks a leading tone, -V does not tend very actively toward I. This makes it ineffective in immediate V-I progressions and in situations where the expectation of I becomes a factor—in half and deceptive cadences, for example. In all such cases, the major form of V (+V, with raised $\hat{7}$) helps to define the tonality much more clearly. Until now, therefore, we have employed V in minor only as a major triad derived from the harmonic and ascending melodic forms of the mode.

It would be quite wrong to conclude, however, that minor V plays no role in composition and has only a kind of theoretical significance. On the contrary, situations arise in which this chord is permitted and even required. Minor V can form a very good support for natural $\hat{7}$ as a descending passing tone, usually leading from I to VI. As Example 16-16 indicates, linear rather than chordal considerations determine whether -V must occur, for the chord progression as such permits either a major or a minor triad on $\hat{5}$. But the augmented 2nd, $\sharp\hat{7}$-$\flat\hat{6}$, is unmelodic and should be avoided; in a descending stepwise line, therefore, $\hat{7}$ will occur in its lowered form, and V will be in minor.

16-16

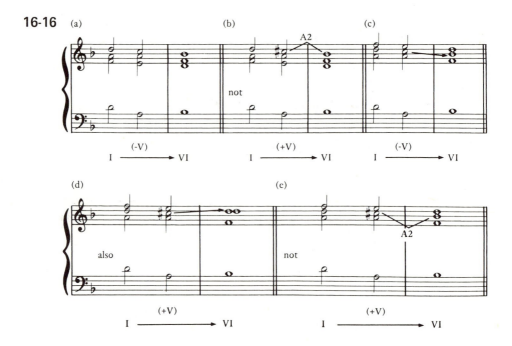

We can observe the application of this principle to composition by comparing two of Bach's settings of the same chorale phrase (Example 16-17). Note that the settings are identical up to the third beat of the first bar; even after the upper voices begin to diverge, the bass lines remain the same. Both settings have the same harmonic framework: I (prolonged contrapuntally)-II⁶-V. In the first setting, the VI (bar 2, downbeat) leads from the prolonged I to the cadential II⁶ in a progression of descending 3rds. The V (bar 1, fourth beat) supports the passing tone, C♯, of the soprano and forestalls 5ths (bass and alto) between I and VI. Although this V is not a functionally harmonic dominant, Bach uses raised $\hat{7}$, thus making it a major triad, because of the *ascending* tenor progression $\hat{7}$-$\hat{1}$.

In the other setting, the corresponding V chord is minor, with A♮; this is because the alto line *descends* from A to G and F♯. This version, far more than the other one, is permeated by the motivic figure of a rising 3rd (see brackets in the example). A consequence of the motivic design is the substitution of IV⁶ for the more usual VI on the downbeat of the second bar.

16-17

(a) Bach, Chorale 62

(b) Bach, Chorale 104

We have included the second phrase of Chorale 62 to show another function of the minor V; here it prepares for a brief tonicization of III. In the further course of the book, we will cover other important functions of the minor dominant.

POINTS FOR REVIEW

1. In the progression of descending 5ths (I-IV-VII-III-VI-II-V-I), the bass line usually alternates descending 5ths and ascending 4ths.

2. The progression of ascending 5ths, which is much less goal-oriented than that of descending 5ths, is basically a rising step-wise line: C $\overset{(G)}{\diagup}$ D $\overset{(A)}{\diagup}$ E. The complete series I-I is virtually never used.

3. Another important type of progression is bass motion by 3rds (bass arpeggio). Motion by descending 3rds (I-VI-IV, for example) is much more goal-oriented than motion by ascending 3rds.

4. A chord can be expanded by motion to its upper 5th. For example, II can expand V and I can expand IV.

5. Similarly, a chord can be expanded by motion to its upper 3rd—IV can expand II and VI can expand IV, etc.

6. Chords can be used as voice-leading correctives (to break up parallel 5ths or octaves). Such a chord is especially useful between chords with roots a 2nd apart, for example, I-(VI)-II.

7. Chords can be used to support passing tones in the soprano. Here is an important example: $\hat{4}$ - $\hat{3}$ - $\hat{2}$

    IV-(I)-V.

8. Chords can be used above a passing tone in the bass. In a small-scale progression, $\frac{6}{3}$ and $\frac{6}{4}$ chords are most frequently used for this purpose. In a large-scale progression IV can serve as a passing chord from III to V, and so on (see Example 16-2).

9. Chords can support neighboring tones in the upper voices. Such progressions as I-(IV)-I or V-(I)-V occur very frequently.

10. Chords can occur over neighboring tones in the bass. Over small spans $\frac{6}{3}$ chords are most frequently used; over longer spans $\frac{5}{3}$ chords are more frequent. Most important is VI as upper neighbor to V.

11. An important function of -V is to support $\hat{7}$ as a descending passing tone, where it helps to avoid an augmented 2nd. Minor V also prepares for the tonicization of III.

EXERCISES

1. Preliminaries. Write progressions in different major and minor keys that illustrate the following techniques:

    a. descending 5ths—entire series

    b. descending 5ths—part of the series

    c. ascending 5ths connecting III and IV in minor

    d. descending 3rds connecting III and IV in minor

    e. descending 3rds connecting I and II in major

    f. VI breaking up parallels between I and II

    g. "I" supporting $\hat{3}$ as a passing tone

    h. "IV" supporting $\hat{1}$ as a passing tone

    i. "III" supporting $\hat{7}$ as a passing tone

    j. V going twice to VI in minor, once with V as a minor triad and once with V as a major triad

    k. root-position "I" connecting V$\frac{4}{3}$ and V$\frac{6}{5}$; use two different sopranos

2. Outer voices with unfigured bass. This exercise makes use of V as a minor triad; sometimes you will have to decide whether major or minor V is the better choice.

*don't harmonize any of the sixteenth notes

SEVENTEEN | DIATONIC SEQUENCES

17-1 Bach, Well-Tempered Clavier, I, Prelude 21

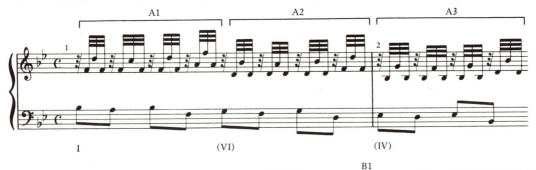

(moving toward tonicized V)

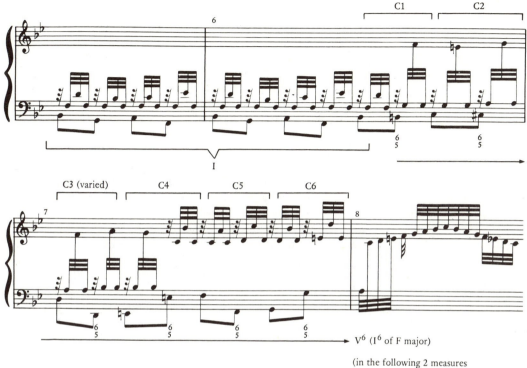

(in the following 2 measures
V is confirmed as a key area)

COMPOSITIONAL FUNCTIONS

1. Repetition. A crucial element—often, indeed, *the* crucial element—in musical design and form is repetition of a melodic or chordal pattern. If such repetitions occur on different scale degrees, the result is called a *sequence.* Maintaining the same musical idea (sometimes with slight variations) establishes a connection between the beginning and the end of the sequential passage and creates the possibility for expansions—some on quite a large scale—of many of the techniques we have already discussed.

The expansional character of sequences is very evident in Example 17-1, which contains three sequential passages, labeled A, B, and C. Sequence A expands the field of motion from a I to a cadential II. This motion—normally a rising 2nd—is expressed as a descending 7th; the 7th is subdivided into three 3rds (B♭-G; G-E♭; E♭-C). The material of the first half-bar is repeated on G and E♭; the descending bass leads to a cadential II-V^7-I.

Much of the remainder of the excerpt forms a transition from the expanded tonic of bars 1-3 to the tonicized F major $^6_3$ chord of bar 8. This transition is effected in two stages (sequences B and C). Sequence B grows out of the tonic of bar 3, each pattern taking up an entire bar. The bass moves up a step with each new bar until the D is reached in bar 5, where the sequence breaks off and the bass returns to the tonic. The stepwise ascent begins once more in sequence C, but with a shorter pattern so that each step lasts only one beat. The bass moves chromatically until D is regained in bar 7. The sequential motion then continues (with varied bass) until it reaches its goal—the F major chord in bar 8. Note that the motion to the tonicized V is achieved in a much more gradual way than in the examples of Unit 14.

Like sequences A and B in the Bach, most sequences contain three statements (or two plus the beginning of a third). More than three can be tedious unless the pattern is very short and simple, as in sequence C (bars 6½-7) of the Bach.

2. Diatonic progressions. Sequences vary in many respects—some use only triads; others use seventh chords, applied dominants, and so on. In this unit we will discuss sequences using $\frac{5}{3}$ and $\frac{6}{3}$ chords only, and will confine ourselves to sequential patterns that appear frequently in composition. Some sequences are completely diatonic; others use chromatic elements. Some remain in one key; others effect a change of tonal center. We will discuss chromatic and modulating sequences in later units; here we will work with diatonic ones, like the first sequence in the Bach prelude. This passage demonstrates an important principle: when the pattern repeats in a diatonic sequence, the qualities of chords and melodic intervals will sometimes change. Thus the first statement begins with a B♭ major chord, the second with a G *minor* chord; the first melodic progression of the bass is a half step, but its repetition is a *whole* step. The lesson is clear: to keep a sequence diatonic use only tones that belong to the key; avoid accidentals (except for the customary inflections of $\hat{6}$ and $\hat{7}$ in minor).

3. Classification of sequences. Most diatonic chordal sequences fall into one of the following categories:

1. sequences with descending 5ths
2. sequences with ascending 5ths
3. sequences using ascending 5-6 technique
4. sequences falling in 3rds (descending 5-6 technique)

Example 17-2 shows these basic types in four-voice settings. You will find it helpful to compare this example both with the excerpts from the literature in this unit and with your own written work.

17-2   basic sequence types

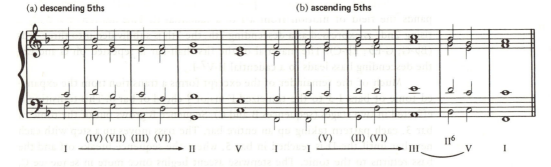

(a) descending 5ths   (b) ascending 5ths

I ——→ (IV) (VII) (III) (VI) ——→ II   V   I   I ——→ (V) (II) (VI) ——→ III   II⁶   V   I

(c) rising by step (ascending 5-6)

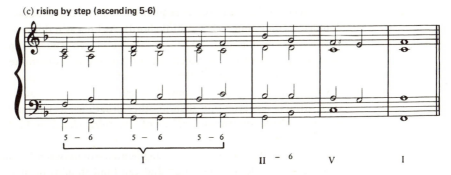

(d) falling in 3rds (descending 5-6)

Each of these basic types of sequence can fulfill various functions in a composition, depending on how the composer uses it. The progressions of Example 17-2 illustrate, in abstract form, three important ways in which a sequence functions:

1. To form a transition between the beginning of a motion and its goal, perhaps the most frequent function. In 17-2b and d, the sequences lead from the opening tonic to III and IV, respectively.
2. To contain both the transition and the goal, as in the progression of descending 5ths in 17-2a, which moves from the initial tonic through intervening chords to the cadential II-V-I (here emphasized by the broadened rhythmic values).
3. To expand a single chord—most often the tonic. In 17-2c the sequence expands the initial tonic (moving from I to I⁶) of the progression I-II-V-I.

Sequences frequently contain a prominent scalewise line in the bass or the soprano—sometimes, in fact, in both. This scalewise component helps the sequence to fulfill its basic function, that of forming a transition between two relatively stable points.

4. Voice-leading implications. Normally, as in the Bach prelude, *all* the voices above a sequential bass are themselves sequential. And with any repetitive patterns where all the voices participate, 5ths and octaves may become a problem. Therefore, voice-leading chords play an essential role in sequential passages. In sequence A of the Bach, the chord on the fourth eighth note prevents 5ths between successive strong beats in the bass and middle voice. And in the third sequence, the $^6_5$ chords also break up 5ths.

Keeping the upper voices sequential, as in 17-2, will occasionally produce a doubled leading tone (17-2a, third chord). As long as it does not appear before a goal tonic, this doubling is perfectly acceptable. In sequential passages based on descending 5ths or on the ascending 5-6 technique, a diminished triad in $\frac{5}{3}$ position will sometimes appear. When it forms part of a repetitive pattern and when the progression as a whole conveys a sense of forward motion, the diminished triad attracts less attention than in other situations; its harshness is considerably softened. (Note the smooth effect of the third chord in 17-2a.) In sequences based on descending 5ths, a melodic augmented 4th or diminished 5th will appear in one of the voices (see the augmented 4th between IV and VII in 17-2a). However the melodic augmented 2nd can (and should) be avoided in four-part vocal writing.

SEQUENCES WITH DESCENDING 5THS

5. Harmonic and contrapuntal implications. Example 17-3a illustrates the first basic type of sequence—the one based on descending 5ths. In this type of sequence, the chords are grouped in twos (see the brackets in 17-3a), and each repetition of the two-chord pattern is one step lower than the preceding statement. The bass line reflects this grouping, for it is also arranged in groups of two—down a 5th, up a 4th (or vice versa)—so that it forms two stepwise lines, such as:

One of these two lines will usually predominate, such factors as rhythm and register throwing it into relief. The stepwise relationships that occur in a series of descending 5ths add a strong contrapuntal implication to this typically harmonic progression.

17-3   (a) Handel, Bourrée   (from *Royal Fireworks Music*)

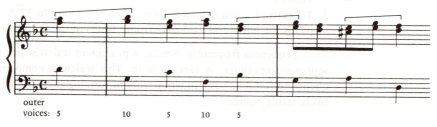

outer
voices: 5   10   5   10   5

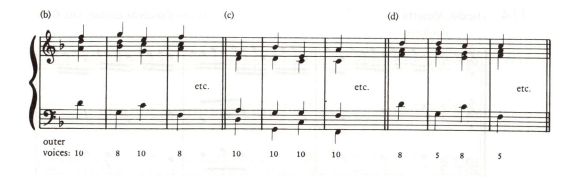

In a sequential series of descending 5ths, as in the nonsequential ones discussed in the preceding unit, some of the chords may receive more emphasis than others. The last three chords of a complete series are often important because they form a cadence II-V-I. Thus the fundamental motion of the Handel excerpt is from the opening I to IV (first strong beat, highest soprano tone) through a passing chord (III) to the cadence II⁶-V⁷-I. The VII and VI have a harmonic role as part of the series of 5ths; in addition the VII functions as a voice-leading chord that prevents parallel octaves in the stepwise descent from IV to III. Notice how the cadential II⁶ is further set off by the rhythmic change in the upper voices.

Sequential patterns are often characterized by the intervallic relationships between the outer voices. In the Handel the bass and soprano alternate 5ths and 10ths (intervallic pattern 5-10, 5-10). The progressions of 15-3b, c, and d show some other possibilities. The combinations that contain imperfect consonances (5-10, 10-8, and 10-10) are usually preferable to the 8-5 pattern, which may sound empty unless decorated.

It is by no means necessary to use the complete series of descending 5ths (I-IV-VII-III-VI-II-V-I); shorter segments may also occur, but one must be careful with diminished triads. They ought not to occur at the very beginning or end of such progressions, where they are likely to be too exposed.

6. $\frac{5}{3}$-$\frac{6}{3}$ **pattern.** The descending 5th pattern is often modified so that $\frac{6}{3}$ chords alternate with $\frac{5}{3}$. This procedure tends to enhance one of the stepwise bass lines. In another Handel excerpt, Example 17-4, the $\frac{5}{3}$ chords support the bass descent C-B♭-A♭; the $\frac{6}{3}$'s are clearly subordinate until the cadential II⁶ arrives in bar 88. Notice how the register change in the top voice helps to emphasize the importance of this chord.

17-4 **Handel, Musette** (from *Concerto Grosso*, Op. 6/6)

In Example 17-5, on the other hand, the series of descending 5ths *begins* with a $^6_3$ chord, the $^5_3$'s coming in on the second half of the measure. This sequence leads from I^6 through V^6 to I with the $^6_3$ chords predominating. As in the Handel Musette (17-4), the last chord of the sequence is a goal, but the two sequences function quite differently. The sequence of 17-4 connects the opening I to a cadential II^6, while the one in 17-5 moves between different positions of the same chord, I^6 to I.

17-5   Mozart, Piano Sonata, K. 545, I

G: I^6 (IV)   (VII^6)   (III)

(VI^6)   (II)   (V^6)   I

II^6

V$^6_4$ 7   I

SEQUENCES WITH ASCENDING 5THS

7. Harmonic and contrapuntal implications. Another Handel excerpt (Example 17-6) illustrates the second basic type of sequence—the one that contains ascending 5ths. This pattern rises, unlike the progression of descending 5ths, where the basic tendency is downward. As 17-6 shows, some of the ascending 5ths may be expressed as descending 4ths. In Unit 16, we saw that a succession of $\frac{5}{3}$ chords whose roots rise by 5ths normally grows out of an ascending stepwise line. Review Example 16-2, where a nonsequential passage with ascending 5ths elaborates a rising stepwise line that moves from III through a passing IV to V. The Handel Adagio contains the same progression, but expressed sequentially. The motion III-IV-V is expanded into a series of ascending 5ths—III-VII-IV-I-V. The VII and I prevent parallel octaves and support incomplete neighbors in the soprano (see the accompanying reduction). An interesting feature of this excerpt is the use of suspensions alternating between the soprano and the tenor.

17-6 **Handel, Adagio**   (from *Harpsichord Suite No. 2*)

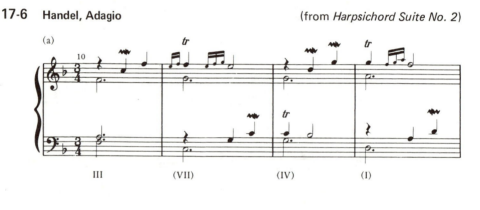

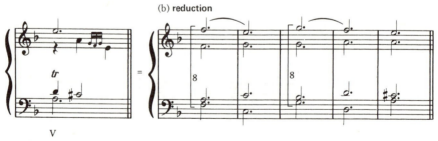

8. Omitting a step in the ascent. Like the Handel Adagio, an excerpt from Beethoven's "Waldstein" Sonata (Example 17-7) contains a rising sequence with ascending 5ths. In the Beethoven, however, the ascent skips over one step, the pair of chords III-VII on $\hat{3}$. In this way, a diminished triad (VII) is avoided. Omitting a step in the ascent is very frequent, usually to avoid the diminished triad; for an illustration in minor, see Example 17-22.

17-7   Beethoven, "Waldstein" Sonata, Op. 53, III

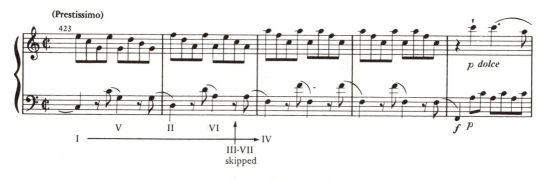

9. $\frac{5\text{-}6}{3\text{-}3}$ **pattern.** As with descending 5ths, $\frac{6}{3}$ chords may alternate with $\frac{5}{3}$'s (Example 17-8). As in the "Waldstein" excerpt, a step in the ascent is left out. Here, however, the bass tone that follows the skip is not a goal but an incomplete neighbor resolving to I^6 (see reduction). In this way the initial tonic is prolonged, the span between I and I^6 filled in by a passing tone and decorated by an incomplete neighbor. The stepwise bass motion Gb-Ab-Bb continues beyond the sequence through the $\frac{6}{5}$ chord on Cb to the cadential $\frac{6}{4}$ on Db (bar 33). (The chords on Gb and Cb are applied dominants, which will be explained in Volume 2. If the reduction [17-8b] is played *without* these accidentals it will still make sense.)

17-8   Chopin, Etude, Op. 25/9

(b) reduction

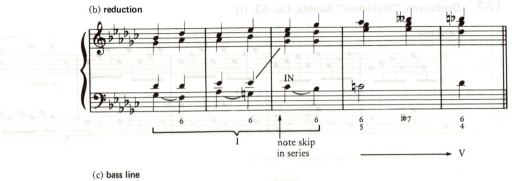

I   note skip
in series   V

(c) bass line

I   V

SEQUENCES USING THE ASCENDING 5-6 TECHNIQUE

10. Syncopes. Example 17-9 shows the familiar procedure whereby a $^6_3$ chord arises out of contrapuntal motion (5 to 6) over a single bass tone.

17-9

This technique can be extended over a stepwise ascending bass, producing a series of 5-6 progressions. In such a series the 6ths normally appear on weaker beats than the 5ths. The motion 5-6 emphasizes the weak beats so that the voice in which it appears sounds syncopated; for this reason, 5-6 progressions in such a series are often called *syncopes*. Example 17-10 demonstrates the 5-6 series in two and three voices. In three voices, 3rds or 10ths are added either above or below the 5-6 syncopes.

17-10

(a)   **(b)**   **(c)**

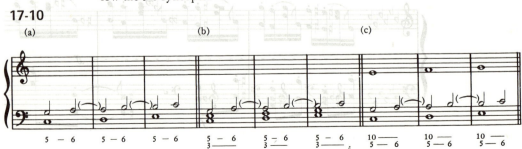

The 5-6 series occurs most naturally in a texture of three voices, but with careful attention to doubling, four voices are also possible (Example 17-11).

17-11 (a)   (b)

The use of 5-6 in a series is an old contrapuntal technique and one that occurs very frequently in composition. Often it serves to prevent parallel 5ths, as we can see in Example 17-12, which presents a particularly beautiful use of 5-6 technique in a fragment from an "Ave Maria" by the great Renaissance composer Josquin des Pres. Here the outer voices move by step in parallel 10ths, forming a sequence in rising 2nds. The tenor forms a 5-6 series with the bass, avoiding a series of parallel 5ths.

17-12 Josquin, Ave Maria

translation: [Hail to thee, whose conception] full of solemn
rejoicing, would fill heaven and earth with new joy.

In the Josquin, the 5-6's occur within a larger sequential pattern. Often, however, as in Example 17-13, the 5-6 series itself helps to form a sequence in rising 2nds; in this example, the top voice decorates the sequential pattern. The 5-6 technique lends itself easily to all kinds of sequential elaborations, ranging from the simple to the very complex. Variants using seventh chords and applied dominants (as in the third sequence of Example 17-1) occur very frequently; we will take them up in later units.

5-6 series in major often contain a diminished triad in root position (VII$_3^5$), as in bar 260 of 17-13. This diminished chord does not create a disturbing effect if the tonic follows soon after, as it does in the A major chord of bar 261. The importance of this chord as the goal of the passage is underscored—not contradicted—by the rest that precedes it.

17-13 Mozart, Piano Concerto, K. 488, I

11. Root-position variant of ascending 5-6. Example 17-14 shows an important variant of the 5-6 technique; the bass leaps down in 3rds and transforms the $\frac{6}{3}$ chords into $\frac{5}{3}$'s. Bars 3-5 of Example 17-1 also illustrate this procedure.

17-14

5-6 becomes 5-8

SEQUENCES FALLING IN 3RDS (DESCENDING 5-6)

12. Harmonic and contrapuntal implications. The fourth important type of sequence (17-2d) also alternates 5ths and 6ths, but in a very different manner. Here the 5th and 6th do not share a common bass tone. Instead, they alternate above a bass descending by step; each new interval pair (5-6) occurs a 3rd below the one before it, so that the sequence is organized in descending 3rds. Example 17-15 illustrates this very important sequential pattern. In the Mozart the descending bass line is expressed by the first and third eighth notes of the left-hand piano part; the second and fourth eighths represent an inner voice. The descending bass, supporting $\frac{5}{3}$ and $\frac{6}{3}$ chords in alternation, leads from I to the goal chord, II^6. The melody is in the right-hand part of the piano; it clearly shows the sequential repetition at the lower 3rd. The violin part—actually an "alto" voice—has a simpler line, a stepwise descent in parallel 10ths above the bass.

17-15 **Mozart, Violin Sonata, K. 379, II**

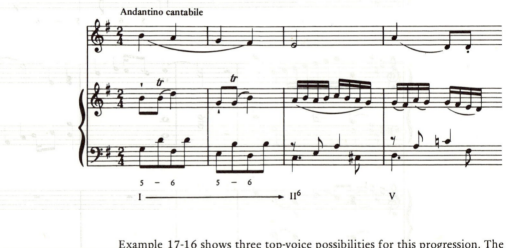

Example 17-16 shows three top-voice possibilities for this progression. The first two resemble the right-hand piano part and the violin part of the Mozart excerpt.

17-16

(a)   (b)   (c)

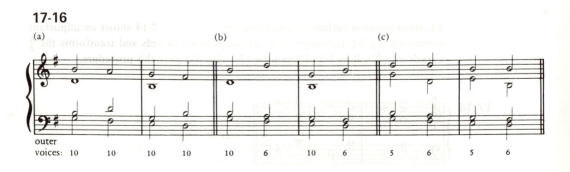

outer
voices: 10   10   10   10   10   6   10   6   5   6   5   6

An excerpt from Handel (Example 17-17) also makes use of a descending 5-6 sequence; the violin parts elaborate a motion in parallel 10ths above the bass. The function of this sequence is quite different from that in 17-16. By carrying the bass line one step further, Handel makes a connection between the opening tonic and its first inversion; the bass then continues by step, but in quicker time values, to complete the octave descent. In the Handel, therefore, the sequence expands the initial tonic, whereas Mozart's sequence forms a bridge from I to the cadential II^6. (Note the minor "V^6" in the first bar of the Handel, resulting from the normal use of the descending melodic form of minor.)

17-17 Handel, Allegro   (from *Concerto Grosso,* Op. 6/12)

13. Root-position variant of descending 5-6. Example 17-18 is the opening of the first variation (for piano alone) of the same Mozart sonata movement as Example 17-15; it shows an important derivative of the descending 5-6 sequence. Here the bass leaps down in 4ths and transforms the $^6_3$ chords of the basic progression into $^5_3$'s. The disjunct bass emphasizes the organization in descending 3rds of this type of sequence.

17-18   Mozart, Violin Sonata, K. 379, II

A more elaborate form of the same sequential progression occurs in bars 1-2 of our Bach prelude (Example 17-1) where the first $^5_3$ chord in each group is embellished by its lower neighbor. See the reductions in Example 17-19 and compare them with the original example.

17-19

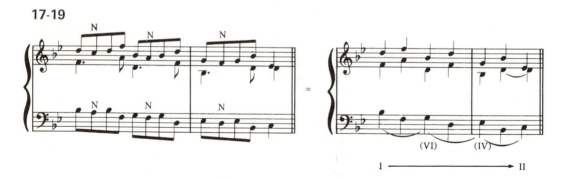

LESS FREQUENT SEQUENTIAL PATTERNS

14. Ascending by step with voice-leading $^5_3$ chords. Example 17-20 shows another way to produce a sequence rising by step; in this respect it resembles the rising sequence with ascending 5ths and the 5-6 syncope technique. Here, the bass moves alternately up a 4th and down a 3rd, all with root-position triads. The first chords of each pair are the principal ones; the second ones function as voice-leading correctives, breaking up parallel 5ths and octaves. In this excerpt the sequence forms a stepwise transition from I to V. Note that the change of rhythm and the breaking off of the sequential pattern do not occur at the same time.

17-20 Mozart, Two-Piano Sonata, K. 448, III

15. Descending sequence with 6-5 syncopes. The interval succession 6-5 over a single bass tone can occur in series thus producing a descending sequence. This procedure is the reverse of the ascending 5-6 series discussed earlier. In Example 17-21, the bass moves from I down to a cadential $\frac{6}{4}$. The bass remains sequential for three complete steps except for the chromatic A♯-A♮ in the bass. The right-hand part, at first sequential, is altered in bar 18 to allow for the chromatic bass; a leap to A would produce an ugly effect. Two neighboring chords separate the cadential $\frac{6}{4}$ from its resolution, a possibility that we shall explore in Unit 19.

17-21 Brahms, Intermezzo, Op. 117/3

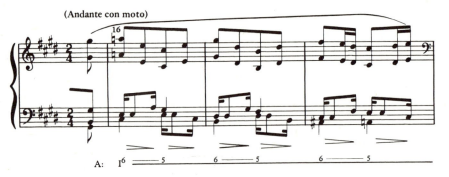

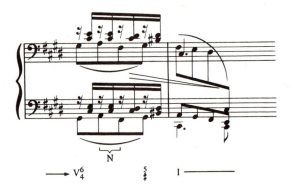

SEQUENCES IN MINOR

16. Descending motion. If you use your ear, you will soon discover that not all diatonic sequences that work well in major can be used successfully in minor. Two factors limit the possibilities for sequential treatment in minor: the diminished triad on II and possible difficulties in approaching the leading tone. Descending 5ths, the descending 5-6 succession, and their variants are the easiest to use. In the complete series of descending 5ths, from I to I, $\hat{7}$ need not be raised until the cadential V is reached (see Example 17-3a). In a sequence by descending 5ths, the diminished triad on II is good; it forms part of the cadential II-V-I and its approach from VI sounds natural. In the descending 5-6 progression, the natural form of minor will be used for the bass (Example 17-17). This progression also presents few problems in moving down from I. The approach to II, however, is less convincing than with descending 5ths; usually VII[6] or II[7] is used instead (thus modifying or breaking off the sequence; again see 17-17).

17. Moving up from I. In minor, moving up from I is much more difficult than moving down because of the diminished triad on II. In a rising sequence with ascending 5ths, the pair of chords II-VI can be left out to avoid this triad, a technique discussed in section 8. Example 17-22 illustrates. The bass ascends from I to IV (skipping II), the soprano moving in 10ths above the bass. In bar 4, a voice exchange between soprano and bass transforms IV to IV⁶; the IV⁶ leads to V in a Phrygian cadence. The major V in the second half of bar 1 is typical; raised $\hat{7}$ intensifies the connection with the tonic.

17-22 **Corelli, Allemanda**   (from *Trio Sonata,* Op. 4/8)

The ascending 5-6 series can move up from I without skipping II (Example 17-23a). The diminished triad is approached by step and is less harsh than when preceded by a leap. Moreover it "resolves" into the next $\frac{5}{3}$ chord, III (compare section 10). The tonal meaning of this progression, however, can be ambiguous; the III will tend to sound like the tonic (of the "relative major") unless followed by a progression leading to I as in 17-23b.

17-23

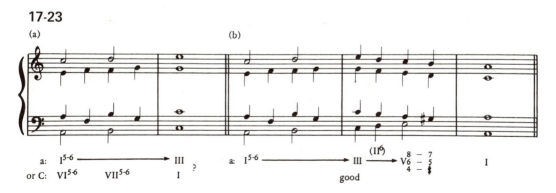

This series can be convincingly extended to the next step IV-II⁶ and on to V⁽⁷⁾ or V$\frac{4}{2}$. Be sure to avoid the augmented 2nd in moving on to V. Example 17-24 shows several voice-leading possibilities.

17-24

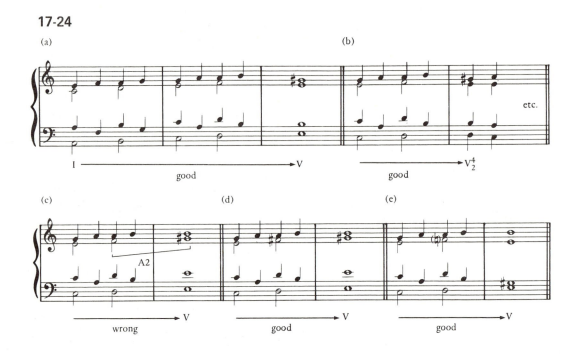

18. Moving up from III. III is the most frequent point of origin for rising sequences in minor and the easiest to use, as difficulties with the diminished triad or with the approach to the leading tone are unlikely. Because of the tendency of the minor mode to gravitate to III, this chord makes a logical beginning for a sequence, as we have already seen in Example 17-6, where the progression from III to V is accomplished by ascending 5ths. Ascending 5ths cannot continue beyond V. The next chord would be the weak, unconvincing diminished triad on II. However the 5-6 series can extend to VI (Example 17-25a) or even to natural VII (17-25b). The chords will be exactly the same as those contained between I and IV or V of the "relative major"; consequently a key-defining progression (leading to I or tonicizing III) must follow the VI or VII.

17-25 (a)

(b)

III ⟶ VII

19. Moving up from V. The remainder of the minor scale—from V or VI to I—is almost unusable in a diatonic setting. $\hat{7}$ must be raised in order to move to the goal tonic, but raising $\hat{6}$ to avoid the augmented 2nd produces two diminished $\frac{5}{3}$ chords in close succession, a less than euphonious combination. Therefore, for the time being, avoid ascending sequences between V and I in minor.

POINTS FOR REVIEW

1. The following are simple four-part progressions showing the most important types of sequences in major, with typical variants.

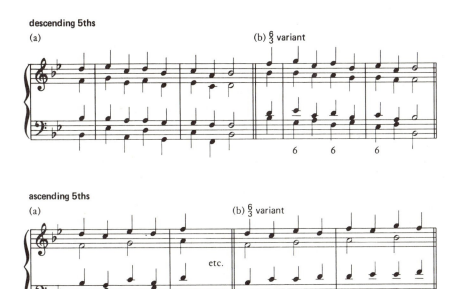

2. In minor, the easiest sequences to use are those that move down—the descending-5th and descending-3rd types.

3. Remember the following points when using ascending sequences in minor:

   a. When moving up from I by ascending 5ths, omit the step II-VI to avoid the diminished triad on II.

   b. When moving up from III by ascending 5ths, stop at V to avoid the diminished triad on II; using the ascending 5-6 series, however, makes it possible to continue to VI or natural VII.

   c. Moving up from V requires chromatic inflection, so avoid for the present.

EXERCISES

NOTE. From now on, you should be aware of sequential repetitions in a given melody or bass, and you should preserve the sequence in your harmonization. Remember that scale patterns in the soprano or bass can often be set sequentially, and that melodic repetition by stepwise descent in the soprano often indicates a sequence with descending 5ths (as in Example 17-3).

1. Preliminaries.
   a. Write a short progression in major using 5-6 technique over an ascending bass (in whole notes), lead to IV, and make a cadence.
   b. Using the following pattern, continue to II^7 and make a cadence. Do the same thing in the key of G♯ minor.

   c. Using the following pattern, continue to V. Extend V by a deceptive cadence before going on to I.

2. Figured bass.

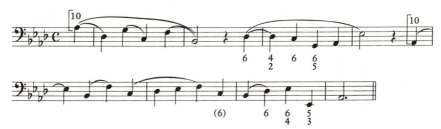

3. Melody.

4. Melody.

*don't harmonize anticipation

EIGHTEEN | $\frac{6}{3}$=CHORD TECHNIQUES

18-1 Dufay, Ave Maris Stella

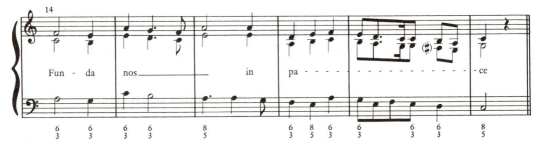

translation: Settle us in peace.

18-2 Mendelssohn, Song without Words, Op. 53/3

$^6_3$ CHORDS IN PARALLEL MOTION

1. Transitional passages in $^6_3$ chords. A casual glance would reveal little if any similarity between the two excerpts in Examples 18-1 and 18-2, the first from a hymn by Dufay (c. 1400-1474), the other from a piano piece by Mendelssohn (1809-1847). The pieces represent vastly different styles; they display a contrast in texture and sound that could hardly be greater. Nevertheless the two passages have one significant element in common: both are based on the use of $^6_3$ chords in extended parallel motion. The Dufay excerpt bears witness to the fact that the use of parallel $^6_3$ chords is a very old technique, dating back to the early Renaissance. Originally a device characteristic of both improvisational practice (*fauxbourdon,* English discant) and composition, it remained an important technique throughout the history of triadic music.

   $^6_3$ chords form perhaps the ideal sonority for extended parallel motion. In close position they do not contain the interval of the 5th; parallel 5ths, therefore, need not be a stumbling block, as they must inevitably be if a series of $^5_3$ chords appears in parallel motion. Furthermore, in a passage of extended parallel motion, the single chords tend to lose their individual identity and merge into a continuous linear flow. Such a passage, therefore, like the sequences discussed in the last unit, can function appropriately as a transition from one stable point to another. The characteristic interval of the 6th gives the $^6_3$ chord a more fluid, less stable sound than the $^5_3$, a quality particularly well suited to passages of a transitional nature.

The fluid character of passages in $\frac{6}{3}$ chords is evident in both of our excerpts. In the Dufay, the $\frac{6}{3}$'s provide a sense of motion and the $\frac{8}{3}$'s (bars 16 and 19) sound like goals. In the Mendelssohn, the $\frac{6}{3}$'s form a bridge from the tonic of bar 95 to the cadential II^6 of bar 101. This transition is a contrapuntal, not a harmonic one. Because the individual chords do not stand out, it would be misleading to describe what happens in such a series as a "harmonic" progression: for example, I-I^6-VII^6-VI^6-V^6, and so on. Only the beginning and the end of the series will normally receive enough emphasis to form a point of articulation. In the Mendelssohn, the I^6 that begins the series is important as an expansion of the initial tonic; the II^6 at the end is important because of its cadential function.

2. 6ths between the outer voices. Just as consecutive or recurrent 10ths help to organize the relationship between the outer voices, so do 6ths. 6ths between the outer voices do not appear in as many kinds of progressions as 10ths, but an extended series of parallel $\frac{6}{3}$ chords will have 6ths, not 10ths, between the bass and soprano. In the Dufay excerpt, the outer voices move in 6ths, and the two upper voices in parallel 4ths. (These parallel 4ths are absolutely correct.) The Mendelssohn does the same thing in a more elaborate manner (see reduction, Example 18-3). The soprano line is a "polyphonic melody" that implies two voices that move in parallel 4ths, as in the Dufay.

18-3

As Example 18-4 shows, a series of parallel $\frac{6}{3}$ chords will not normally have 10ths between the outer voices because of the 5ths that would occur between the two top parts.

18-4

3. Parallel $\frac{6}{3}$ chords in four voices. The Dufay and Mendelssohn excerpts indicate that the use of parallel $\frac{6}{3}$ chords is essentially a three-voice technique. (The Dufay is obviously written in three voices; the reduction in 18-3 shows that the Mendelssohn, too, has only three real voices, the other tones being merely doublings.) With careful attention to doubling, a series of parallel $\frac{6}{3}$'s can occur in four-part writing. The main problem is avoiding parallel octaves; the solution is to allow one of the voices to forego parallel motion and to alternate doublings. Example 18-5 shows a number of possibilities. Of its ten progressions, all but 18-5e and j contain recurrent patterns of alternate doublings, and all ten are good; the choice often depends on the doubling that sounds best in the emphasized last chord. Remember not to double the leading tone if the tonic triad follows, and to avoid the melodic augmented 2nd in minor.

Series of parallel $^6_3$ chords can both descend (18-5a-e) and ascend (18-5f-j). However, descending progressions are much more frequent.

18-5

4. **Variants in the use of parallel $^6_3$ chords.** Quite often a passage mostly in parallel $^6_3$ chords will contain one or more $^5_3$ chords, will depart momentarily from parallel motion, or will show other "irregularities." Thus Example 18-6 is a variant of the progression shown in 18-5e. Instead of maintaining parallel motion, however, the soprano has a voice exchange with the bass that shifts it into a higher register

and allows it to end an octave higher. A consequence of this voice exchange is the $\frac{5}{3}$ chord on the third beat. If nothing but $\frac{6}{3}$ chords were used, the 10ths between the outer voices would lead to parallel 5ths (Example 18-4). This danger exists even in a succession of only two chords unless one of the 5ths is diminished.

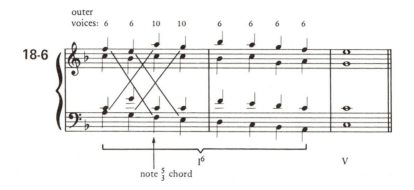

Example 18-7 shows four excerpts from the third movement of Handel's Concerto Grosso, Op. 3, No. 1, in which the use of parallel $\frac{6}{3}$ chords is exceptionally clear and instructive. Note that in all the excerpts, the texture is in three voices. Composers will often change to three voices for passages using parallel $\frac{6}{3}$ chords, an option not available to you in exercises in four-part vocal style, but possible when you are working in a free keyboard or other instrumental style.

18-7a, the opening of the movement, contains two phrases. The first, characterized by imitation between the outer voices, contains $\frac{6}{3}$ usages familiar from previous units (such as VII^6 passing from I^6 to I). The second phrase, like the first, begins with imitation; however the last soprano tone of bar 3 becomes F♮ to allow a stepwise descent in parallel $\frac{6}{3}$'s. The motion in $\frac{6}{3}$'s continues until V^7 arrives in bar 4. The chord just before V^7 is IV^6, emphasized by longer duration and by the suspension (7-6) that delays its 6th, C.

18-7b uses a variant of the same theme, but in the mediant, B♭ major. This time the descending 6ths do not continue beyond two eighth notes. Instead the soprano shifts to a higher position, forming a pair of 10ths with the bass, as in 18-6. To avoid 5ths and, at the same time, to emphasize the subdominant, a $\frac{5}{3}$ chord appears on the downbeat (the continuo player would complete this chord); on the second beat the soprano moves up once more, regaining the interval of a 6th, but now an octave higher. An interesting feature of the voice leading is the continuation of the parallel 10ths in the middle part.

18-7c is in D minor, the key of the minor dominant. It contains two voice exchanges, after which the parallel 6ths continue. Since the first chord in bar 21 contains a diminished 5th, Handel can write two consecutive $\frac{6}{3}$ chords with 10ths between the outer voices.

18-7d shows the conclusion of the movement. Like the opening statement, it consists of two phrases. Here, however, there is no imitation in the second phrase; instead the outer voices move in 10ths filled in by the descending 5-6 progression familiar to us from Unit 17.

18-7   Handel, Concerto Grosso, Op. 3/1, III

(a)

(b)

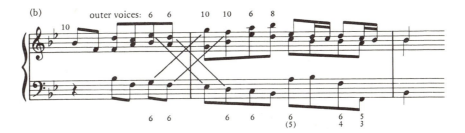

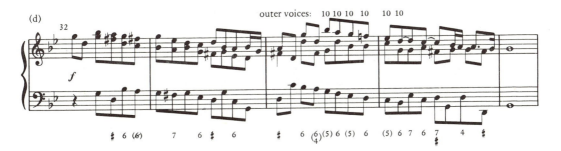

OTHER USES OF $\frac{6}{3}$ CHORDS

Most of the techniques described in connection with $\frac{5}{3}$ chords in Unit 16 can be applied to $\frac{6}{3}$ chords as well. Because the techniques are mostly familiar, we will describe these $\frac{6}{3}$ usages rather briefly, summing them up in the last example of this unit.

5. **The neighboring $\frac{6}{3}$.** We are already very familiar with the most important neighboring $\frac{6}{3}$ chords: V[6] as N or IN to I. Between other scale degrees, a neighbor in the bass works best when the melodic progression is a half step. Thus I[6] as N to IV is usually better in major than in minor, where I[6] is generally altered to form an applied dominant, V[6] of IV. Example 18-8 shows some possibilities.

18-8 **Michael Praetorius (1571-1621), Bransle Gentil**

(a)

(b)   (c)

6. **The passing $\frac{6}{3}$.** Most often a passing $\frac{6}{3}$ connects a root-position triad with its first inversion, as in the familiar progressions I-VII[6]-I[6], V-IV[6]-V[6], and II-I[6]-II[6]. On other scale degrees, the passing $\frac{6}{3}$ is usually altered to form an "applied" VII[6] unless the effect of a leading-tone chord occurs naturally as in III-II[6]-III[6] in minor, which briefly tonicizes III (Example 18-9).

18-9

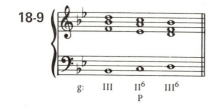

Sometimes a $\frac{6}{3}$ chord will connect two root-position triads a 3rd apart, as in Example 18-10.

18-10   Praetorius, Bransle Gentil

7. Motion in 3rds. Parallel $\frac{6}{3}$ chords normally occur in stepwise motion, as in the earlier examples of this unit. Parallel $\frac{6}{3}$'s can also leap in 3rds, though not very frequently and never for very long (Example 18-11a). Sometimes a stepwise progression will conceal an underlying motion in 3rds. Thus the Mendelssohn excerpt in Example 18-1 contains a two-bar pattern, repeated sequentially in descending 3rds: I-(VI⁶)-(IV⁶)-II⁶ (Example 18-11b).

18-11   (a)

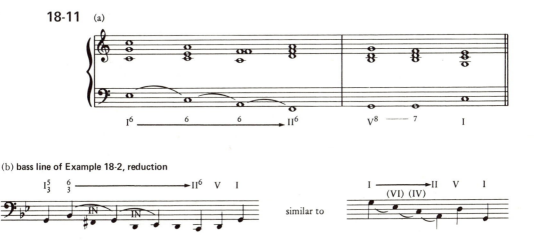

(b) **bass line of Example 18-2, reduction**

8. "VI⁶" and "III⁶" representing I and V. Excerpts from compositions by Chopin and Brahms (Examples 18-12 and 18-13) seem to feature VI⁶ as their opening chord. In the Chopin, however, the 6th above the bass decorates the 5th, and in the Brahms, the 6th substitutes for the 5th; the chords function as *tonics*, not submediants (compare Example 4-10). In the Chopin, the apparent "VI⁶" results from a neighboring motion; the C♯ of the accompaniment moves directly to the B that follows; in a manner less immediately apparent, it continues the first note of the melodic line. In the Brahms, the 6th displaces the 5th entirely. However, we hear the bass tone of bar 1 as a tonic—an impression confirmed as correct by the subsequent course of the music in which the 5th, A, is implied as the point of departure for this 6th.

18-12 Chopin, Nocturne, Op. 62/2

18-13 Brahms, Piano Concerto, Op. 15, I

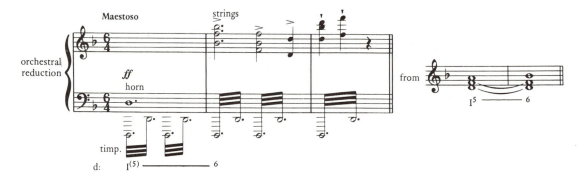

$^6_3$ chords can embellish or substitute for $^5_3$'s on any degree of the scale. These possibilities, however, are most significant in connection with the tonic and dominant degrees; $\hat{1}$ and $\hat{5}$ are such strong scale degrees that their harmonic force can be felt even when they do not support a $^5_3$ chord. Just as "VI^6" is often a variant of I rather than an inversion of VI, so, too, "III^6" can function as a decoration of or substitute for V. In Example 18-14, bars 14 and 15 form an expansion of V. In the course of this expansion, the melody moves up from $\hat{2}$ to $\hat{4}$, the E of bar 14 functioning as a passing tone. The G in the bass that supports this passing tone functions as V; the chord, therefore, is not a III^6 but part of an expanded dominant. In Example 18-15, the top voice of bar 7 duplicates that of bar 3. The 6th above the bass makes this repetition possible without at all contradicting the impression of a V-I cadence.

18-14   Bach, Chorale 11

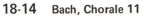

18-15   Haydn, Symphony No. 101, IV

If a 6th decorates or substitutes for a 5th over V in minor, an apparent augmented triad (in $\frac{6}{3}$ position) will result. Most instances of "augmented III" in minor are examples of this usage; as far as their function is concerned, these are not III chords at all, but V's (Example 18-16).

18-16   Bach, Air   (from *Suite No. 3*)

9. Synopsis of $\frac{6}{3}$ functions. Example 18-17 lists the important contrapuntal functions of $\frac{6}{3}$ chords. All these functions have been explained in either this or a preceding unit (especially Unit 16). Thus, although a few of the progressions may be unfamiliar, you should have no difficulty in understanding their significance.

18-17

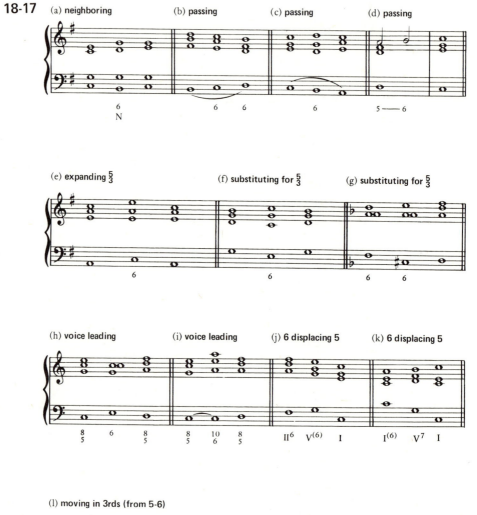

POINTS FOR REVIEW

1. Extended passages in parallel motion in which the outer voices typically move in 6ths are characteristic of $\frac{6}{3}$ chords. In four voices, careful doubling is necessary to avoid parallel octaves (Example 18-5).

2. 10ths between the outer voices are not suitable for extended motion (danger of 5ths), but brief segments may occur, often as the result of voice exchange and often involving the use of a $\frac{5}{3}$ chord (Examples 18-6 and 18-7).

3. Other contrapuntal uses of $\frac{6}{3}$ chords are as
   a. neighboring chords (Examples 18-8)
   b. passing chords (Examples 18-9 and 18-10)
   c. chords allowing motion in 3rds (Example 18-11)

4. "VI^6" and "III^6" usually stand for I and V (Examples 18-12, 18-13, and 18-14).

EXERCISES

NOTE. In instrumental textures, including figured-bass realizations, passages in parallel $\frac{6}{3}$ chords are often set for three voices. However, it would be a good idea for you to use four voices in these exercises to gain practice in working out the doublings.

1. Preliminaries: figured-bass fragments.

2. Figured bass (adapted from Handel). Because of the high register of Handel's bass, vocal ranges need not be strictly observed.

3. Figured bass (adapted from Handel).

4. Melody (adapted from Handel).

*don't harmonize

NINETEEN | $\frac{6}{4}$-CHORD TECHNIQUES

19-1 Beethoven, String Quartet, Op. 18/2, II

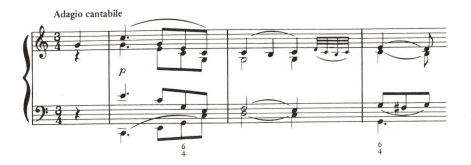

1. The double nature of the $\frac{6}{4}$ chord. The $\frac{6}{4}$ chord G-C-E occurs twice with identical spacing and doubling in the first three bars of a string quartet movement by Beethoven (Example 19-1). But although they contain the same tones, the two $\frac{6}{4}$ chords function in very different ways. The first arises out of arpeggiations within tonic harmony. It functions as an inversion of I$\frac{5}{3}$ and is treated by the composer as a consonance; both the bass tone and the 4th, C, are approached and left by leap. The second $\frac{6}{4}$, of course, is the cadential type familiar since Unit 10; in this chord the 4th is a dissonance, resolving to B by stepwise descent.

This excerpt illustrates the most striking feature of the $\frac{6}{4}$ chord; unlike any other chord, it is sometimes consonant and sometimes dissonant. Whether it is one or the other does not depend on the chord itself—as we saw, in the Beethoven the $\frac{6}{4}$'s are identical—but on how it functions *in context*. The double nature of the $\frac{6}{4}$ results from the double nature of its most characteristic interval—the perfect 4th—which itself is sometimes consonant, sometimes dissonant (Unit 2, section 11). So in order to understand the various ways in which $\frac{6}{4}$ chords can come about, let's look at some of the ways a 4th might appear in two-part texture (Example 19-2).

19-2

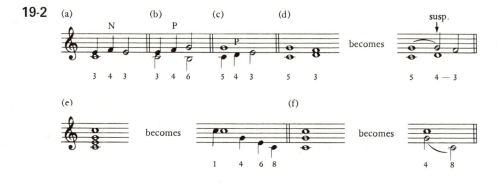

19-2a shows the 4th as a neighboring tone; in 19-2b and c the 4th is a passing tone. Note that sometimes it is the motion of the upper voice that produces the 4th (19-2a and b) while at other times (19-2c) it is the motion of the lower voice. In 19-2d the 4th is a suspension, as frequently occurs in familiar cadential $\frac{6}{4}$'s. In all four of these progressions the 4th is heard as a dissonance and is resolved by step.

In other situations, however, the 4th can be heard as consonant. If a triad (19-2e) or triadic interval (19-2f) is arpeggiated in the bass, for example, the 4th that might arise is consonant because it forms part of the unfolding of a consonant chord; the first $\frac{6}{4}$ chord of our Beethoven excerpt relates directly to the technique illustrated in 19-2e.

Example 19-3 shows the procedures described above in four-voice settings; here the 4ths of Example 19-2 become $\frac{6}{4}$ chords of various types, all of which we will discuss in the following pages.

19-3

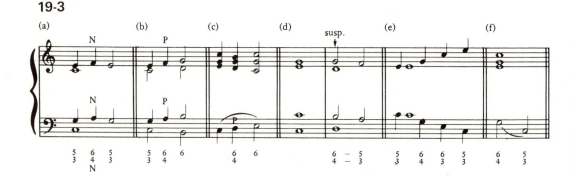

DISSONANT $\frac{6}{4}$ CHORDS

2. Three main types. Most dissonant $\frac{6}{4}$ chords belong to one of three main categories: the accented $\frac{6}{4}$ ($\frac{6\text{-}5}{4\text{-}3}$), the neighboring $\frac{6}{4}$, and the passing $\frac{6}{4}$. Since these chords derive their meaning completely from their relation to a larger context, and since even a slight difference in context can alter their significance, it is impossible (and unnecessary) to categorize every conceivable situation in which $\frac{6}{4}$ chords might appear. We will present only the most typical and important usages and a few particularly suggestive exceptional cases. If you understand the principles discussed in this unit, you will have a good basis for understanding other $\frac{6}{4}$ usages you may encounter.

19-4   Mozart, Piano Sonata, K. 330, II

3. Accented $\frac{6}{4}$ chords. Example 19-4 contains four $\frac{6}{4}$ chords. One of them (bar 2, beat 3) is a passing $\frac{6}{4}$ and will be discussed later. The other three are metrically accented relative to the chords of resolution—that is, they all resolve (over a stationary bass) from a stronger to a weaker beat. Two of these accented $\frac{6}{4}$'s are examples of the familiar cadential $\frac{6}{4}$ (bars 4 and 7). The one that begins bar 2, however, does not occur at a cadence, nor does it resolve to a dominant. But in all other respects it resembles the cadential $\frac{6}{4}$. The 6th and 4th, metrically accented, move down by step to the 5th and 3rd of the chord of resolution—in this case, VI. We use the term *accented* $\frac{6}{4}$ for chords of this type—those that are metrically accented and that resolve over a stationary bass. The cadential $\frac{6}{4}$ is the most important type but, as the Mozart excerpt shows, it is by no means the only possibility. Other accented $\frac{6}{4}$'s closely resemble the cadential type. The principles of doubling and of voice leading are the same (review Unit 10); so is the chord's basic function—to delay the arrival of an expected melodic or harmonic event. Accented $\frac{6}{4}$'s—including cadential ones—depend on their chords of resolution; they do not function as inversions of a root-position triad. This fact should be reflected in any chordal analysis. In bar 2 of the Mozart, therefore, the correct labeling is as shown, *not* II$\frac{6}{4}$-VI.

Accented $\frac{6}{4}$'s can occur on several scale degrees, $\hat{6}$ in major, as in the Mozart, being a particularly frequent choice. On other scale degrees, avoid a "resolution" to a diminished $\frac{5}{3}$ except in three-part texture. On $\hat{7}$ in major and raised $\hat{7}$ in minor, doubling the 6th of the $\frac{6}{4}$ and resolving to V$\frac{6}{5}$ rather than to VII$\frac{5}{3}$ will prevent such a resolution. Example 19-5a shows this possibility in major. In minor (19-5b), the $\frac{6}{4}$ contains a diminished 4th. Such a $\frac{6}{4}$ appears to be the second inversion of an augmented triad, but since the accented $\frac{6}{4}$ results from melodic motion rather than inversion, the "augmented" triad is nonfunctional here.

19-5   Schubert, Nacht und Träume

(a)   *Sehr langsam*

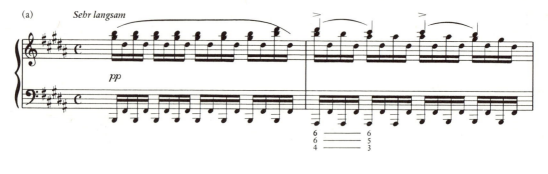

(b) in minor

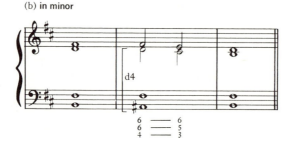

4. Neighboring $\frac{6}{4}$ chords. Example 19-6 illustrates the second important type of dissonant $\frac{6}{4}$, the *neighboring* $\frac{6}{4}$. In this excerpt neighboring figures 5-6-5 and 3-4-3 decorate the 5th and 3rd of tonic harmony. This type of $\frac{6}{4}$ arises out of neighboring motions performed above a stationary bass by two upper voices that typically move in parallel 3rds, 6ths, or 10ths.

19-6   Beethoven, Variations, Op. 34

Usually the soprano will take one of the neighboring figures—either 5-6-5 (as in the Beethoven) or 3-4-3, as in Example 19-7.

19-7   Brahms, Variations on a Theme by Haydn, Op. 56a

The bass of the neighboring $\frac{6}{4}$ is generally doubled. Usually this type of $\frac{6}{4}$ is unaccented, falling on a metrically weaker place than the $\frac{5}{3}$ that precedes it, thus forming a kind of opposite to the accented $\frac{6}{4}$. Sometimes the neighboring $\frac{6}{4}$ is repeated on the next strong beat, as in bar 2 of Example 19-8, the beginning of a theory exercise written by Mozart for one of his students.

19-8   Mozart, Exercise for Barbara Ployer

As with the accented $\frac{6}{4}$, the neighboring type functions best when the $\frac{5}{3}$ chord it decorates is not diminished.

5. **Passing $\frac{6}{4}$ chords (above a moving bass).** Of the various types of passing $\frac{6}{4}$'s, the most important is $V\frac{6}{4}$ connecting I and I^6, as in Example 19-4 in the last half of bar 2, where $V\frac{6}{4}$ forms a stepwise connection between I^6 and $I\frac{5}{3}$ (compare VII^6 and $V\frac{4}{3}$). The passing function of this chord is obvious. In this usage the 4th above the bass is a stable tone, the 5th of the tonic chord within which the $\frac{6}{4}$ moves. The active, dissonant element in this type of $\frac{6}{4}$ chord, therefore, is not the 4th but the bass tone. When a passing $\frac{6}{4}$ is used in this way, a voice exchange frequently occurs between the bass and one of the upper voices (usually the soprano), as is evident in the Mozart excerpt. Such an exchange will often cause a doubling of the bass tone of the $\frac{6}{4}$, but the consonant 4th is also a possible doubling. Passing $\frac{6}{4}$'s can appear either on unaccented (most frequent) or accented beats or parts of beats.

Example 19-9 shows two other possibilities: expanding II and IV. The passing $\frac{6}{4}$ can also serve to expand seventh chords (Example 19-10).

19-9 (a) (b)

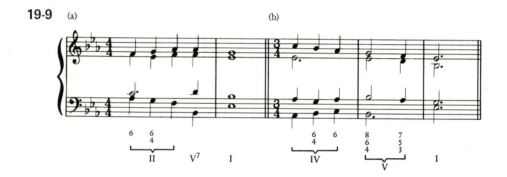

19-10 Mendelssohn, Trio, Op. 49, I

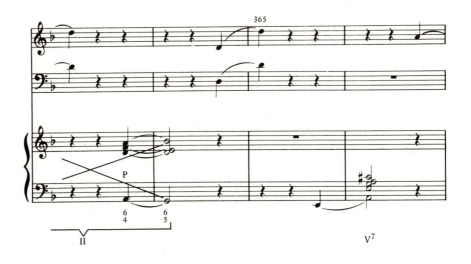

A passing $\frac{6}{4}$ between IV^6 and II$^6_5$ (less often II^6) is *very frequent*; the outer-voice motion is usually in 6ths (Example 19-11).

19-11   Bach, Chorale   (from *Motet, Jesu, meine Freude*)

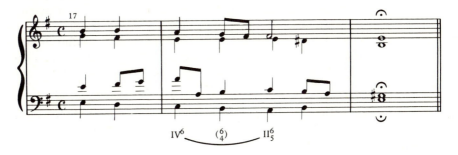

Sometimes a passing $\frac{6}{4}$ occurs above a descending bass without any motion in the upper voices (Example 19-12). Because of the preponderance of common tones, we do not really hear a change of chord at the entrance of the $\frac{6}{4}$; such $\frac{6}{4}$'s have little vertical identity and hardly count as chords, unless the composer emphasizes them by long duration.

19-12

6. Passing $\frac{6}{4}$ chords (above a sustained bass). Sometimes a $\frac{6}{4}$ formation results from passing tones in parallel 3rds, 6ths, or 10ths moving up from the 5th and 3rd of a $\frac{5}{3}$ chord. In this type of $\frac{5\text{-}6}{3\text{-}4}$, the $\frac{6}{4}$ is virtually always metrically weak (Example 19-13). In many ways this type of passing $\frac{6}{4}$ resembles the neighboring $\frac{6}{4}$.

19-13

(a) Bach, Geistliche Lieder, No. 47

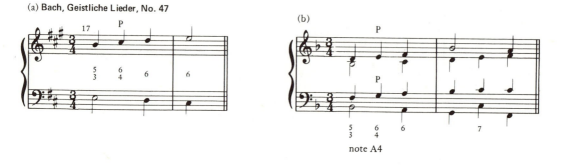

A passing $\frac{6}{4}$ above a sustained dominant can connect V^7 with V^5_3, as in Example 19-14. In such cases, the motion to the $\frac{6}{4}$ does *not* resolve the 7th of V^7, despite the downward motion. The 6th of the $\frac{6}{4}$ is a passing tone, not a goal tone; therefore it does not form an appropriate resolution of the dissonance. Normally a resolution of the 7th will follow the dominant. In the aria from which our illustration is taken, the resolution appears several bars later, transferred to another voice (bass, bars 63-64).

19-14   Mozart, Mi tradì   (from *Don Giovanni*, K. 527)

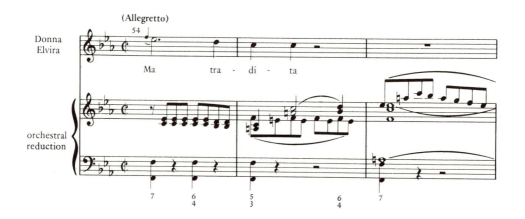

translation: But betrayed and abandoned,
[I still pity him.]

7. Elaborated $\frac{6}{4}$ chords (above a sustained bass); the progression $\frac{8\text{-}7\text{-}6\text{-}5}{6\text{-}5\text{-}4\text{-}3}$. Passing or neighboring $\frac{6}{4}$'s over a held bass can be elaborated in various ways. In Example 19-15a, the first-violin part (bar 3) is "polyphonic"; the single melodic line suggests two voices—$\hat{7}$-$\hat{8}$ and $\hat{4}$-$\hat{3}$. This creates the possibility for two $\frac{6}{4}$'s above the sustained bass.

19-15   Haydn, String Quartet, Op. 76/5, II

Very frequently a voice exchange accompanies a soprano line like the one in Example 19-15; Example 19-16 illustrates.

19-16

Example 19-17 illustrates another frequent possibility: two upper voices can descend in parallel 3rds, 6ths, or 10ths, creating the interval progression $\frac{8\text{-}7\text{-}6\text{-}5}{6\text{-}5\text{-}4\text{-}3}$. This progression can have various meanings. Here it elaborates the resolution of a neighboring $\frac{6}{4}$ over an extended I.

19-17   Mozart, Eine kleine Nachtmusik, K. 525, II

8. $\frac{6}{4}$ chords as incomplete neighbors (above a sustained bass). This is similar to both the passing $\frac{6}{4}$ (section 6) and the neighboring $\frac{6}{4}$ (section 4); Example 19-18 illustrates. Following such a $\frac{5\text{-}6}{3\text{-}4}$ by an accented $\frac{6\text{-}5}{4\text{-}3}$, usually with root motion by ascending 5th, produces one of the few progressions where two $\frac{6}{4}$ chords follow each other immediately (19-18b).

19-18 (a)   (b)

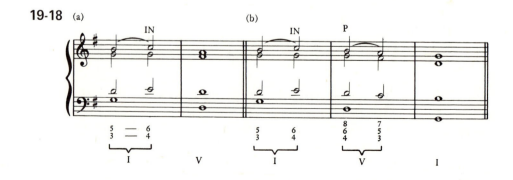

SPECIAL TREATMENT OF CADENTIAL $\frac{6}{4}$ CHORDS

9. Unprepared 4ths; transferred resolution of the 4th. In four-part vocal style, the dissonant character of the cadential $\frac{6}{4}$ imposes certain restrictions on its use—restrictions we discussed in Unit 10. In principle these restrictions hold good for instrumental music as well. However, departures from the norms of voice leading and dissonance treatment occur fairly often with cadential $\frac{6}{4}$ chords in instrumental style. Sometimes the 4th—normally a suspension or an accented passing tone—will enter by leap, as in Example 19-19. Such a leap to the 4th often results from the decoration of a stepwise line; thus the voice leading is not really as exceptional as it might at first seem.

19-19   Mozart, Wind Serenade, K. 388, I

Sometimes composers will treat the *resolution* of the 4th with a certain freedom. In Example 19-20, the 4th is stated in the soprano and its resolution transferred into the alto. This allows the soprano to ascend after the 4th and to express the melodic motion of a 3rd—an important element in this piece. Motion upward from the 4th (the resolution transferred to another voice) occurs quite often in music of the classical period—especially in Mozart's.

19-20   Beethoven, Bagatelle, Op. 119/11

Example 19-21 shows another type of transferred resolution—into the bass, producing a V$^6_5$. Such progressions occur rather frequently, though not where a strong V-I cadence (with root-position V immediately before I) is needed.

19-21 **Mozart, String Quintet, K. 516, I**

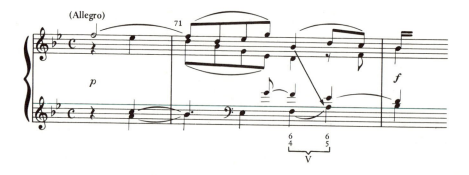

In free textures, composers will sometimes let an inner voice double a 4th that appears in the soprano (see Example 19-4, bar 7). One of these 4ths will have to move up; if both resolved down, parallel octaves would result.

10. Expanding the cadential $^6_4$. The tension created by the cadential $^6_4$ can be enhanced by expanding it. In Example 19-22, a bass arpeggio causes the expansion.

19-22 **Mozart, Der Hölle Rache** (from *Die Zauberflöte*)

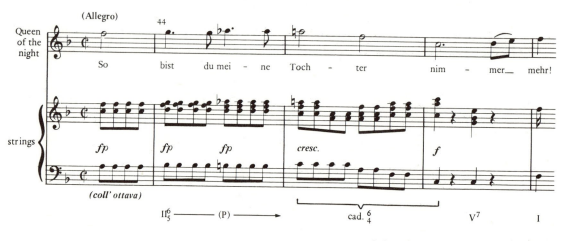

translation: Then you are no more my daughter!

At the end of Brahms' *Ein deutsches Requiem* (Example 19-23), a double neighbor prolongs the bass of the $^6_4$; compare the Brahms excerpt in Example 17-21.

19-23 Brahms, Ein deutsches Requiem, Op. 45, VII

(winds and brass omitted)

translation: [Blessed] are the dead, who die in the Lord.

11. Interpolations between the $\frac{6}{4}$ and its resolution. Frequently a neighboring chord separates the $\frac{6}{4}$ from its resolution (Example 19-24).

19-24   Bach, Chorale 220

An expansion of this same principle—interpolating material between a cadential $\frac{6}{4}$ and the dominant to which it resolves—forms the basis for the cadenza in classical concerto movements. The very word *cadenza*—which simply means "cadence" in Italian—indicates its cadential function. A cadenza from a concerto would be too long to quote here, but the principle is very well illustrated by the miniature cadenza from the first movement of Beethoven's Piano Sonata, Op. 2, No. 3, a sonata movement that is written to sound very much like a concerto (Example 19-25).

19-25   Beethoven, Piano Sonata, Op. 2/3, I

12. Metrically weak cadential $\frac{6}{4}$ chords. $\frac{6}{4}$ chords that resolve to cadential dominants are virtually always metrically strong. Occasionally, however, we encounter
such $\frac{6}{4}$'s on the weak beat preceding the dominant. Most of these "deviant" $\frac{6}{4}$
chords come about through an anticipation of V in the bass that coincides with a
passing tone in one of the upper parts. In such a case, the $\frac{6}{4}$—instead of resulting
from a delaying progression in one of the upper voices—results from a bass that
arrives at its goal just before the strong beat where it is expected. Example 19-26,
from a Schubert lied, illustrates.

19-26   Schubert, Die Liebe hat gelogen

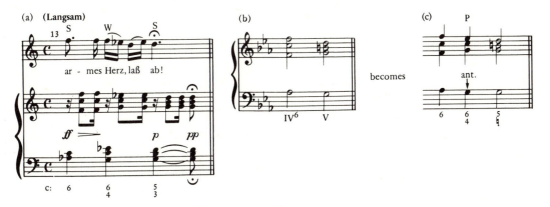

Of the great composers, Schubert and Chopin probably used these "anticipating" $\frac{6}{4}$'s the most. Review Example 14-5, bars 6-7. There the metric irregularity results in part from motivic design: the repetition of the rising 4th in the bass,
D♯-G♯, G♯-C♯.

CONSONANT $\frac{6}{4}$ CHORDS

13. The arpeggio $\frac{6}{4}$. Review Example 19-1 and you will easily see that the first
$\frac{6}{4}$ chord (bar 1) has a fundamentally different meaning from any of the dissonant
$\frac{6}{4}$'s we have been discussing. The obvious fact that all the voices approach and

leave the chord by leap points up this difference in meaning. The bass arpeggiates the tonic triad; the $\frac{6}{4}$ results from the arpeggiation. Because it arises out of and derives from the root position of the triad, this $\frac{6}{4}$ is heard as *consonant*. Consonant $\frac{6}{4}$'s tend to occur in music with considerable rhythmic activity and where at least some of the chords persist for a long time. Thus, such $\frac{6}{4}$'s occur infrequently in chorale style, where chords change on almost every beat. Most consonant $\frac{6}{4}$'s are tonics, for the I is the chord most often expanded by arpeggiation. The bass tone is frequently doubled; however, doubling the root or (less often) the 3rd is also possible.

14. The consonant $\frac{6\text{-}5}{4\text{-}3}$. Most often the arpeggio $\frac{6}{4}$ appears after the $\frac{5}{3}$ chord that makes it consonant. However in the music of some composers (Brahms in particular) the $\frac{6}{4}$ will sometimes appear first; it is then stabilized "retrospectively" by a $\frac{5}{3}$ that follows it (Example 19-27). In such cases the $\frac{6}{4}$ can represent the upper voices of a $\frac{5}{3}$ chord whose bass is delayed.

19-27 **Schumann, Albumblätter, Op. 99, V**

15. The oscillating $\frac{6}{4}$ (waltz or march type). In Examples 19-1 and 19-27, the consonant $\frac{6}{4}$'s appear *above* the bass of the governing $\frac{5}{3}$ chords; in context, therefore, the bass of the $\frac{6}{4}$ functions as an inner-voice tone of the $\frac{5}{3}$. But sometimes the bass of the $\frac{6}{4}$ appears *below* that of the $\frac{5}{3}$. This is particularly frequent in instrumental accompaniment patterns, such as those in waltzes or marches, where the bass of I oscillates between $\hat{1}$ and the $\hat{5}$ below it. The $\frac{6}{4}$'s appear on weak beats; if, as in waltzes, the bass normally moves in whole bars, the $\frac{6}{4}$'s will appear on the metrically weak bars. The descending motion from $\hat{1}$ to $\hat{5}$ emphasizes the strong-weak metric pattern—hence the popularity of this idiom for dances and marches. The repeated $\hat{5}$'s seldom form part of the main bass line; they serve to extend the governing chord and to provide a characteristic rhythmic pattern. The $\frac{6}{4}$ chords they produce are heard as consonant and dependent on the preceding $\frac{5}{3}$'s. Example 19-28 illustrates.

19-28 (a) Chopin, Valse, Op. 34/1

(b) Mozart, Piano Sonata, K. 282, Menuetto II

SOME EXCEPTIONAL CASES

16. $\frac{6}{4}$ chords by voice exchange. $\frac{6}{4}$ chords often result from a kind of extended voice exchange in which two two-note figures ($\hat{4}$-$\hat{3}$ and $\hat{6}$-$\hat{5}$) are interchanged. Depending on the larger context, the $\frac{6}{4}$ chord thus produced will be either consonant or dissonant. In Example 19-29, the bass of the opening tonic—emphasized by its low register—persists in the listener's memory through the voice exchange. Thus the voice exchange represents an extended tonic embellished by subdominant neighbors; the $\frac{6}{4}$ is stable—a consonant inversion of I.

19-29   Mozart, String Quintet, K. 614, II

In Example 19-30 the "I$_4^6$" is an unstable passing chord within an expansion of IV—not a consonant inversion of I.

19-30 Mozart, Piano Sonata, K. 311, II

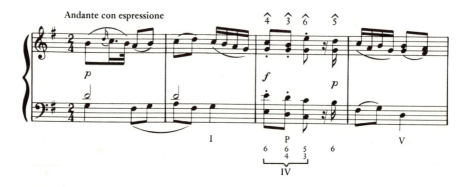

17. **$\frac{6}{4}$ chords with augmented 4th ("VII$_4^6$").** Sometimes one encounters a $\frac{6}{4}$ chord with an augmented 4th, built on $\hat{4}$ as bass tone. (In major, the augmented 4th lies between $\hat{4}$ and $\hat{7}$; in minor, between $\hat{4}$ and raised $\hat{7}$.) A literal analysis of these chords as "VII$_4^6$" would be correct as far as it goes but not particularly revealing of their function. As example 19-31 indicates, these $\frac{6}{4}$'s function as incomplete V$_2^4$ chords; they normally occur only in three-part texture which explains their incomplete state. In music with a figured-bass accompaniment (Baroque trio sonatas, for example) the continuo player would most probably complete the $\frac{4}{2}$ chord.

19-31 Mozart, Piano Concerto, K. 453, II

18. **Dissonant or consonant: V or I?** The two excerpts quoted in Example 19-32 illustrate how much the meaning of a $\frac{6}{4}$ chord depends on context. In the Chopin, the E♭ minor $\frac{6}{4}$ "ought to" resolve to a V (the excerpt shows the final cadence of the piece). Most exceptionally, the V chord does not appear—an instance of harmonic elision. But the bass progression suggests IV-V-I so unmistakably that the

cadential function of this $^6_4$ can hardly be questioned; it stands for the embellishment of a V that is not literally present but that is nonetheless strongly implied.

In the Schumann excerpt, an E♭ major $^6_4$ appears *after* the cadential V; it is, in fact, the last chord in the piece. This $^6_4$ stands for I, not for V. In order to avoid a definite conclusion that would be out of keeping with the dreamy nature of Eusebius (a character Schumann invented who represented the poetic, gentle side of his personality), Schumann lets the inconclusive I$^6_4$ substitute for a final I. This consonant $^6_4$—unlike those discussed in sections 13-15—is stabilized not by its own root position, but by the harmonic implications of the context in which it occurs.

19-32

(a) **Chopin, Prelude, Op. 28/14**

(b) **Schumann, Eusebius**   (from *Carnaval,* Op. 9)

POINTS FOR REVIEW

1. $\frac{6}{4}$ chords are sometimes dissonant and sometimes consonant.

2. The main types of dissonant $\frac{6}{4}$ chords are accented ($\frac{6\text{-}5}{4\text{-}3}$), neighboring, and passing.

3. Accented $\frac{6}{4}$ chords include the familiar cadential type ($V^{6\text{-}5}_{4\text{-}3}$). On other scale degrees, accented $\frac{6}{4}$'s resemble the cadential type (same doubling, same metric position, same descending resolution). They are particularly frequent on $\hat{6}$ in major.

4. Neighboring $\frac{6}{4}$ chords (usually unaccented) result from the progression $\frac{5\text{-}6\text{-}5}{3\text{-}4\text{-}3}$ above a stationary bass. The bass is usually doubled.

5. Passing $\frac{6}{4}$ chords (above a moving bass) typically connect $\frac{5}{3}$ and $\frac{6}{3}$ positions of the same triad, often with voice exchange between the bass and an upper voice. The most frequent progression is V^{6}_{4} connecting I and I^6, in which V^{6}_{4} resembles VII^6 and V^4_3.

6. Other passing $\frac{6}{4}$'s connect two positions of a seventh chord or connect a triad with a seventh chord. *Important usage:* $\frac{6}{4}$ passing between IV^6 and II^6_5, with the outer voices usually in 6ths.

7. Passing $\frac{6}{4}$ chords (above a sustained bass) sometimes result from passing tones moving up from the 5th and 3rd of a $\frac{5}{3}$ chord. Another type is the $\frac{6}{4}$ that connects V^7 and V^5_3.

8. Possibilities above a sustained dominant bass include the progression $\frac{8\text{-}7\text{-}6\text{-}5}{6\text{-}5\text{-}4\text{-}3}$ and the voice exchange $\hat{4}\text{-}\hat{3}$, $\hat{7}\text{-}\hat{8}$.

9. The cadential $\frac{6}{4}$ is often treated irregularly in instrumental style. (See sections 9-12.)

10. Consonant $\frac{6}{4}$ chords include the arpeggio type, which results from a complete or incomplete arpeggio in the bass. This chord usually prolongs tonic harmony, with I^5_3 preceding I^6_4. Another consonant $\frac{6}{4}$ is the oscillating (waltz or march) type.

11. $\frac{6}{4}$ chords produced by voice exchange ($\hat{4}\text{-}\hat{3}$, $\hat{6}\text{-}\hat{5}$) often help to expand IV.

12. $\frac{6}{4}$ chords with an augmented 4th on $\hat{7}$ in major or raised $\hat{7}$ in minor can substitute for V^4_2 in three-voice texture.

EXERCISES

NOTE. From now on, be prepared to explain the function of every $\frac{6}{4}$ chord you use. In setting melodies, never use a $\frac{6}{4}$ chord unless you have a clear idea of how it functions; sprinkling an exercise with $\frac{6}{4}$'s unrelated to their surroundings is one of the surest ways to botch your work.

1. Preliminaries. Using a different key for each progression, write an example of each of the following $\frac{6}{4}$ usages:

a. $\frac{6\text{-}5}{4\text{-}3}$ on $\hat{6}$ in major

b. $\frac{6\text{-}6}{6\text{-}5}$ $\frac{}{4\text{-}3}$ in minor. Which scale degree is appropriate?

c. Passing $\frac{6}{4}$ (bass moves) between I^6 and I in major

d. Passing $\frac{6}{4}$ (bass moves) between II^6_5 and II^7 in minor

e. Passing $\frac{6}{4}$ (bass moves) between IV^6 and II^6_5 in major

f. Neighboring $^6_4$ (upper voices move) in minor
g. Passing $^6_4$ (upper voices move) in major
h. $^6_4$ arising out of bass arpeggiation in minor
i. $^6_4$ resulting from voice exchange ($\hat{6}$-$\hat{5}$ and $\hat{4}$-$\hat{3}$)
j. $^6_4$'s resulting from voice exchange over V in bass
2. Figured bass.

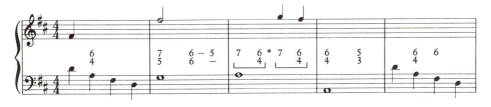

*voice exchange between soprano and tenor

3. Melody. Use one neighboring $^6_4$ and at least two passing $^6_4$'s—one between IV^6 and II$^6_5$:

4. Figured bass. (Keyboard style is possible.)

*voice exchange between bass and soprano

5. Melody and bass.

*If you harmonize this B♮ as a seventh chord, you will need two quarter notes in the tenor in the first half of bar 2 to avoid 5ths. Or you can treat the B♮ as a passing tone and not harmonize it.

APPENDIX | KEYBOARD PROGRESSIONS

The following progressions illustrate the most important techniques covered in Units 6-19. They are designed to be played at the piano and are notated in C throughout for your convenience in transposition. Your goal should be to get them well enough into your head and fingers to be able to play them fluently through at least the first four sharp and flat keys, major and minor.

We have not attempted to include every possible soprano voice; finding other possibilities will be good practice for you. You can incorporate some of the shorter progressions into longer and more continuous ones (as we did in *d* of Unit 8, for example); in this way, you will gain experience in improvising phrases and phrase groups.

Unit 6: I, V, and V⁷

Don't forget to raise $\hat{7}$ in minor! In *e-h*, pay particular attention to the resolution of the 7th.

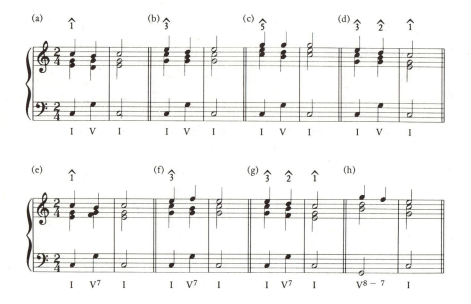

Unit 7: I⁶, V⁶, and VII⁶

Progressions *a* and *b* can function as expanded initial tonics and can lead to a V-I cadence; *c* can continue to a final I.

Unit 8: Inversions of V⁷

Many other sopranos are possible. Use these progressions to expand I, then lead to either an authentic cadence or a semicadence.

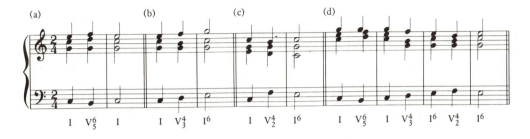

Unit 9: Leading to V: IV, II, and II⁶

The initial tonics of *a-d* can be expanded by the progressions of Units 7 and 8; cadences using IV and II can follow.

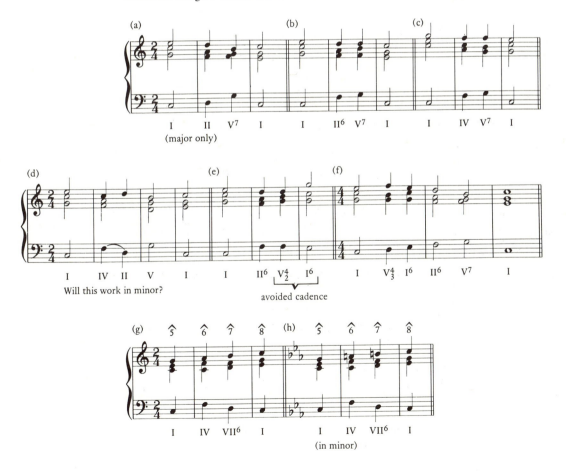

Unit 10: The Cadential $\frac{6}{4}$

Using progressions learned in Units 7, 8, and 9, play antecedent-consequent phrase groups; both semi- and authentic cadences should feature $\frac{6}{4}$ on V.

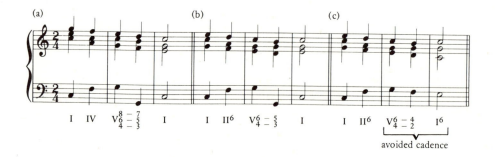

Unit 11: VI and IV^6

Other sopranos are possible for *a* and *e*. Expand the initial tonic of *a* and *b*; incorporate *c, d,* and *e* into longer progressions.

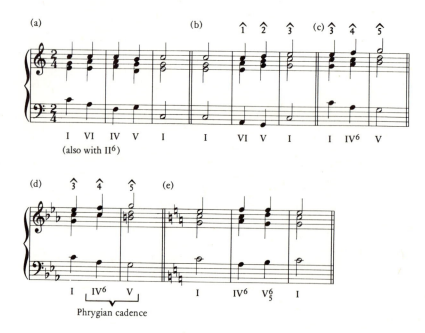

Unit 12: Supertonic and Subdominant Seventh Chords

Practice *a, b,* and *c* with other sopranos; *e, f,* and *g* can lead to cadential progressions.

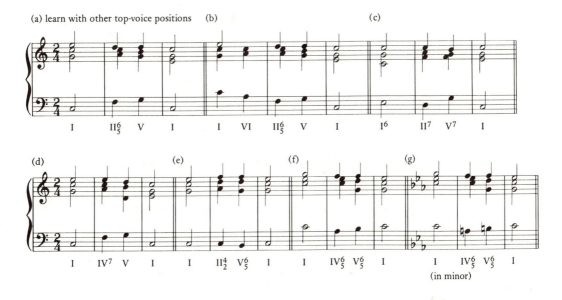

Unit 13: Other Uses of IV, IV^6, and VI

After the deceptive cadences, play authentic ones to complete the progressions. In addition to the progressions given here, practice the scale harmonizations in Examples 13-18 and 13-19.

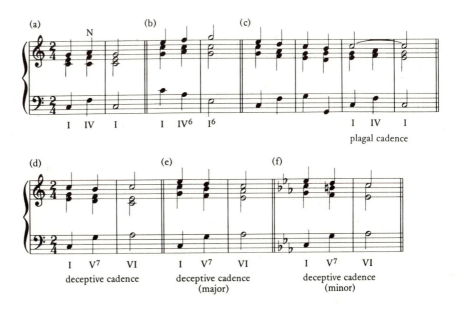

Unit 14: V as a Key Area

Many other possibilities exist for progressions that tonicize V and return to I. Invent progressions using other pivot chords than the ones used here.

Unit 15: III and VII

The progression given here works only in minor. In addition, practice the scale harmonization in Example 15-11.

Unit 16: ⅝-Chord Techniques

Keyboard progressions using only ⅝ chords are most common in sequences; they will therefore be presented in the following group.

Unit 17: Diatonic Sequences

Other sopranos are possible for some of these progressions, especially *a, c, d, e,* and *g.* In *d,* the progression is easier in four voices if the left hand plays the tenor; alternatively, the tenor may be omitted.

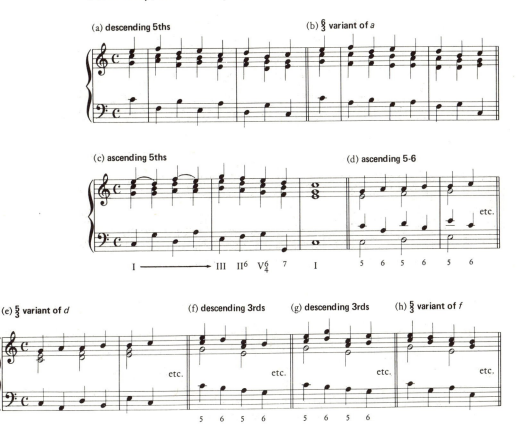

Unit 18: $\frac{6}{3}$-Chord Techniques

These progressions show the alternating doublings characteristic of parallel $\frac{6}{3}$ chords in four voices. Performance in three voices is also possible, omitting the tenor, but be sure to include the 3rd in $\frac{5}{3}$ chords.

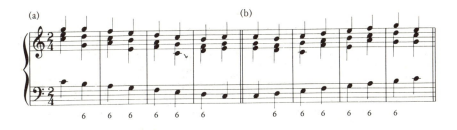

Unit 19: $\frac{6}{4}$-Chord Techniques

The most important $\frac{6}{4}$ usages are summarized in these progressions.

(a) accented $\frac{6}{4}$

(b) neighboring $\frac{6}{4}$

(c) consonant and passing $\frac{6}{4}$ (d) passing $\frac{6}{4}$

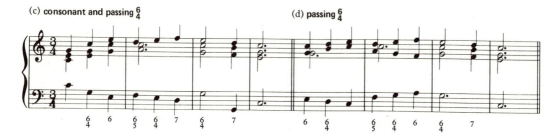

INDEX OF MUSICAL EXAMPLES

SUBJECT INDEX

A 8
B 9
C 0
D 1
E 2
F 3
G 4
H 5
I 6
J 7